A Cultural History of Famine

The term "food security" does not immediately signal research done in humanities disciplines. It refers to a complex, contested issue, whose currency and significance are hardly debatable given present concerns about environmental change, resource management, and sustainability.

The subject is thus largely studied within science and social science disciplines in current or very recent historical contexts. This book brings together perspectives on food security and related environmental concerns from experts in the disciplines of literary studies, history, science, and social sciences. It allows readers to compare past and contemporary attitudes towards the issue in India and Britain – the economic, social, and environmental histories of these two nations have been closely connected ever since British travellers began to visit India in the latter half of the sixteenth century. The chapters in this book discuss themes such as climate, harvest failure, trade, technological improvements, transport networks, charity measures, and popular protest, which affected food security in both countries from the seventeenth century onwards. The authors cover a range of disciplinary and interdisciplinary approaches, and their chapters allow readers to understand and compare different methodologies as well as different contexts of time and place relevant to the topic.

This book will be of great interest to students and researchers of economic and social history, environmental history, literary studies, and South Asian studies.

Ayesha Mukherjee is a Senior Lecturer in the Department of English at the University of Exeter, UK.

A Cultural History of Famine

Food Security and the Environment in
India and Britain

**Edited by
Ayesha Mukherjee**

Routledge
Taylor & Francis Group

LONDON AND NEW YORK

earthscan
from Routledge

First published 2019
by Routledge
2 Park Square, Milton Park, Abingdon, Oxon OX14 4RN

and by Routledge
52 Vanderbilt Avenue, New York, NY 10017

First issued in paperback 2020

Routledge is an imprint of the Taylor & Francis Group, an informa business

British Library Cataloguing-in-Publication Data
A catalogue record for this book is available from the British Library

Library of Congress Cataloging-in-Publication Data
A catalog record has been requested for this book

ISBN 13: 978-0-367-66285-1 (pbk)
ISBN 13: 978-1-138-23092-7 (hbk)

Typeset in Baskerville
by Wearset Ltd, Boldon, Tyne and Wear

Contents

Figures

Tables

Contributors

Rob Allan leads the Atmospheric Circulation Reconstructions over the Earth (ACRE) initiative at the Met Office Hadley Centre for Climate Science and Services. He is an expert on climatic variability and climate change, especially with regard to the El Niño Southern Oscillation (ENSO) phenomenon.

Ujjayan Bhattacharya is Professor of History and Dean of the Faculty of Arts at Vidyasagar University, in Midnapur, India. His current research interests are focussed on the history of the Portuguese in early modern Bengal, and on water management, floods, fiscal regimes, and the rural economy in eighteenth-century Bengal.

Vinita Damodaran is Professor of South Asian History and Director of the Centre for World Environmental History at the University of Sussex. She leads a project on the *Botanical and Meteorological History of the Indian Ocean*, and has recently co-edited *East India Company and the Natural World* (2014), and *Climate Change and the Humanities* (2017).

Amlan Das Gupta is Professor of English and Director of the School of Cultural Texts and Records, Jadavpur University, Calcutta. His research areas are classical and early modern European literature and Digital Humanities. He was Co-Investigator on the AHRC project *Famine and Dearth in India and Britain, 1550–1800: Connected Cultural Histories of Food Security*.

Rajat Datta is Professor of History at the Centre for Historical Studies, Jawaharlal Nehru University, New Delhi. He is author of *Society, Economy and the Market: Commercialization in Rural Bengal* (2000), and has edited *Rethinking a Millennium: Perspectives on Indian History from the Eighth to the Eighteenth Century* (2008). His monograph *Market, Subsistence and Transition in Early Modern India* is forthcoming.

James Hamilton is a post-graduate researcher who has worked for a number of years with Professor Vinita Damodaran at the Centre for World Environmental History at the University of Sussex. His primary areas of study are historical human, animal, and environment inter-relations in East Africa and India.

Julie Hudson completed her PhD at Warwick University in 2018, with a thesis titled "The Environment on Stage: Scenery or Shapeshifter?" Her publications include "'If You Want to Be Green Hold Your Breath': Climate Change in British Theatre", *NTQ* 111 (2012), and *Food Policy and the Environmental Credit Crunch: From Soup to Nuts* (with Paul Dono-van, 2013).

Ayesha Mukherjee is Senior Lecturer in the Department of English, University of Exeter. She is author of *Penury into Plenty: Dearth and the Making of Knowledge in Early Modern England* (2015), and was Principal Investigator on the AHRC-funded project *Famine and Dearth in India and Britain, 1550–1800: Connected Cultural Histories of Food Security*.

Lesa Scholl is Head of Kathleen Lumley College, University of Adelaide. Her publications include *Translation, Authorship and the Victorian Profes-sional Woman* (2011), *Hunger Movements in Early Victorian Literature: Want, Riots, Migration* (2016), and *Medicine, Health and Being Human* (2018).

Sanjay Sharma is Professor of History at Ambedkar University Delhi. He is author of *Famine, Philanthropy and the Colonial State: North India in the Early Nineteenth Century* (2001), and his research focuses on the history of famines in North India, notions of philanthropy, and indigenous sur-vival practices during food shortages.

John Walter is Emeritus Professor of History at the University of Essex. His publications include *Famine, Disease and the Social Order in Early Modern Society* (with Roger Schofield, 1989), *Understanding Popular Violence in the English Revolution* (1999), *Negotiating Power in Early Modern Society* (with Michael Braddick, 2001), *Crowds and Popular Politics in early Modern Eng-land* (2006), and *Covenanting Citizens: The Protestation Oath and Popular Political Culture in the English Revolution* (2017).

Michael Winter, OBE, is Professor of Land Economy and Society in the Department of Politics, University of Exeter. His research focuses on the governance of sustainable agro-food systems; historical and con-temporary sociology of West Country agriculture; and farmer environ-mental attitudes and decision-making.

Acknowledgements

I would like to thank the Arts and Humanities Research Council, UK, for funding our project workshop, "Food Security and the Environment in India and Britain" (2015), which first brought together the contributors to this book. I am also grateful to the Smith School of Enterprise and the Environment, University of Oxford, who provided us with a venue and supported our workshop discussions in many ways. Thank you, all participants who contributed to the workshop. *A Cultural History of Famine* has evolved from these discussions, and the exchanges and debates that continued beyond our first meeting. I am deeply grateful to colleagues who have contributed chapters, for their sustained enthusiasm, time, and patience.

At the University of Exeter, I would like to thank colleagues in the Department of English, the Centre for South Asia Research, and the Digital Humanities team; and at Jadavpur University and Aligarh Muslim University, colleagues in the English and History departments and the Institute of Persian Research. This book has benefited from their encouragement and support.

It has been a pleasure to work again with Routledge; many thanks, from all contributors, to Leila Walker, Rebecca Brennan and Steve Turrington for their wonderful and patient assistance.

Ayesha Mukherjee

Abbreviations

BCP	Proceedings of the Board of Customs (WBSA)
BR	Board of Revenue
BRC	Bengal Revenue Consultations (British Library)
BRP (G)	Proceedings of the Board of Revenue, Grain (WBSA)
BRP (M)	Proceedings of the Board of Revenue, Miscellaneous (WBSA)
CCC	Controlling Committee of Commerce
CCRM	Controlling Committee of Revenue, Murshidabad
COA	Commissioner's Office, Allahabad
COF	Commissioner's Office, Faizabad
COR	Commissioner's Office, Rohilkhand
IOR	India Office Records (British Library)
IPCC	Intergovernmental Panel on Climate Change
OIOC	Oriental and India Office Collections (British Library)
PCR	Provincial Council of Revenue
UPRAA	Uttar Pradesh Regional Archives, Allahabad
WBSA	West Bengal State Archives

Introduction

A cultural history of famine

Ayesha Mukherjee

In, arguably, his most macabre comment on famine, 'Abd Al-Ḥamīd Lāhawrī (d.1654), court historian of the Mughal emperor Shah Jahan (1592–1666), describing the effects of the notorious Gujarat famine of 1630–32, wrote:

گوشت فرزند را شیرین تر از مهر او می‌دانستند

[*gosht-i farzand-rā shirin tar az mehr-i ou midānistand*]

The flesh of a son was considered sweeter than his love.

(Lāhawrī, I: 362)

This line was translated by Sir Henry Miers Elliot in his edition of excerpts as "the flesh of a son was preferred to his love" (1875: 26). Elliot's translation obscures, in my opinion, the deliberate poeticism of

شیرین تر از مهر او (sweeter than his love),

and Lāhawrī's self-conscious shift to the poetic register of the macabre and grotesque from the factual register of chronicling events. In early modern accounts of famine, this kind of rhetorical shift is frequent, and cuts across place, language, and literary mode or genre. Reports of famine-induced cannibalism and desperate forms of eating abound in travelogues, poems, and chronicles, across time and space. Lāhawrī's predecessor, Abul Fazl, the court historian of Shah Jahan's grandfather, the emperor Akbar, described men eating each other in desperation during a famine (1554–56) that had inaugurated Akbar's reign (Fazl, 1907–39, II: 30). The East India Company (EIC) factor Peter Mundy, whose recording of the Gujarat famine during Shah Jahan's reign will be discussed later in this book, noticed people who looked like human "annatomies", sifting through the dung of travellers' horses in hopes of finding undigested grain (Mundy, 1907–36, II: 44). In quite a different context, Piero Campo-resi's famous studies of hunger (1989, 1996) give numerous examples, from early modern Italy, of extreme forms of eating. One of Camporesi's examples is Giovan Battista Spaccini's *Cronaca modenese* which described how, in 1601 in the town of Reggio, neighbours discovered three young boys, whose parents had fled the famine: "they found two of the sons dead, and the third dying with straw in his mouth, and on the fire there was a pot with straw inside which was being boiled in order to make it softer for eating" (1919, vol. 2: 177; Camporesi, 1989: 85). After the four-year period of dearth and famine in 1590s England, the poetry anthology *Englands Parnassus* (1600) personified Dearth and Famine as cannibals, whose "greedie gorge" consumed their "owne deere babes", as well as their own flesh (256; Mukherjee, A., 2015: 1–3). *A Cultural History of Famine* attends to such modes of representing famine and dearth, and their historical contexts.

To regard such accounts as sensational disruptions of the narration of factual evidence of famines would be to undermine the complex function of the Mughal chronicle (or other literary writing) as a cultural document. Lāhawrī was allegedly asked by Shah Jahan to model his chronicle on the style of Abul Fazl. Thus, continuity of rhetorical tradition and style was as important for Mughal imperial "self-fashioning"[1] as the consistent recording of key events across a temporal continuum that connected emperors to their ancestry. Yet, to return to Lāhawrī's trope, there seem to be few accounts of famine cannibalism which utilised the macabre and the grotesque to such devastatingly succinct effect. This was rhetorically achieved by words that selectively evoked fundamental things in human life: flesh, sweet, love, son. Readers were asked to imagine the unimaginable: in what condition of physiological deprivation and mental aberration would the flesh of your son taste sweeter than his love? The horror of famine was literally and physically tasted in this trope, which used ironic exaggeration to signal the absolute breakdown of closest kinship ties and moral agency among human beings. What is also underlined here is the realisation that, beyond a point, famine sufferers, physiologically and mentally, inhabit a different zone from the rest of humanity. When we encounter representations of hunger-driven extremes, whether in Lāhawrī, or Spaccini, or – to consider another representational mode and timeframe – in Zainul Abedin's remarkable sketches of the 1943 Bengal famine (Sen, 1944), which blended the horrific and the mundane, these demand extreme ways of imagining human degradation and the breakdown of kinship, humanity, and morality.[2]

Forms of representing famine, despite similarities in their rhetorical strategies, are distinct and relate to their specific contexts. There are many degrees of horror in the different types of famine representation and reportage: not all are as brilliantly sensational as Lāhawrī. But even the most factual kinds of reporting, such as official EIC correspondence, are often emotive, beneath the surface of official structure. The sifting of fact from fiction, in the strictest sense, is frequently difficult, because the reporting itself is coloured by human perceptions, imagination, a sense of duty or loyalty, and politics. In seeking to understand how "a cultural history of famine" might be constituted, this book considers how famines (and their remedies) have been imagined, or, for that matter, misunderstood or forgotten, as part of the construction of famine history. Famines are not only about sensational extremities – they are also linked with periods of dearth, in differing degrees, so that the point at which "dearth" slips into "famine" can be highly context specific and tricky to identify or generalise.[3] Indeed, in human memory and in literary sources, famine and dearth are often conceived as interchangeable conditions, as in the similar personifications of Dearth and Famine in *Englands Parnassus*. Moreover, habits of economy and mundane life work alongside conditions of dearth and famine (Thirsk, 1967, 2007; Mukherjee, A., 2015: 145–94). Both conditions affect social norms, patterns of economic exchange, political behaviour, and the moral life of human beings. *A Cultural History of Famine* thus calls for an approach that looks at, but also beyond, causalities, such as climate change, or market prices, or political events like wars and rebellions, and towards human responses in times of dearth and famine.

Time and space

Concerns about what we might today call "food security", or the long-term availability, quality, and distribution of food, have a cultural history that can be traced far back. This is not only a history of economics and agricultural or technological development at points of time; it is equally a history of human responses, resilience, and representations in the long term.[4] In this book, authors, whose expertise covers different disciplines, geographical areas, and time periods (from the early modern to the present day), aim to stimulate readers to think about famine and food security as long-term questions, whose specific shapes have altered over time. The term "food security" may have been invented in the twentieth century, but not the problem itself or the debates about possible solutions.[5] By bringing together disciplinary perspectives on famine, the book highlights fundamental debates about historical, literary, and social science approaches to the topic, and explores ways of connecting these perspectives. The authors also contend with questions of geographical breadth and depth. In other words, both spatial and temporal complexities affect the book's approach because food, famine, and dearth are not issues that are, or have been, problematic for the "Third World" alone. The Western world too has a long history of coping with food crises, which have impacted on the wider world.[6] We have elected to focus on India and Britain since the wider political and cultural histories of the two nations, and their famine histories, in particular, are closely connected.

Famine and dearth featured with remarkable persistence in the histories of early modern (sixteenth- to eighteenth-century) Britain and India.

Table I.1 Famine and dearth chronology

India	Britain
1554–56	1555–57
1596–1600	1596–1600
1630–32	1630–32
–	1647–49
1658–63	1658–61
1691–97	1693–97
–	1709–10
–	1727–28
1732–37	–
1752–55	1756–57
1767–70	–
1777–79	–
1783–84	–
1787–93	–

Sources: Hoskins (1964, 1968); Walter and Schofield (1989); Habib (1999); Moosvi (1987, 2008); Datta (2000); Grove and Chapell (2000).

In Britain, their effects and intensities varied locally, but in some cases (for example, in the 1590s) the crises were experienced across the nation (Hoskins, 1968; Appleby, 1978; Walter, 1989). In India, famines occurred throughout the Mughal period in the Northern provinces, Bengal, and the south (Habib, 1999; Moosvi, 2008; Datta, 2000; Subrahmanyam, 1990). The famine chronologies of the two countries in this early period are uncannily parallel, matched almost decade by decade, until the mid-eighteenth century. After this, famines seem to no longer afflict Britain, although they continue unabated in India, as Walter and Datta demonstrate in the first two chapters of this book.

It may be argued that the reasons for this remarkable parallelism were climatic: the links between severe El Niño events, the coldest periods of the Little Ice Age, and droughts in tropical regions, have long been the subject of investigation and debate among climate scientists and historians (Grove, 1994; Grove and Chapell, 2000).[7] Table I.1 shows the most acute points of crisis, as represented in the existing historiography of famine and dearth for both nations, covering the period 1550–1800.[8] Climatologists have shown that difficult winters and poor crops in European regions have coincided with El Niño events, and archival data uncovered by historians suggests that from the seventeenth to the nineteenth centuries, a number of El Niños had wider and more intense global effects than those of the twentieth century (Lamb, 1977; Grove and Chappell, 2000, 7–20; Quinn *et al.*, 1987; Ortlieb, 1998). But whether coincidence is evidence remains a question. As Damodaran and her colleagues argue, in Chapter 3, finding answers to such questions requires "more detailed mining of documentary and paleo sources" across time and space. Nevertheless, the congruence, this book suggests, shapes cultural evidence regarding famine and dearth, especially if we consider this in relation to socio-economic exchanges between the selected nations.

Forms of exchange

Grove and Chappell comment that

> it was at precisely the time that the European powers strengthened their commercial and revenue grip on Asia, that the stress of increasingly severe climatic events with associated disease and famine contributed to the vulnerability of Asian agricultural societies, especially between 1590 and 1800.
>
> (2000: 13)

They suggest that these stresses may have facilitated European expansion. India and Britain thus offer a useful case study of how pre-colonial experiences of famine and dearth impacted on later crises during the course of colonial expansion, when famines and their memories had arguably become more remote in Britain itself, and were perceived as issues affecting its distant colonies.[9] Despite differences in scale and local ecologies, from the sixteenth to the eighteenth centuries, both contexts register chronic instabilities, sharp contrasts, and fears generated by the close proximity of plenty and dearth. National and local economies struggled to build physical infrastructures to cope with uncertainties of climate and create a secure agricultural environment. This was a formative period for cultural interactions between the two countries. British emissaries travelled frequently through famine-ridden Indian terrain along with local migrants displaced by shortages. One such example is Peter Mundy, discussed in Chapter 4, who travelled from Surat to Agra and back during the Gujarat famine (1630–32), possibly caused by moderate El Niños which led to acute drought in this and other Asian regions (Quinn, 1992; Grove and Chappell, 2000: 15). The experience of constant mobility and unsettledness was shared by Company men and local populations. Indeed, British travellers to India were familiar with negative ecological consequences of dearth-driven vagrancy and displacement in their own national context (see, for example, Fumerton, 2006).

Conditions for the exchange and interaction of cultural understandings of famine, dearth, and ecological ethics were thus created. Early modern and pre-colonial contexts of what these economic and environmental issues meant, and how they were addressed *across* seemingly separate cultural zones, are yet to be properly examined. At the same time, despite the existence of many valuable historical studies of famines in Indian colonial and post-colonial contexts, there is a need for more reflection, first, on how this shared early modern and pre-colonial history of famine and dearth may have impacted colonial famine and food security policies; and, second, on how internal British concerns about food shortage, in key contexts such as the institution of the Poor Laws, or post-war food shortages, may have played out in relation to remedial (or exploitative) actions undertaken in the colonies. In its engagement with such questions, this book is concerned with the ways in which the past relates to the present: how we might understand the lessons of the past (temporally remote contexts), or learn from the experience of other communities (geographically remote contexts).

Comprehensive coverage of five centuries of famine history, in two countries, and in a single volume, is therefore not the purpose here. The chapters engage with methodological debates, and bring fresh perspectives often by highlighting regional, micro-level conditions which had a wider impact. In Part I, "Historical interpretations", John Walter offers a vital overview of responses to famine and dearth in early modern England, arguing that the "infrapolitics" of the people tried to maintain, in the face of economic and intellectual change and exchange, forms of social and governmental responses offering protection against the crisis of dearth. In his reassessment of moral economy and the English social order, Walter points out that, despite demographic evidence of crisis mortality and the "silent violence" of dearth, famine was regionally selective; and the reciprocities of "commonwealth", rather than profits of commodity, continued to be significant in the mental world of early modern society, especially during harvest failure. In this context, he examines the role of popular protest, characterised by a disciplined (frequently symbolic) violence, preferring negotiation, rather than reflecting the elite stereotypes of thievery, random violence, and disorder. In the next chapter, Rajat Datta shifts focus from the social and moral economy of food crisis to questions of evaluating "subsistence crises" as economic history; the context also shifts from early modern England to pre-colonial Bengal. However, Datta, like Walter, raises wider interpretative issues. He explores how we might construct an economic history of subsistence crises, which are often seen as severe dislocations in the "normal" run of things, whose economic consequences were considered "excess" points – excess starvation, excess mortality, and so on. Addressing a different kind of (historiographic) silence around the interims between excess points, Datta demonstrates how a serious scarcity (even if not a full blown famine) dismantled economic structures of subsistence in pre-colonial systems, reliant on production, circulation, and consumption. Based on his data on eighteenth-century Bengal, Datta advocates constructing an economic history of subsistence focused on variables such as market networks, money, exchange mechanisms, and price fluctuations.

While Walter's and Datta's introductions to the moral and subsistence economies suggest ways of understanding human agency during famine and dearth, in Chapter 3, Vinita Damodaran, James Hamilton, and Rob Allan consider another possible agent – global climate change. By examining the links between climate signals, environment, and livelihoods in the long seventeenth century in India, this chapter assesses the claim that the synchronicity of the many disorders of mid-seventeenth century Eurasia was no accident but associated with climatic conditions between 1610 and the winter of 1708–09. These conditions, as the historian Geoffrey Parker (2013) argued, led to natural forces combining in this period to generate cooler temperatures and greater climatic variability, reduced solar energy, increased volcanic activity, and a greater frequency of El Niño. The El Niño southern oscillation also disrupted the Asian monsoons and North American rainfall. The idea of a "global crisis" in the seventeenth century, as Damodaran and her colleagues affirm, is here to stay, but their chapter queries whether climate change was the primary agent of seventeenth-century demographic change, and makes the case for an approach which would focus on regional and national differences and the resilience of agricultural production in the face of population pressure, exogenous shocks, and environmental change.

As Part I of the book sets up fundamental debates about historical interpretations of food crises, their causes, and human responses, it also discusses particular instances of famine in early modern Britain and India – such as the famines in Gujarat in the 1630s, in Bengal in the 1770s, in England in the 1590s and early seventeenth century. The chapters that follow revisit some of these examples in more detail, and explore ways of combining or modifying the approaches critically examined in the first Part. Part II on "Roads and rivers" pays close attention to regional contexts, taking up the intersecting issues of navigation, settlement, mobility, and representation in the selected local environments, and considering their impact on agriculture, food supply, and distribution. Chapter 4 attends to individual, local, and state-guided discourses of famine and dearth in seventeenth-century India and Britain, which expressed concerns about climate, place, and mobility. The chapter thus focuses on perceptions of space and place as driving factors for British and Mughal understandings of alternating dearth and plenty in India. East India Company men, such as Peter Mundy, were constantly on the move, whether by sea or on land, and their accounts of travel and economic crisis in India, Ayesha Mukherjee argues, adapted the developing modes of representing domestic mobility in Britain. Using Mundy's text and narration during the notorious Gujarat famine of 1630–32 as a case study, the chapter shows how themes and principles in British domestic travel writing familiar to Mundy were adapted by him to describe the topography, climate, politics, local resilience, and travel experiences during the Gujarat famine. This is compared with the politics of representing the famine in Mughal official and courtly accounts. Mukherjee suggests that, in the process of narrating subsistence crises, seventeenth-century English travel journals and Mughal chronicles recorded the beginnings of a global discourse of food security, which must be recovered in its own terms.

In Chapter 5, Ujjayan Bhattacharya observes that rivers in the region of Bengal, by the nature of their seasonal flooding, and volatile change in their courses of flow, determined the scale of ecological impact on agrarian society. Changes in the direction of river flow altered ecological zones, creating new deltaic spaces for expansion of agriculture, rendering the older zones moribund. He identifies that channels of the Damodar in 1770 and the Teesta and Karatoya in 1787–89 had gone through rapid changes in character, causing significant ecological shifts in western and north-eastern Bengal, and argues that long-term changes resulting from the considerable impact of inundations and the system of watercourses were crucial for food security and the evolution of new agrarian settlements. Moving on from the well-known Bengal famine of 1770, Bhattacharya focuses on official records and government responses to the flood and famine situations in 1787 and 1790s. Though we may argue the evidence of climate change, on a global scale, still needs to be fully discovered and collated, the case of Bengal in 1787–90 suggests that this process can be aided by considering the micro-dynamics of responses to specific climatic events, evidenced in holdings of local archives which allow us to reconstruct famine conditions from below. Bhattacharya's detailed reconstruction demonstrates how changes in local climate and ecology, market exchanges, and conflicted notions of moral economy (from the Company's perspective) worked in tandem to determine the precise shape of a food crisis.

Discourses, narratives, and memories

On the one hand, the issues raised in "Roads and rivers" link back to questions of commercial, environmental, and moral response (raised in Part I), with an emphasis on the recovery of local detail through varied (often conflicting) sources – local administration records, travel accounts, imperial histories, and popular culture. On the other hand, the chapters point forward to the tensions between state-centred responses to famine situations and localised perceptions and experiences of mobility and terrain in such situations. Such tensions surrounding the coping practices and moral responsibilities of the state and individuals appear to have reached a climactic point in the colonial period, by which time, as Walter shows, famines had all but disappeared from England; nevertheless, food and subsistence crises took increasingly complex shapes in colonies like India. Part III, "Politics of climate and relief", shows how this altered balance of famine events shaped *discourses* of extreme weather, political economy, charity, and relief in the colonial period. Food and consumption were embedded in ideas of justice, charity, and their administration in colonial India and Victorian Britain. These ideas had their roots in the early modern history of the poor law and charity, resurrecting categorisations of the "deserving and undeserving poor" in Britain, discussed in earlier chapters by Walter and Mukherjee. The two chapters here consider the disjunctions, competing voices, and disruptions that resulted when principles of political economy, charity, and relief were codified and put into practice in the context of famine during a period of colonisation.

Lesa Scholl closely reads selections from a relatively lesser known text, Harriet Martineau's *Illustrations of Political Economy* (1832–34). Both lauded and condemned for her mission to make the precepts of classical political economy accessible to all, Martineau was established by her contemporaries as a proponent of political economy. However, Scholl argues, such renderings must be interrogated through the strong counter-narratives of chaos, dispossession, and conflict within the series that unflinchingly challenge the tenets espoused by early political economists. This chapter draws out Martineau's more complex relationship to political economy by focusing on the dialogic nature of her tales – the way she uses the chaotic force of weather disturbances to critique the seeming stability of economic theory. Martineau's characters (in the 1833 volumes *French Wines and Politics*, *Sowers Not Reapers*, and *Cinnamon and Pearls*) who express political economy's ideals became increasingly problematic figures in the light of environmental devastation. The intervention of uncontrollable climatic forces of the hurricane, drought, and monsoon mirrored, in these narratives, hunger and economic turbulence and, most crucially, as the chapter demonstrates, spoke to the visceral trauma of the community. In the next chapter, Sanjay Sharma describes a different kind of subversive force which resisted the state's construction of power and authority through famine relief measures in colonial North India. Poorhouses, established in India in the second half of the nineteenth century, provided opportunities for colonial administrators to devise and test their principles of governance on a subject population located in a defined space. One of these principles, the provision of cooked food for recipients of famine relief, became the desirable norm and means of measuring real need. Poorhouses (like prisons) were enclosed sites in the colonial administrative imagination. In these spaces, Sharma points out, the inmates' acceptance or rejection of cooked food meant to meet their subsistence and nutritional requirements became a way of enforcing authority and reiterating humanitarian claims. Sharma's close examination of official narratives reveals conflicting voices at different layers of the colonial regime – district-level administrators, higher bureaucracy, policy-makers, and medical practitioners – whose views were often couched in the language of political economy and prevailing ideas of nutrition, disease, and health. Despite humanitarian rhetoric, this chapter argues, colonial poorhouses were designed to minimise responsibility, discourage indolence, and ensure discipline, eventually producing a discourse of governance that reinforced administrative and paternal hierarchies.

Prototypes of such institutions existed in nineteenth-century industrialising Britain, where debates on how to set the poor to work, dissuade indolence, and curb vagrancy and misuse of charity were at the heart of the New Poor Law and establishment of workhouses.[10] Similar questions informed the agenda of the colonial state in famine situations in a different context where death and disease pushed the state to assume greater responsibility for its subject population (Arnold, 1993). These responsibilities were shaped by conflicts between the tenets of market-driven political economy (already under critical scrutiny in the 1830s, as Scholl's account of Martineau demonstrates) and the imperatives of humanitarian concern (cf. Brewis, 2010). Sharma and Scholl reveal how both were tested by climatic disruptions and attitudes to charity and relief. They illustrate contradictory pulls, as relief/reform policies sought to discipline needy subjects and also strengthen the claims of welfare and responsibility by the colonial state, which were, in turn, contested by the state's own functionaries.

In the final Part IV of the book, "Contemporary voices and memories", narratives of the notorious Bengal famine of 1943 are placed alongside the politics of farming in war-time and post-war Britain. From the 1870s to 1939, Britain's food security depended on its ability to import food from around the world, as a colonial and a trading nation, while domestic agriculture suffered. The 1939–45 war began with Britain producing barely a third of its own food, after 20 years of agricultural depression and a rapid process of restructuring land ownership and occupation. Farmers remembered the "great betrayal" of the government's sudden removal of the protectionist price policy in 1920, and it was clear that increasing food production, vital to the war effort, would require firm assurances that the government would not walk away from the agricultural industry at the end of the war. However, the nature of the state–agriculture relationship in the post-war period was deeply contested; some advocated land nationalisation, others a new social contract between the state and farmers, and many a market solution with price guarantees (Friedmann, 1978; Cox *et al.*, 1986, 1991; Griffiths, 2010; Brassley *et al.*, 2012). In Chapter 8, Michael Winter argues that out of this turbulence and debate, the idea of family farming emerged in literary representations in the 1930s to the 1950s, as a political project (to circumvent class-based politics of landed capitalist agriculture), as a socio-economic reality (resulting from the fixity of landholding structures, mechanisation, and the declining size of the hired labour force), and as a cultural ideal. The chapter examines the works of three farming writers (George Henderson, Clifton Reynolds, and Frances Donaldson) who related their personal experiences of farming. These "working farmers" set out to inspire, inform, and warn would-be farmers. Two of them (Henderson and Reynolds) also had strongly articulated political and moral views of agriculture which, in different ways, were at odds with the corporatist policy "consensus" between government and the leading political representatives of the farming industry that emerged in this period. Their divergent voices offer an insight into the drive for food security in war-time and post-war Britain, and Winter's analysis suggests that alternative visions for agriculture were articulated in the 1940s and 1950s, even if these have often been forgotten in conventional agrarian histories of the period.

At the same time, attempts to sustain the war effort created extraordinary challenges in one of Britain's colonies, as Amlan Das Gupta notes in his study of literary representations of the 1943 Bengal famine, in Chapter 9. This infamous famine, which occurred in pre-partition British India during the Second World War after the Japanese occupation of Burma, reportedly resulted in the death of more than 3 million people, largely from rural Bengal.[11] The winter rice crop of 1942 was affected by a cyclone in October, followed by flooding and fungus diseases. Rice imports from Burma were cut off. The wholesale price of rice rose from Rs 13/14 per *maund* in December 1942 to Rs 37 in August 1943, while in the retail market of Dhaka rice was being sold at Rs 105 per *maund* in October (Sen, 1981a: 52–5). Amartya Sen identifies the period from March to November 1943 as the phase of maximum starvation deaths (55). The famine was perceived and experienced differently in the districts and in Calcutta. District officers described hunger marches, property crimes, paddy looting, towns filling with starving beggars, and the disposal of dead bodies becoming a problem for civic authorities. In Calcutta, while official policy developed schemes to ensure essential food supplies in the "industrial area", rural destitutes arrived in masses, filled the city streets, relying on personal or ad hoc charity until relief for them became official policy in August. It was estimated that, just for October, starving and sick migrants amounted to at least 100,000, while 3363 unattended dead bodies were disposed of by relief organisers (Sen, 1981a: 57; Famine Inquiry Commission, 1945a; *The Calcutta Gazette*, various Supplements[12]).

The famine is near enough in time to endure in memory and oral testimonies: it also inspired volumes of literature, including some of the most powerful works of modern Bengali fiction. Das Gupta examines ethical questions that arose from the experience of deprivation, migration, and death during this famine, many of which related to long-established norms of conduct within settled communities. While Winter demonstrates how the active intervention of communal enterprise, such as family farming, tried to address the challenge of food security in Britain, Das Gupta queries the extent to which what P. R. Greenough called "the implicit rules for crisis conduct" in settled communities were able – if at all – to come to terms with the enormity of the events of 1943–44 in India. The chapter revisits these events through their representations in memorial reconstructions of people who lived through the crisis, and in works by Bibhutibhushan Bandyopadhyay (1894–1950) and Manik Bandyopadhyay (1908–56), major authors in the modern Bengali literary canon, who felt they had (in Das Gupta's terms) "a duty of response".

Winter and Das Gupta both raise, in distinct but not unrelated contexts, the question of public memory and understanding of food shortage. This is also studied in the final chapter by Julie Hudson, who examines the reception of food security issues in modern performances of an early modern English play to understand how present audiences might read, own, or disown past environmental and food production challenges. Hudson asks to what extent people living in the resource-intensive societies typical of developed countries in the present day recognise that the persistent over-use of natural resources by an expanding global population is a recipe for being "performed by" dearth. Her chapter explores the relationship between people and food (in)security from an eco-theatrical perspective, in the context of live theatrical performance in conventional theatre spaces. It considers plays that first came to the stage at a time of dearth and that also directly thematised dearth, finally focusing on Shakespeare's *Coriolanus*, written *c*.1608/09 and first performed *c*.1609/10, drawing on experiences of the Midlands Revolt – a series of peasant riots over enclosure in 1607. As Hudson explores modern performance archives for evidence of food insecurity awareness, her discussion reflects on whether the ecological threads of meaning, embedded in noteworthy food insecurity scenes in the play texts, are fully included or occluded in modern-day productions. She argues that modern production teams and audiences can thus be seen as an indicator of societal readiness (or otherwise) for the cultural and behavioural changes needed to fend off the next dearth, or famine.

The chronological arrangement of chapters in *A Cultural History of Famine* is thus used to interrogate the perception that hunger and famine have a neat teleological trajectory, allowing us to chart the agricultural and socio-economic "progress" of affected nations. Famines may have disappeared from England after the seventeenth century, but it may be argued that they were merely displaced to other areas over which Britain had evolved administrative sway, and responsibilities of governance. Moreover, there are cases and contexts, as Cameron Muir recently noted, where agriculture has repeatedly served as a "strategic asset", and progress defined by increasing yields has "failed to address the inequitable distribution of food and the long-term health of the environment" (2014: 185). As many of our authors show, local concerns with agricultural development, issues arising from the application of colonial European technologies, ideologies, and remedies, and pressures of global markets and policies, have at different points in history created complexities (exacerbated during severe famines) that make linear narratives of agricultural and economic progress problematic.[13] It may be still more difficult to deduce from the charting of agricultural and socio-economic progress a different model of development – of social memory and moral consciousness, where modern understandings of hunger, famine, and welfare ideologies are seen as "improvements" upon the past.

In his study of the modern history of hunger, James Vernon tracks the transformation of "hunger" from the late-eighteenth to the mid-twentieth centuries. He argues that the political economy of Smith and Malthus "established hunger as an avoidable, man-made phenomenon", as opposed to the early modern understanding of it as a "curse of nature or providence". This laid the ground for neo-Malthusian arguments blaming the continuation of famine on "the laziness and moral weakness of the hungry"; and there emerged what he terms "the humanitarian discovery of hunger" in British liberal politics. Nationalists in Ireland and India, and the suffragettes and the unemployed in Britain, stimulated sympathy by turning hunger into an object of political outrage and "a symbol of the failure of British liberalism" and colonial states (Vernon, 2007: 273).[14] Social and nutritional scientists evolved techniques to measure hunger and its social costs, and proposed reforms of social welfare (ibid.: 118–58; cf. Gangulee, 1940; Bourne, 1943); and, Vernon sums up, "Humanitarians, political activists, and social and nutritional scientists subsequently fostered a more democratic social view of hunger as the responsibility of society as a whole" (2007: 274). However, early modern or pre-colonial providential accounts of famine were simultaneously open to both manipulation by the authorities and to challenges by the hungry, destitute, and unemployed; and the motivations of charitable and humanitarian activity have been underpinned by complex and frequently contested political desires.[15] This destabilises the notion of "more democratic" ideas of welfare and social responsibility developing over time. Jenny Edkins' observation, that the human desire for certainty and completeness "drives the discursive and social practices surrounding famine relief and food aid" and the technologising of modern famines (2000: 156), is notable because it was precisely the desire for certain ends, connected to discourses of power and authority, that many early modern discursive practices surrounding famine and dearth were engaged in debating and resisting. Do famines persist, and remain tied to violence and power relations, due to an unproductive solidifying of discourses of certain ends in the course of time?

It is useful to consider the role of memory in this regard: the memorialising of past hunger was a crucial tactic in criticisms of colonial governance and in the evolution of post-war British social democracy, still used in the later decades of the twentieth century (Vernon, 2007: 236–71; cf. Webster, 1982; Thorpe, 1992: 4; Baxendale and Pawling, 1996). Vernon quotes from Bessie Braddock, the first female MP of Liverpool, speaking eloquently in the House of Commons in November 1947 (incidentally, three months after Indian independence, and three years after the Bengal famine) to celebrate the demise of the abhorred Poor Law: "Let us remember the queues outside the Poor Law relief offices, the destitute people, badly clothed, badly shod, lining up with their prams ... for the week's rations of black treacle and bread" (Hansard, *Commons*, 1947: vol.

444, col. 1632). While Braddock's rhetorical emphasis on memory may have aimed to legitimise the gains (however precarious) of social democracy and the labour movement, it is also worth drawing attention to her equal emphasis on forgetting, which comes after a caveat about ensuring the continued efficacy of the new schemes:

> I hope that the working class movement will be able now to forget the horrors of the past in the joy of realising that we are living in a country that is going to produce for the benefit of the citizens as a whole.
>
> (Ibid.: col. 1636)

One hopes there might have been some irony here, in this call to memory to serve the latent desire of forgetting, at a moment when the horrors of famine smarted afresh among citizens of a recently relinquished colonial state.

Indeed, the famine in Bengal received strikingly scant attention in Britain (though the Indian national press and its special correspondents reported it vividly[16]) where focus had shifted to the "humanitarian crisis" and acute food shortages in occupied Europe (Walker, 1941; Famine Relief Committee, 1942, 1943). However, the Bengal famine became the first site of nutritional experimentation with the notorious F-Treatment (intravenous administering of protein hydrolysates) which, after its spectacular failure in Bengal, was used again for emergency feeding during the "Hunger Winter" (1944–45) in Holland, where it also failed (Drummond, 1946, 1948; van der Zee, 1982). In Belsen, the apparatus triggered patients' memories of the implements of torture, and apparently, the starving, in both contexts, wanted food and not "capsules". This, too, was not a straightforward matter because, as a *Times of India* special correspondent, complaining of woefully inadequate medical treatment in relief camps, reported on 23 November 1943, "Improved food supplies may for a time wreak havoc because once a certain stage of emaciation has been reached long treatment is essential before a person can assimilate solid food." The correspondent added that the majority of the starving reacted against treatments as far as their strength permitted, tried to run away from the hospitals, "and sell the very sheets that cover them for a meal of rice – a meal which is likely to kill them" (4). In the same month, the Bengali newspaper *Jugāntar* ("New Age") published regular counts of sick and dying destitutes in local hospitals, reports of parliamentary discussions, and subversive cartoons (7: 47 (6 November 1943), 48 (7 November 1943), 49 (8 November 1943), 52 (11 November 1943), 75 (4 December 1943)). The newspaper's weekly comic strip called *Śeỹāl Paṇḍit* ("Learned Fox") produced a parody titled *Cāñḍāpushṭa!* ("Plumped by Charity") on 6 November 1943. The Learned Fox, a familiar figure of Bengali oral tales, could be used in political parodies to satirise the "cunning" of colonial rulers or of those who were seen to imbibe this through blind emulation.[17]

Seyāl Paṇḍit appeared in this cartoon series as an ambivalent and clever trickster. In the 6 November version, a pair of skeletal and scruffy-looking stray cats, one with a harmonium strapped round his neck, appear below *Seyāl Paṇḍit*'s window. They sing a song of complaint in rhyming verse: they claim they can no longer bear the pangs of hunger (জঠরের জ্বালা সহেনা আর [*jaṭharer jwālā sahenā ār*]) and are prepared to sing in praise of *Seyāl* for a good meal (খাবার আগে বলরে দাদা/জয় শেয়ালের জয় [*khābār āge balore dādā/jai Seyāler jai*]). At the top left corner of the frame, *Seyāl*'s snout is just visible as he peers out of the window and dumps a pile of left-over fish bones into the bin below. The cats dive in and gorge themselves, having eked out this charitable donation from the proverbial trickster himself by means of their sycophantic singing. The final frame shows the cats prostrated by the bin with bulging bellies; they sing out a warning, that if they ask for such charity when they are hungry *again* (খেতে পাইনি বোলে চাঁদা চাইলে পুনর্ব্বার; [*khete paini bole cāṁdā/cāile punarbār*]), they will be thrown out by the scruff of their necks, or simply beaten (গলা ধাক্কা দেবে কিম্বা/স্রেফ লাগাবে মার [*galā dhākkā debe kimbā/sreph lāgābe mār*]) (*Jugantar*, 7.47 (6 November 1943): 7).[18] A week later, on 11 November, another caricature appeared, this time more visibly on centre front page, above a report on the Commons debate on the famine.[19] The cartoon, titled "পার্লামেন্টে দুর্ভিক্ষ [Famine in Parliament]", showed an abandoned parliament session, with empty seats and a few scattered figures weeping helplessly into their handkerchiefs. Signs in the background say "Members: 600" and "Present: 35". A placard lies flat on the table which reads "বাঙলায় দুর্ভিক্ষের জন্য বিশেষ অধিবেশন [Special Session for the Famine in Bengal]" (*Jugāntar*, 7.52 (11 November 1943): 1). Such representations do not simply suggest nationalist outrage and demand for welfare from a colonial state that appeared brutally forgetful, but a concerted scrutiny and interrogation of the paradoxes driving this famine, often with self-directed irony.

Amidst the contesting perspectives of relief workers, doctors, nutrition scientists, journalists, cartoonists, nationalists, and politicians, the expectation of a magic solution was sharply satirised in a sketch in the 7 November 1943 edition of *The Hindustan Times*. The illustration showed half-naked skeletal figures of natives queuing before a rotund officer (strangely reminiscent, despite his modern suit, of *Oliver Twist*'s Mr Bumble), who, elevated upon a stool, holds a large bottle in one hand, and with the other administers drops of the miraculous medicine straight into open starving mouths, with a look of benevolent assuredness. At the other end of this production line, the bodies of the starving emerge transformed into a state of obesity. Behind the official, in a corner, a Chinese man in traditional dress holds out his hand, with a speech bubble, "Spare one for me, Brother". The caption above the sketch mockingly reported that "masses of walking skeletons" in Bengal would be turned into "living masses of flesh" by means of "Vitamin 'A' pills … coming from London".

Meanwhile, in Britain, the controversies of post-war food rationing and austerity policy and practice were imminent (Zweiniger-Bargielowska, 2000), and old and familiar arguments about "cultures of dependency", "loss of self-reliance", and "the value of work" were about to resurface in ways that might be worthy of representation in the mode of Dickensian macabre. Perhaps the value of our shared ghosts of famines past lies in their capacity to recall lessons in food insecurity that are yet to be learnt, and to suggest that "hunger's demise" is not only a slow but an uncertain end.

Notes

1 I use the term "self-fashioning" in Stephen Greenblatt's sense of the "fashioning of human identity as a manipulable, artful process" (1980: 2). While Greenblatt and others have applied this to English and European contexts in particular, it is also applicable (bearing in mind cultural specificities) to literary contexts outside Europe.

2 As the Bengali journalist Tushar Kanti Ghosh observed while reporting on the 1943 Bengal famine, "A child here or there, dead or dying from starvation, has been removed from the pavement. Had the child parents? ... What hunger can do to break the most sacred and loving ties well-fed people cannot imagine" (1944: 35).

3 See Datta, Chapter 2 of this book, where he itemises degrees of shortage across the eighteenth century, for Bengal; Bhattacharya, Chapter 5, identifies the Company official's call for state relief as the indicator marking the turning point from acute dearth to a famine situation. On the issues that arise while attempting distinctions, especially in the early modern world, where precise data is hard to find, see Hoskins (1964); Walter and Schofield (1989).

4 In the early modern English context, for example, the history and literature of famine and dearth was shaped by wider social issues, such as marriages, kinship patterns, formal welfare provision through poor laws, informal structures of charity, household management, and popular protest (Kussmaul, 1985: 1–30; Wrigley and Schofield, 1981: 421–2; Wrightson, 1980: 176–91; Sharpe, 1998: 62; Hindle, 2004: 21; 2008; Mukherjee, A., 2015).

5 The changing definitions of "food security" can be traced through the following documents. It was defined in 1974 in the *Universal Declaration on the Eradication of Hunger and Malnutrition* at the first World Food Conference convened by the UN. For further definitions that have evolved since, see *World Food Summits* (FAO, 1996 and 2002), *Declaration of the World Summit on Food Security* (FAO, 2009), FAO *et al.*, *The State of Food Insecurity in the World* (2012).

6 On European famines, there are recent, thought-provoking overviews by Cormac Ó Gráda (2010, 2015), and Alfani and Ó Gráda (2017). On famines as accelerators of disparity and the creation of the "Third World", see David Arnold (1988) and Mike Davis (2002).

7 A recent investigation of the documentation of famine and dearth in historical and literary sources corroborates this striking correlation between India and Britain across two and a half centuries: *Famine and Dearth* (2016).

8 On famine mortality and climate in India, post-1800, see especially the figures in Davis (2002: 2, 247).

9 On the better-known nineteenth-century famines, see Davis, 2002; Arnold, 1988, 1993; Sharma, 2001; Mukherjee, U., 2013. The experience of food

shortage, however, did not disappear from Britain, as demonstrated in studies of the history of hunger (Newman, 1990, rev. 1995: 213–80; Schofield in Rotberg and Rabb, 1985: 67–93; Scholl, 2016; Vernon, 2007).

10 Among many studies of this topic, see reflections in Driver (1993) and Englander (2013).

11 The figure is similar to the estimated deaths in Gujarat in the early 1630s, though considerably less than the estimated deaths of 10 million in Bengal during the dearth and famine years of 1769–72.

12 See especially *The Calcutta Gazette*, Supplements, 1943: 13 (1 April), pp. 295–300, 14 (8 April), pp. 319–22, 15 (15 April), pp. 353–6, 16 (22 April), pp. 379–98; 17 (29 April), pp. 509–10, 27 (8 July), pp. 1333–6, 34 (26 August), pp. 1501–4, 36 (16 September), pp. 1529–34).

13 In the collection of essays, *Hunger in History*, Kates and Millman suggest a "middle ground" approach which seeks "hunger's demise", while acknowledging that "further progress will require fundamental change in structures, institutions, and values" (1995: 406). The question is whether the fundamental values that define progress itself need to change.

14 For other arguments on the emergence of hunger as a moral imperative, see Laqueur, 1989; Haskell, 1992; Boltanski, 1999: 170–92; Edkins, 2000.

15 See useful discussion on humanitarian action and desire in Boltanski, esp. 188–90.

16 *The Statesman* newspaper in Calcutta published some of the earliest photographs (22 August 1943), and some of the special correspondents' narratives were printed as books: Freda Bedi, *Bengal Lamenting* (1944); K. Santhanam, *The Cry of Distress* (1944); Santosh Kumar Chaterjee, *The Starving Millions* (1944). An account of the famine, *The Bengal Tragedy*, by the editor of *Jugāntar* and *Amrita Bazar Patrika*, Tushar Kanti Ghosh, was also published in 1944. As Ghosh complained, despite the rapidly increasing deaths, "not a mouse stirs in London or Washington" (1944: 35).

17 See, for example, the well-known Bengali author Bankim Chandra Chattopadhyay's dark parody of the creation of the modern Bengali intellectual (imbued, by the "redbearded savant" Creator, with "slyness from the fox", among other qualities) in his essay *Anukaran* ("Imitation", 1872), in *Bankim Rachanavali*, II: 198–207.

18 On ways in which "local town humour" drew upon a Bengali satirical literary tradition of self-directed irony, see Kaviraj, 2000.

19 The *Jugāntar* report, titled "কমন্স সভায় ভারত প্রসঙ্গ: দুর্ভিক্ষ সম্পর্কে মিঃ আমেরিকে প্রশ্ন [India Matters in the Commons Session: Questions to Mr Amery [Secretary of State for India] regarding the famine]", summarised the discussion in the House of Commons on 11 November 1943 (see Hansard, *Commons*, 1943, vol. 393, cols. 1278–81, nos. 40–4).

Part I

Historical interpretations

1 Famine and food security in early modern England

Popular agency and the politics of dearth

John Walter

Famine had been a recurring reality in medieval England, and it was an ever-present fear in early modern (sixteenth- and seventeenth-century) England. A state that lacked a standing army and professional police force feared the disorder that dearth was inevitably thought to bring in a world in which, it was proverbially believed, "hunger will break through stone walls" (Tilley, 1950: 333). Nevertheless, despite demographic evidence of the reality of crisis mortality, England in this period did not experience a breakdown in the social order. Famine was regionally selective and of diminishing impact after the crisis of 1622/23; a social economy continued to operate in which for the fortunate a preference for food security was written into many economic relationships; the reciprocities of "commonwealth", not the profits of commodity, retained diminishing, but at times of harvest failure, continuing importance in the mental and normative world of early modern society, upholding the importance of charity and informal relief and regulating, to some degree, an economy in which rising agricultural productivity underwrote a surprisingly responsive system of crisis relief. Famously (and controversially) a moral economy shared between Crown and crowd meant that popular protests were fewer than expected and that in their disciplined exercise of (often symbolic) violence and preference for negotiation they failed to conform to the elite-inspired stereotype of collective theft with violence. In offering an overview of responses to problems of food security in early modern England, this chapter argues for the importance of popular agency in the politics of dearth in maintaining in the face of economic and social change forms of societal and governmental responses that offered protection against subsistence crises.

Famine and social and economic change in early modern England

In 1965, Peter Laslett famously asked: did the English peasant really starve? (Laslett, 1965). Like elsewhere in Europe, England had a history of famine which extended back into the Middle Ages. An imbalance between the pressure of population growth and an insufficiently responsive food supply precipitated the Great Famine of 1315–17. This was perhaps the worst subsistence crisis in England's recorded history in which an estimated half a million people, something like 10 per cent of the population, died (Ó Gráda, 2015: 9–5; Dyer, 1998: 61). Renewed population growth, accelerating by the later sixteenth century, caused renewed subsistence crises. These peaked nationally in the 1590s, when in the harvest year 1596/97, a year which witnessed the most severe increase in food prices for the entire period 1541–1871, mortality was some 25 per cent above trend, and continued in some regions into the 1620s (Walter and Schofield, 1989: 34).

Subsequent work has shown, however, that the answer to Laslett's original question was more complicated and nuanced than once thought. By the period at which parochial registration of vital events begins (the midsixteenth century), years of high food prices were already not always years of mortality crises.[1] Famine had always been regionally pronounced. It became increasingly so. For example, in the crisis of 1596/97, only a little under a fifth of parishes under observation registered mortality crises (Wrigley and Schofield, 1981: 319–35, 645–93).[2] By the time of the next major crisis, in 1623–24, communities registering harvest-related mortality crises were now confined to the northern section of England's highland zone (north Lancashire, Cumberland and Westmorland) (Appleby, 1978; Hoyle, 2010). Thus, by the mid-seventeenth century, England's experience diverged from other famine-prone regions in the British Isles, in Scotland and Ireland and in continental Europe as the relationship between harvest failure and crisis mortality weakened. Despite three successive years of harvest failure, the death rate was actually below trend in the later 1640s, and this despite England being engaged in civil war. Although there was evidence of widespread suffering among the region's poor, even those areas scarred by crises of subsistence were now free of such crises, including the previously vulnerable north-west, which were no longer registering crises of subsistence (Healey, 2014). By the "hungry 1690s", a period of harvest-related crisis throughout Europe, the relationship between high food prices and mortality in England had become muted. In a decade with some of the sharpest falls in a 300 year index of real wages, death rates never rose more than 6 per cent above, and actually fell below, trend in the years at the end of that decade (Walter and Schofield, 1989: 35–6).

If England escaped famine, then in the longer term economic changes played the larger role in explaining that escape. Improvements in agricultural productivity, storage and distribution, helped to lift the threat of national famines by stabilising food prices and moderating the exogenous shock of extreme weather events (Wrightson, 2000). By the mid-seventeenth century, better crop mixes had broken the symmetrical price structure in which harvest failure usually brought a sharp increase in the price of all grains (Appleby, 1979). At the same time, expanding international trade made it possible to access foreign, notably east European, grain (Zins, 1972; Federowicz, 1980).

But in the short run this was a period marked by paradox. In a transitional period, economic change undermined traditional practices whose logic had in part been to ensure resilience in agricultural output. The increasing commercialisation of agriculture and consequent commodity relations undercut practices designed to secure subsistence security and so exposed producers and consumers to economic, as well as "natural", risk. Thus, economic change, while ultimately increasing agricultural productivity to the point that later seventeenth century England could become a net exporter of grain, also *increased* the vulnerability of some regions. That famine was most marked and lasted longest in England's highland, above all north-western, zone was a product of *new* patterns of regional specialisation attendant upon agrarian capitalism. Years of harvest failure, penalising the region's focus on livestock production and dependence on bought-in grain, brought a collapse in trade entitlements (Appleby, 1978). Nationally, the growth in the number of land-poor and landless now forced to buy their food in the market made food security a pressing problem, making them more vulnerable to the doubling or even trebling of food prices that harvest failure brought in this period of transition.

At the same time, a more gradual change, which emphasised the *economic* imperative in relationships between landlord and tenant, master and employees, producers and consumers, threatened to undercut traditional practices that had offered the harvest-sensitive access to food independent of the market. In altering the calculus of the rates of exchange embedded within these relationships, this weakened resources on which the harvest-sensitive had been able to draw to meet the challenge of harvest failure. For an increasing number, poverty and landlessness threatened their very participation in these circuits of exchange. At the same time, a challenge to traditional thinking about the role of charity and hospitality also threatened to deny the poor what protection these had offered in the face of harvest failure. All of these changes took place gradually and none of them were universally complete by the end of the early modern period (Waddell, 2012). In the face of these changes it was popular pressure within the politics of subsistence that was important in maintaining relationships and strategies by which the harvest sensitive could continue to access food at times of harvest failure.

Food security, risk insurance and the social economy of dearth

If famine, defined demographically as subsistence crises, was absent at an early date from many areas in England, and no longer even a regional problem after the mid-seventeenth century, this did not mean that the *fear* of famine had receded. Although the death rate proved surprisingly unresponsive in the crisis of the 1690s, it was not until the mid-1740s that the link between prices and mortality finally disappeared. Harvest failure remained a recurring risk, one whose occurrence could be anticipated but never accurately predicted (Hoskins, 1964, 1968; Harrison, 1971). Denied the twenty-twenty vision of the historian's hindsight, it was therefore the memory of *past* famines (and, for a society that knew its bible, biblical famines) that informed the thinking of both early modern government and people about the problem of food security.

The harvest was the heartbeat of the early modern economy and society. Its economic consequences were extensive in a pre-industrialised economy where agriculture was the major source of income for the majority of the population and the harvest the major determinant of levels of demand for non-agricultural production. It determined levels of prosperity and poverty. Chroniclers (and individuals) remembered and recorded events by reference to past famines, while almanacs and proverbial lore claimed to offer ways of predicting future scarcity. Diarists and writers of annals anxiously noted unusual weather patterns – in the temperate zone, in what has been called the Little Ice Age, it was predominantly cold springs and wet summers, rather than drought, that delayed and damaged the harvest. In a society which prayed "give us this day our daily bread" and where bread remained literally the staff of life, contemporaries recorded with alarm spiralling prices in the market. In a discourse of dearth, poets and dramatists reflected the psychic hold harvest failure had on contemporaries and the threat hunger posed to both individuals and society (Mukherjee, A., 2015).

Contemporaries were sensitive to the role played by the weather in creating scarcity, but both government and people focussed more on the role of human agency, in causing dearth and threatening or ameliorating famine. In this period, as both the church and its puritan critics preached, extreme weather was believed to be a providentialist intervention by an angry God intended to punish human failings and to call the people to repentance and reformation (Walsham, 1999). But if the weather caused scarcity, both government and people believed it was human action that threatened to turn scarcity into famine. High food prices were believed to be the result of covetousness and corrupt practices in the storing, movement and marketing of grain. These contravened laws to police the grain market and disregarded the moral code that sought to uphold, in the face of changing economic imperatives, a Christian ethic that was meant to regulate personal and communal relationships. This held that it was a God-given duty to place poor before profit.[3] Reinforced by civic humanism, the protean idea of society and polity as a commonwealth made monarchs and magistrates responsible for the well-being of fellow men and women. Hence, harvest failure in early modern England was the focus of a politics of subsistence in which both the causes and consequences of dearth (and even the discourses within which this politics was conducted) were contested. Thus, it was contemporary *beliefs* about the causes and character of dearth that informed policies and practices to prevent or ameliorate famine.

At the beginning of the early modern period, there was a surprising degree of consensus between government and people about the causes of dearth and the policies for its prevention and mitigation. Both subscribed to an explanation of dearth that moralised its causes. They placed the emphasis on malpractices in the marketing of grain by those the government labelled "greedy cormorants" that produced, in the contemporary phrase, "want amidst plenty". E. P. Thompson famously wrote about the "moral economy" of the eighteenth-century crowd, "a popular consensus as to what were legitimate and what were illegitimate practices" in the marketing and processing of grain which "can be said to constitute the moral economy of the poor" (Thompson, 1971: 78–9). In the early modern period, this was a view of the proper ordering of the economy shared by both government and people.

Nevertheless, differing priorities meant that there was always a potential tension in the relationship between government and people over the question of food security. For governments and for elites, who continued to believe that harvest failure automatically threatened to mobilise "the many-headed monster" of the people in "revolts of the belly", questions of food security remained central to the maintenance of the political and social order. For the poor and harvest-sensitive, the threat of hunger in years of harvest failure (with its causal link to trade depression) ensured that food security remained a pressing problem. Over time, there was a shift in government economic policy in pursuit of national food security from prohibitive to permissive, permitting enclosure and land re-organisation in agriculture and promoting a free market in grain. This increased tensions between government and people.

Given the recurring reality of harvest failure, food security was problematic in a society where surpluses offered a narrow margin between sufficiency and want, where the storage of grain was problematic, and the possibilities of carry-over from good to bad years therefore limited. That harvest time was usually a time of higher wages, better food and extravagant commensality in food and drink made the inversion of harvest failure harder to bear. In the face of the threat of famine, contemporaries had to pursue a range of survival strategies. Food substitution – trading down in grains and making use of grain substitutes, such as lentils and beans, usually used as animal feed – was perhaps the most common adaptive strategy. As a contemporary proverb had it, "hunger setteth his first foot into the horse manger" (Harrison, 1587: 133). But the result was that it was the cheapest grains that recorded the highest rise in prices.

Doubtless, the poor were driven to eat foods otherwise proscribed by the contemporary dietary code. But in comparison with other famine-prone societies, and particularly England's Celtic neighbours, we know less about the tradition of "need foods". This perhaps reflects the earlier escape from famine in England. That bread was baked from a meal ground from amongst other things from acorns and roots offers some evidence of their use (Camporesi, 1989; Lucas, 1959; Mukherjee, A., 2015: 162–3; Platt, 1596: A4r, B2r, C1v; Sayce, 1953/54). It also serves as a reminder that dearth and famine were also experienced as a cultural shock. Early modern England fell into the broader north European farinaceous dietary zone in which bread formed the largest part of the daily diet in a Christian culture in which people prayed, "give us this day our daily bread". Given the intimate relationship between human identity and culturally valorised foods, complaints from the poor about being forced to consume food normally fed to animals, or breaking unwritten, but important, taboos on eating pets, to eat cats and dogs, as well as reports of cannibalism in *past* famines, served to express the people's anger at their treatment and to underscore the unnaturalness of their condition (The National Archives, SP 12/188/47; Thomas, 1983: 115–16; Marvin, 1998). Food security was measured on a cultural as well as a calorific scale.

Food security and risk-insurance informed many of what can be seen as traditional subsistence practices that were to be labelled by later agricultural improvers as inefficient. For example, the logic of open-field agriculture with communal organisation of the agricultural calendar and farming practices, crop diversification and dispersal of individual holdings in multiples strips across all soil types and sowing seasons, might be seen in terms of a subsistence-sufficiency orientation. Now thought to be potentially more productive than contemporary critics and earlier historians thought, traditional agricultural practice sought the minimisation of risk, rather than the maximisation of profit (Walter, 1989: 93–4).

Beyond this, a variety of societal practices within what might be called the social economy of dearth offered some insulation against harvest failure, providing varying degrees of privileged access to food independent of the market. Within this social economy, rates of exchange in what would now be seen as economic relations reflected their value as forms of "life insurance". To the extent they survived the shock of harvest failure, all offered a degree of protection against the failure in exchange entitlements that Amartya Sen has argued prevents the poor from securing food, even in famines in which it was human action, rather than absolute scarcity, that caused problems of food availability (Sen, 1981a). The access to food these practices offered meant that even in commercialising economies like early modern England the impact of dearth cannot simply be read off from the indices of wage rates and price series.

Within the manorial system, the "right" of the poor to glean for grain after the harvest and of skilled specialists in husbandry to cultivate small amounts of land on which to grow food or to a share of the animals they raised were valuable perquisites. More generally, the ability to purchase food at concessionary, "farm-gate" prices, to take wages partly in kind, or for live-in servants in husbandry (perhaps some 40 per cent of the rural labour force) to be fed at their employer's table, mitigated the impact of dearth. Credit, in which the *social* credit of the recipient often determined its availability, might also allow some to ride out the crisis of harvest failure: rent remittance or carry-over of arrears for fortunate tenants, or neighbourly loans in kind for others. Food could be exchanged on credit for later repayment or future labour (Walter, 1989: 96–105, 112).

Informal relief was also important and potentially available to more people. The provision of grain or bread in times of dearth was part of an expected relationship between elite and poor, in a society in which in which the importance of charity was upheld by the church and claims to liberality and magnanimity were considered a defining characteristic of their status by members of the landed class (Heal, 1990; Heal and Holmes, 1994). Promptings of church and conscience, as well as government recommendations for the gentry to return to their estates to exercise hospitality among their tenants and the poor, upheld charity as a Christian duty. Though we should not mistake prescription of noble charity as evidence for its practice, it was apparently more common in years of harvest failure, and where it was practiced examples suggest that in conditions of dearth its value to the harvest-sensitive could be very important (Walter, 1989: 106–10).

The continuing importance of charity, insistently urged in preaching campaigns ordered by the government in years of harvest failure, help to explain why, for example, in years of dearth there was some loosening of prohibitions on begging. Similarly, the ordering of collective ceremonies of repentance and (weekly) fasting to propitiate a jealous God, the *primum mobile* of weather shocks, was also designed to save grain with which to feed the poor (Hindle, 2001; Walter, 1989: 112–13). Such actions were doubtless intended as symbolic statements intended to assert social cohesion in the face of the stark inequalities that harvest failure revealed. But that the government expected to be able to recommend days when households should fast and on which householders should invite their poorer neighbours to eat with them underlines the continuing force of such ideas. By its very nature, informal relief is hard to quantify, but examples multiplied in years of dearth, and some indication of its overall importance is suggested by the fact that up until the later eighteenth century charity perhaps provided as much relief as the poor law (Slack, 1990: 41–4).

It was a contemporary trope, to be found in a literature of complaint that ran from popular verse to godly sermons, that compared to a previous (and mythical) golden age charity was in decline. Perhaps it had been ever thus. But while some contemporaries believed this, moralists and governments continued to urge the importance of charity in combatting dearth. In years of dearth the people were then able to exploit the social consensus, upheld by the actions of the state and the preachings of the church, that required the rich to relieve the poor. In a period in which some questioned the appropriateness of indiscriminatory aid, and where there was a trend towards making its application both discretionary and discrim-inatory, popular pressure drew on the force of such ideas to help the propertied "remember" their Christian duties (and past food crises) at a moment of maximum pressure on their own resources. That such entreaties appealed to commonly-held norms made them harder to resist. But there were additional sanctions. In the mental world of early modern England, it was still widely believed that God would intervene to punish those who failed to relieve the poor. Divine judgements on covetous and greedy hoarders of grain were the subject of both sermons and popular ballads. Their common message was that God hears *and* answers "the poor's moan" (Walter, 2001).

Appeals for relief couched in the language of moral obligation could take a variety of forms. Wherever food was in circulation, for example the market place or mill (or even at household doors at meal times), this created sens-itive sites where public grumbling by the poor could air their grievances and bring pressure to bear on the controllers of surpluses. Contemporary descrip-tions of market places in conditions of scarcity record the disorderly snatch-ing and unruliness and verbal spats between sellers and frustrated purchasers and hint at the latent violence present there. Grumbling critical of the magis-trates' inactivity or the rich's lack of charity might shade into verbal or written threats, while petitions also hinted at the threat of violence which – of course – the petitioners claimed to want to prevent (Walter, 2001: 128–46). The cir-culation of written libels, what E. P. Thompson called the "crime of ano-nymity", left in sensitive sites like the local parish church, allowed threats of violence to be made more explicit (Thompson, 1975). As Hugh Platt, author of *Sundry New and Artificial Remedies against Famine* counselled, if Christian charity was not sufficient reason to remember the poor,

> yet reason and civill policy might prevaile so much with us for our selves and those which are deare unto us, that we should not stay so long until our neighbours flames take holde of our owne houses, nor try the extremities that hunger, and famine may work amongst us.
>
> (Platt, 1596: A3v)

Such threats had to be negotiated by controllers of food surpluses in years of dearth when tensions were high and protection for property holders limited and in a society where the church and state continued to under-write the right to subsistence in language stressing both compassion and obligation.

The politics of harvest failure: protest, popular agency and state intervention

The micro-politics of dearth might secure the defence of the protection afforded by relationships and practice within the social economy locally.

But if the poor and harvest-sensitive were not to starve then this needed a redistribution of surplus in quantities that required the active intervention of authorities. It was fear of the *political* threat that hunger posed to the social and political order that gave the people their political leverage. That the poor would riot in the face of harvest failure was a commonplace in early modern society. "Nothing will sooner lead men to sedition than dearth of victuals", observed Elizabeth I's leading minister (Walter, 1989: 76). "Necessity hath no law" ran a popular proverb (Tilley, 1950: 493). This was a statement seemingly validated in this period by the evidence of a sharp increase in prosecuted crime in years of harvest failure. These thefts of often pathetically small amounts of food by vulnerable men and women probably underestimated the "dark figure" of appropriation occurring in years of dearth, reflecting as they did an uneasy balance between the desire to use the sanction of the law to protect property against the need to avoid the unpopularity that recourse to law threatened (Walter and Wrightson, 1976: 24–5; Lawson, 1986). But they offered an uncomfortable reminder of the belief, once strong in medieval scholastic circles but occasionally surfacing in this period, that hunger and a God-given right to subsistence dissolved rights of property (Swanson, 1997).

It was the threat that hunger would lead to revolt which provided the strongest incentive to try to relieve the poor. The later British famine codes in India used outbreaks of disorder as an early warning signal for famine. In its description of past famines, the 1880 Indian Famine Commission Report gives many examples of public unrest. In 1836, in the Western Provinces, for example, "violent agrarian disturbances and robberies of grain carts and grain stores were so rife that troops had in several cases to be called out" (Part 1: 11).[4] Similar worries appear to have prevailed and influenced famine policy in early modern England. While episodes involving crowds usually saw the central government's call for their punishment tempered by the local authority's desire not to further exacerbate tensions, they invariably led to orders to see the poor relieved. Despite the fact that explanations of dearth, held by the people and endorsed by the government, highlighted hoarding, it was the movement of grain out of the local economy against which collective protests were directed (Boshstedt, 2010; Clark, 1976; Hipkin, 2008; Walter, 2006: chs. 2–3; Walter, 2015). Individuals who turn up in criminal records prosecuted for trying to turn the crowds' anger against the rich and to lead attacks on their houses and granaries found few followers. Crowd actions over food sought to defend local priorities in the marketing of grain.

There was a patterning to the geography of crowd actions over food. In some regions crowds were noticeably absent, either because their local ecology did not produce grain surpluses or promote the movement of grain against which crowd actions were directed, or because the popular explanation for dearth in some regions, like the English Midlands, focused on enclosure in agriculture, against which protests were directed, rather than the activities of middlemen in the market. Where crowds did appear this reflected the weaknesses in a developing but as yet immature national market in grain and the points of tension that the commercialisation of agriculture and regional specialisation exposed. Crowd actions were located in regions from or through which grain was moved to feed the larger cities, in particular Bristol in the West Country, Norwich in East Anglia and above all London.[5] They took place in market towns and ports whose local markets were being subverted, becoming bulking centres for larger urban middlemen. By the later seventeenth century, continued urban expansion and new areas of rapid growth like Birmingham in the industrialising Midlands saw lines of urban supply, and with them crowd actions, ripple further out (Beloff, 1963).

Collective protests also took place in areas of rural industrialisation, above all the cloth industry, through which grain was being moved to the cities. Predominantly located in grain deficient pastoral areas, the question of food security was most acute for the large populations of landless or land-poor workers plunged into poverty by harvest failure. Without reserves and dependent on the market for both employment and food, they simultaneously faced high prices and mass unemployment, since the impact of higher food prices on disposable income quickly cut demand for their products and encouraged the withdrawal of mercantile circulating capital, leaving the producers in their cottages to bear the economic brunt of the crisis. To the extent that rural industrial development took place in areas not favoured by the gentry for the location of their households and where, therefore, a magistracy recruited from the landed class was not available to police local markets or to initiate relief measures, this also helps to explain why it was often the crowd in these regions that first took action against what they saw as the causes of dearth (Walter, 2006: 43–4, 71–2).

Crowd actions were an expression of the popular anger and fear that dearth caused. Where crowds assembled, their anger was directed at the corrupt practices which they (and authority) believed sought to create an artificial scarcity in order to profit from their suffering. But crowd actions were rarely a form of self-help. The amount of grain crowd members could have seized was limited and one consequence of such actions might have been to drive away the middlemen on which some harvest-sensitive areas relied for their supply. There was a question of scale here. Since rural industrial workers might also rely on smaller middlemen for the provision of grain, it was the activities of large city middlemen and, above all, foreign merchants, which particularly aroused popular anger.

While crowd actions were, therefore, a form of direct action to attempt to stop an immediate grievance, they were also an attempt to negotiate with authority. Their rhetoric of violence was an invitation to action on the part of the authorities rather than a call to arms. Since public pronouncements appeared to endorse the popular reading of the causes of dearth, the crowds' anger might be directed against the authorities for their failure to take the measures their own explanation of the causes of dearth required. As such, the stereotype of such actions as food riots – collective theft with violence – does scant justice to the complex and often subtle actions employed by the protesting crowds. Middlemen were attacked when it was clear that they were moving grain *out* of the local market or economy; ships' sails were removed and would-be exporters "fined"; grain was seized, rather than stolen, and either sold in a form of *taxation populaire* at below famine prices or returned to the authorities as a pointed reminder that they should have prevented the illicit movement of grain under the policy ordered by the Book of Orders. That these tactics mimicked actions prescribed by the government's dearth policy was deliberate. Crowds drew on authority's own publicly proclaimed policies in order to coerce the authorities and to signal their belief in the legitimacy of their own actions.

Years of harvest failure in early modern England were, however, not marked by frequent and widespread rioting. The absence of a standing army or professional police force with which to repress popular protest meant that early modern English governments were all too aware that they needed to anticipate and, if possible, pre-empt popular protest. Victims of their own belief in the volatility of the people, government and elite feared the "dangerous desperacy" (The National Archives, SP 14/138/35) unrelieved hunger and popular anger would create. If crowd actions were not more common in this period it was then because such was governmental sensitivity to the threat of disorder that actions short of collective violence, and which avoided the sanctions of the law, might trigger relief measures. A tradition of popular petitioning allowed the poor, individually or collectively, in person or in writing, to appeal more formally to magistrates for relief. These petitions, sometimes presented by large and importunate crowds, hinted at the violence that the lack of relief would bring (Hindle, 2008; Walter, 2001: 123–7, 137–9). Skilfully drafted in the language of the public transcript that government and elites advanced to legitimise power in their self-proclaimed duty to protect the subsistence of their subordinates, these sought to embarrass the authorities into taking action (Walter, 2015, 62–4). Such was the sensitivity that even lurid cases of seditious individuals reported to the king's council could trigger orders back into the regions to see the poor relieved.

It was a commonplace throughout early modern Europe that one of the monarch's prime responsibilities was to ensure the subsistence of their subjects. As Louis XIV noted, "the need for food is the first thing a prince should consider" (Tilly, 1975: 447). Failure to do so might see criticism of the monarch memorialised in the naming of episodes of famine after inept kings (Ó Gráda, 2009: 196). When in the 1690s Scotland experienced one of its worst famines, these were labelled "King Williams's Ill years" (Cullen, 2010: 29). Early modern English governments had developed a range of policies by which to police the grain market and, in years of harvest failure, to ensure poorer consumers access to grain (Slack, 1980; 1988: 138–48; Outhwaite, 1991).

Codified by the later sixteenth century in what came to be called "Books of Orders", they clearly predated this. Printed to be distributed to provincial and local authorities, these established an elaborate policy to address the problem of dearth by policing the movement and marketing of grain. Regular reports on food stocks were to be sent to central government (Langelüddecke, 1998). Justices of Peace in the counties and boroughs were to ensure that laws regulating the activities of "badgers" – middlemen in the grain trade – were enforced in order to prevent hoarding or forestalling markets and regrating (purchasing to later sell at a higher price). Magistrates were to conduct grain surveys and to assign those with surpluses to bring specified amounts of grain regularly to local markets. Within price levels set by statute, they were also to prevent the illegal export of grain in years of harvest failure. There the magistrates were to be personally present to ensure that poorer consumers were served first, in quantities small enough for them to purchase, and (more controversial this) at under-market prices.

Not surprisingly, some key aspects of these policies had been anticipated by city or town governments where the conjectural poor, those rendered vulnerable by the impact of harvest failure on both work and prices, might swell the already large body of structural poor to represent over half the urban population. Large urban centres raised funds to establish granaries to carry over stocks from good to bad years, as in the case of London, and in years of dearth to import foreign grain (Leonard, 1900, chs. 3, 7). These stocks might serve as equalisation funds to moderate high prices, but they might also be used to distribute grain at subsidised, under-market prices and in smaller urban centres even free as either grain or sometimes bread to the very poorest. Nevertheless, harvest failure severely tested the ability of the early modern urban authorities to finance these schemes (Nielsen, 1997).

The poor law represented a second resource to mitigate the impact of harvest failure and on which the poor might draw (Hindle, 2004; Slack, 1988, 1990, 1999; Smith, 2011). Again, it is clear that, as with the Book of Orders policy, parishes had been establishing compulsory collection-based provision for the poor from at least the mid-sixteenth century (and in the more prosperous south-east and eastern counties even earlier) (McIntosh, 2014; Smith, 2015). Codified in legislation at the end of the sixteenth century, the poor law established, at least in theory, a national system of a rate-based poor relief and at the local level of the parish a set of officials responsible for collecting the rate and relieving (and disciplining) those designated the poor. In normal years the collection of an annual or bi-annual rate was used mainly to provide occasional payments to the sick, orphans and the elderly and more regular payments to a small group of pensioner poor, in which widows predominated – those groups subsequent research has shown to be most vulnerable to famine. But in dearth years, in the countryside, as well as in the towns, a developing poor law worked alongside the policy of the Book of Orders to make provision for those unable to purchase their food. Poor law collections were used to fund the purchase and distribution of grain or bread to the much larger numbers of harvest-sensitive, left poor by harvest failure and unable to produce or purchase sufficient food. Local records show parishes in years of dearth collecting multiple rates in order to be able to fund such relief.

The patchwork geography to the introduction of local poor law administration meant that, towns aside, it was more fully and earliest developed in the more prosperous south and east. This suggests that the longer persistence of famine in the highland zone may reflect not just weaknesses in local ecologies but also the greater poverty of these regions and consequent absence in some, but not even all of these communities, of what protection the poor law could provide, fatal to that group of insecure subtenants who have been shown to have been the primary victims of famine there (Healey, 2011). It is significant that an older policy of providing relief by permitting local begging by the community's resident poor persisted here after its suppression elsewhere and that, despite this, dearth years were marked by out-migration from these famine-prone areas in search of relief. Nevertheless, the valuable evidence of reports from the provinces to central government under the Book of Orders, as well as surviving local parish records, suggests that incremental improvement meant that by the mid-seventeenth century effective poor law administration had spread much more widely to include previously vulnerable regions (Healey, 2014). By at least the mid-seventeenth century, the resilience of local structures of relief meant that England (but not Scotland or Ireland) avoided for the most part the forced migrations of populations that elsewhere saw a fatal link between the social dislocation that famine produced and crowd diseases that proved far more deadly than outright starvation.

Government policy – the Books of Orders and the poor law – offered therefore an important resource to combat the immediate problem of food security in years of dearth, providing transfer payments between the propertied and the poor (Kelly and Ó Gráda, 2014: 375–8). But policy needed to be implemented, and there were tensions between policy and practice. For example, for early modern governments the priority of feeding and maintaining order in the capital saw them in years of harvest failure willing to ignore their own laws and permit the continuing movement of grain from countryside to city to feed London. A shared concern for the maintenance of order in years of harvest failure therefore saw the central government's priority to privilege feeding the larger towns and cities clash with the concern of provincial magistrates and the rulers of smaller market towns to protect the local market by banning the activities of large-scale urban middlemen in local markets. There were contradictions in implementing the government's dearth policy in a commercialising society with a significant urban sector and developing, but poorly integrated, national market that relied upon middlemen to move grain. These contradictions were compounded in areas of arable specialisation by a policy which required a landed magistracy whose rents and profits rested on the grain trade to implement regulation and ban exports. They might prove initially tardy in the recognition of a crisis and the implementation of the policies laid down under the Book of Orders. In such counties, actions against the middlemen necessary to carrying on a commercial trade in grain might be thought undesirable by both producers and magistracy. The legality of local magistrates setting the price of grain in the market place was also contested.

Popular agency was therefore often critically important in kick-starting the implementation of policies to regulate the markets and relieve the poor. Given the knowledge that harvest failure brought a sharp increase in those needing relief – as one anonymous libel reminded the authorities, "the PORe TheRe is MORe/Then Goes from dore to dore" – it was popular pressure that served to signal to central authority the onset of the occurrence of dearth locally and thus to prompt the implementation of the government's dearth policies (Walter, 2001, 142). It is significant that reports from local magistrates in arable counties like Norfolk, where crowd actions occurred, report the willingness of grain-producing communities to provide for the poor outside of the market and of middlemen in grain to set aside a portion of the grain traded in the market to be sold to the poor at under-market prices.

Conclusion

While weaknesses in local ecologies, vulnerable surpluses and poor and unfavourable market integration explain the occurrence of famine, in the longer run better market integration and improved agricultural yields, when married with the controls on population growth to be found in England's "low-pressure" demographic regime, explain its disappearance. But in the interim the failure of agricultural output to keep pace with renewed population growth exacerbated problems of food security for the harvest-sensitive land-poor and labour-dependant social groups, whose numbers swelled in years of harvest failure. As a telling comparison with the causes of the more deadly medieval English famines makes clear (Slavin, 2014; Smith, 2015), it was the redistribution secured by a combination of the access to food to be found within the social economy of dearth and transfer payments under the poor law and the government's dearth policy that allowed England to escape crises of subsistence.

A recurring theme in the anthropology of famine is the resilience or otherwise of social structures and community relationships under pressure from harvest failure. In this respect it is worth emphasising that a combination of factors ensured that early modern English society survived the strains that atomisation of households and fraying of inter-personal and inter-household relationships that famine might elsewhere cause. Neighbourliness and reciprocity remained important for all because of England's particular, nuclear familial structure which made the community, not kin the immediate resource for those below the elite. The strategies discussed here were only able to work because harvest failure produced not absolute scarcity, but social and spatial shortages. The existence of a surplus, albeit a diminished one, meant that access to food for the harvest-sensitive might still be secured within the circuits of exchange within the social economy. Despite undoubted pressures in years of harvest failure, redistributive charity and other forms of informal relief never faced the uncomfortable challenge that absolute scarcity might have posed. At the same time, the organised transfer of reduced surpluses under the poor law and the government's dearth policy could take place because the structures of provincial and local and communal government were sufficiently developed and sturdy enough to withstand the dislocations that damaged other governments' attempts to manage famine. In the absence of a professional bureaucracy, the English Crown had developed an effective government down to the local level of the parish of self-government at the king's command by co-opting the support and social capital of provincial and local elites. The harvest-sensitive in early modern England survived dearth then by being able to marry together the protection offered by formal relief, charity and the informal practices and exchanges of the social economy which insulated many from the full impact of harvest failure within what has been called "the makeshift economy" by which the poor survived. Where these were challenged, then popular agency had a role to play in defending a "moral economy", prompting elites and government to renew practices and policies, something made easier for them by the fact that harvest failure was always a temporary crisis.

By the later seventeenth century, England had escaped famine. But this was not the case for her immediate neighbours of Scotland and Ireland, to whom it might be argued England successfully exported famine as a result of the unfavourable specialisation its growth prompted there (Crawford, 1989; Drake, 1968; Flinn, 1977). But this did not mean an end to the food insecurities that dearth caused. The disappearance of "crises of subsistence", precisely defined as a demographic measure, should not be allowed to obscure the fact that for many individuals the recurrence of harvest failure meant that hunger remained a very real threat. For England's poor, the silent violence of hidden hunger persisted. The fact that problems of food security continued to raise questions of political legitimacy made food a source of continuing contest between government and people.

Notes

1 Demographically, mortality crises are defined statistically as a sharp increase above the underlying death rate. Wrigley and Schofield (1981) define mortality crises as years with recorded deaths at least 10 per cent above a 25-year moving average.

2 The impact on nuptiality and fertility, it should be noted, was however stronger.

3 On the application of the doctrine of judgements to dearth, see Walter and Wrightson, 1976; and for an analysis of the rhetoric of famine sermons and their blending of Biblical and practical exempla, see discussion of Lavater and Barlow, 1596, in Mukherjee, A., 2015: 21–30.

4 During the Madras Presidency famine of 1854, the Commission further reported that "crowds of applicants [for famine employment and relief] flocked in from the Nizam's dominions" for nine months (Part 1: 11). Similarly, in 1868–69, relief houses in British cantonments in Rajputana struggled to accommodate the numbers of applicants "so great that it was found impossible to exercise proper supervision" (Part 1: 14). Such anxieties about disorder led to the 1880s' codifying of official approaches to addressing famine. Some of the complexities of administering, in India, officially approved forms of relief, based on models developed in early modern England and Victorian Britain, are discussed by Sharma in Chapter 7 of this book.

5 Early modern popular theatre engaged directly with specific instances of regional crowd action. See Fitter (2000) on Shakespeare's *Romeo and Juliet*, dearth and the London riots of the 1590s; and Hindle (2008) on *Coriolanus* and the Midlands Rising of 1607.

2 Subsistence crises and economic history

A study of eighteenth-century Bengal

Rajat Datta

Subsistence crises – dearth and famines – are often seen as exceptional occurrences, as severe dislocations in the "normal" run of things, or as aberrations. Their economic consequences are considered economic "excess" points – excess starvation, excess mortality and excess misery, without clarity about what constitutes the "normal". This distinction, not easily established even for modern eras, becomes more confounding when analysing such crises in the past. Amartya Sen's influential point of view stresses "entitlement" failures to explain these regressive departures from the normal; while Alamgir sees the prelude to starvation as an outcome of a tangible food availability decline, which is materially a more verifiable feature than an entitlement failure (Sen, 1981; Alamgir, 1980).[1] The latter's lack of empirical clarity becomes more accentuated in past (i.e. pre-colonial) contexts where social categories and their economic constituents are not adequately documented. Ó Grada has suggested, following Sen, that recent (modern?) famines differ from historic famines in the enhanced role of distributional shifts or entitlement losses, rather than output declines per se, in producing famine (Ó Grada, 2007: 10). This chapter will suggest that, on the contrary, evidence from the eighteenth century indicates both distributional shifts and entitlement losses wrought by the inability of consumers to buy their sustenance in a shortage-driven food-market.

Further, by highlighting the *economic content* of entitlement failures in more contemporary contexts, the entitlements approach allows an implicit assumption that subsistence crises in pre-colonial periods (broadly speaking) were failures engendered by the collapse of cultural norms of reciprocity, or other loosely non-market phenomena. While some of these features may have prevailed in past societies, this would be an unsustainable proposition during the early modern period (from the fourteenth to the nineteenth centuries) when economic and market networks had assumed remarkable densities across regions (Datta, 2014). In other words, the entitlement approach, while it indicates that famine or dearth induce economic malfunctions, does not suggest ways of studying, first, the exact *economic content* of such malfunctions, and second, the key elements which combined to trigger such abnormalities, and their sequences. The argument that this economic content can be worked out by examining colonial interventions, through devices such as regressive taxation or distorted commercialization, also provides a partial picture (Raj *et al.*, 1985; Damodaran, 2007).

It would be methodologically limiting to treat subsistence crises as the epiphenomena of mainstream economic history. Do subsistence crises have an economic history (like for instance the economic history of commodities or money)? Can they open explanatory vistas for the economic historian? I would argue that a serious scarcity (even if does not translate itself into a full-blown famine) unravels the economic structure in some fundamental ways. These episodes constitute entry points into the inner operations of the economy primarily because of what they reveal about the *economic fundamentals* of the society in the grip of such a crisis. They unpack factors relating to agricultural shocks and their economic context (the frequency and impact of crop failures, for instance) on the one hand, and those relating to human agency (the functioning of markets, war and social upheaval, public action, governance) on the other (Ó Grada, 2007: 6).

This information base then tells us about the economic structures of subsistence: production (because it has for some reason failed), circulation (because food hasn't reached the circulatory stage) and consumption (because not much is available). The three when combined reveal the interstices of the economy from the consumption side, particularly in pre-colonial systems where consumption data are meagre. In other words, *subsistence crises provide information on the economic history of subsistence* (as distinct from a subsistence economy), which has the following variables: market networks, money and exchange mechanisms (together constituting the commercial dimension) and price oscillations (determining purchasing power in real terms). While the largest numbers of famine victims usually came from the weakest sections of the population, the general impact of famine depended on the internal conditions of a place or region and on the specific causal sequences leading to the famine. This chapter will attempt to construct this economic history from the data on subsistence crises in eighteenth-century Bengal. Though the geographical and temporal boundaries are very specific, it is hoped that some of the inferences from the data may have larger resonances, particularly in the understanding the economics of pre-modern or early modern subsistence and consumption.

The context

Historically, famine and dearth were two distinct, though interrelated crises of survival. Famine was typically a situation when a subsistence and mortality crisis became combined in a critical conjuncture lasting for a length of time, which stretched beyond the critical threshold of a food shock. This reveals how famines exacted large death tolls, despite sometimes being regionally uneven in their spread; had weather as their proximate cause; and resulted in considerable loss of output, as reflected in sharp increases in food prices (Ó Grada, 2005: 146). These variables influenced the extent of both excessive starvation and excessive mortality in a famine. Dearth, on the other hand, constituted a more continuous saga of smaller scarcities. Although periods of dearth had lesser impact than famines, they were nevertheless important since their periodicity created major problems of subsistence among the harvest-sensitive strata (the artisans, labourers and the town poor), women and children in the household, as well as among a section of the peasantry, especially those who worked for wages or cultivated lands with inadequate resources (Datta, 1996). It has been suggested that although crises of subsistence have been identified through the combination of high mortality at a time of high prices, prices need not reflect availability if most of the population was not dependent on the market for food, or if there was a decline in purchasing power, or, more generally, exchange entitlement, in Sen's terms (cf. Cotts Watkins and Menken, 1985). This chapter suggests prices did reflect availability, and people starved, or died, because they couldn't afford to buy food at prevailing prices.

In other words, crises of subsistence, both dearth and famines, were severe dislocations in the "normal" run of things. Social perceptions classified various food-crises according to their scale and magnitude. Paul Greenough correctly states that there are cultural perceptions of prosperity, and conversely of adversity. In traditional Bengali society, such perceptions depended on the nature of the current paddy harvest and the ways in which different social groups were allowed access to it (Greenough, 1982: 42–52).[2] Yet, as I have argued elsewhere, dearth and famines were more than rude shocks to established cultural constructs of plenitude ("society's conception of the good life" (Greenough, 1982: 12)) and scarcity. They caused severe economic dislocations. Production faltered, prices soared and people died. Traditional means of support within the community no longer sufficed to maintain social bonds, or to alleviate the sufferings of the famine stricken (Datta, 2000: ch. 3). Table 2.1 shows the number of times the province was affected during the eighteenth century.

In order to contextualize the dynamics of subsistence and surplus consumption in eighteenth-century Bengal, as well as the economic implications of subsistence crises, one has to keep two specific aspects in mind: the first was its highly fluvial environment; the second, its great wet-rice producing economy. In 1656, the French traveller Francois Bernier, while describing the "beauty of Bengale", remarked that:

> throughout a country extending nearly a hundred leagues in length, on both banks of the Ganges, from Raje-Mehale [Rajmahal] to the sea, is an endless number of channels, cut, in bygone ages, from that

Table 2.1 Subsistence crises in eighteenth-century Bengal

Year	Type of calamity	Location	Symptoms
1711	Drought	West Bengal	Scarcity and deaths
1718	Drought	All-Bengal	Scarcity
1727	Drought	Unspecified	Price increase
1728	Drought	Unspecified	Scarcity
1732	Unspecified	Unspecified	Dearth
1734	Drought	All-Bengal	Scarcity
1737	Flood	West Bengal	Scarcity
1741	Flood	West Bengal	Mulberry crop was ruined
1742	Flood	Unspecified	Scarcity
1752–53	Flood	All-Bengal	Scarcity and death
1755	Flood	West Bengal	High price and scarcity
1761	Unspecified	West Bengal	High prices
1763	Flood	East Bengal	Scarcity and deaths
1767	Flood	East Bengal	Partial loss to crops
1767	Drought	West Bengal	Scarcity
1769–70	Drought	Regional	Famine, dearth, high mortality
1773/74	Drought/Flood	Regional	Dearth, high prices
1775	Drought	West Bengal	Partial scarcity high prices
1777	Drought	West Bengal	Harvest failure, dearth, high prices
1779	Drought	West Bengal	Crops destroyed, high prices and a famine panic
1783	Drought/Flood	Regional	Crop failure and "public scarcity"
1787–88	Flood	South and East Bengal	High mortality in the east
1791	Drought	West Bengal	Food shortage, high prices
1793	Drought	West Bengal	Similar symptoms as above

Source: Datta, 2000: 240, 243.

river with immense labour, for the conveyance of merchandise and of the water itself, which is reputed by the Indians to be superior to any in the world. These channels are lined on both sides with towns and villages, thickly peopled with Gentiles; and with extensive fields of rice, sugar, corn, sesame for oil, and small mulberry-trees, two or three feet in height, for the food of silk-worms.

(1972: 442; cf. Mukherjee, T., 2013)

Bernier's statement suggests a significant connection between fluvial-maritime channels of communication and the density of economic activity in seventeenth-century Bengal. The best confirmation of this comes in the mapping of Bengal rivers undertaken by James Rennell and published in the 1793 edition of his *Memoirs of a Map of Hindoostan*. According to Rennell,

The Ganges and the Burrampooter, together with their numerous branches and adjuncts intersect the country of Bengal […] in such a variety of directions, as to form the most complete and easy inland navigation that can be conceived. So equally and admirably diffused are these natural canals, over a country that approaches nearly to a perfect plane, excepting the lands contiguous to Burdwan, Birbhoom, etc. We may safely pronounce that every part of the country has, even in the dry season, some navigable stream within 25 miles at the farthest, and more commonly, within a third part of that distance. Nor will it be wondered at, when it is known, that all the salt and a large portion of the food consumed by ten million people are conveyed by water within the kingdom of Bengal and its dependencies. To these must be added the transport of the commercial exports and imports, probably to the amount of two million sterling per annum; the interchange of manufactures and products, throughout the whole country; the fisheries, and the articles of travelling.

(1793: 335)

One must however keep in mind that rivers changed courses, which could sometimes lead to moribundity in one place and a renewed fluviality in another (cf. Bhattacharya, Chapter 5 of this book). The Ganges shifted often. Its older arms like the Bhairab dried out, but it grew newer limbs in the form of Bhagirathi which was crucial in the ensuing prosperity of central and western Bengal. The Brahmaputra shifted eastwards and enabled the huge recharging of the Ganga-Padma estuary on which so much of Bengal's early modern maritime economy came to depend in the eighteenth century (Mukherjee, 1938: 7–8).

Despite these uncertainties, other observers largely corroborated Bernier and Rennell in underscoring the centrality of fluvial interconnections in Bengal's maritime vibrancy. In the entire belt stretching from Dhaka to Hughli which was subject to "seasonal inundations", the continuity of economic life was maintained by a seamless transfer from land to boats during the monsoon. For James Taylor, writing in 1840, the "abundance of the necessaries of life" in eastern Bengal was significantly due to the ease with which these could be transported to the markets on boats (294). In 1893, Thomas Twining noted how the innumerable rivers and natural canals that intersected the province "afforded a most extensive and convenient communication through the interior in every direction". From the "Jamuna to the Burrampooter" down to the Bay of Bengal, rivers comprised a grid by which "the productions of Europe, of China, and of the numerous islands in the Straits of Malacca" passed on to the "northern parts of Hindostan destined for every part of the world" (469). Walter Hamilton estimated that Bengal's rivers employed more than 300,000 boatmen on a continuous basis, *c.*1828 (186). The numbers would be substantially higher if we factor in those rivers which were only seasonally navigable.

Turning to the second aspect, the province's wet-rice producing economy,[3] we see that under normal circumstances, Bengal produced three rice harvests, *aman, boro* and *aus. Aman* was the winter harvest which was universally sown in the Bengali month of *Assar* (June–July) and harvested in *Agrahan* (November–December). This harvest was generally considered of great market value "bearing a higher price and sought after by all". The other major crop was that of *aus* (spring), sown in *Baisakh* (April–May) and reaped in *Bhadro* (August–September). Compared to the winter crop, the spring harvest was intrinsically inferior, being consumed overwhelmingly by the "lowest and poorest classes". *Boro* rice was an intermediate crop producing the coarsest quality rice, which was sown in *Chaitra* (March–April) on extremely low lands[4] and reaped in either *Assar* (June–July) or *Srawan* (July–August). Therefore, unlike the two major crops which required a gestation period of six months, the *boro* was a quick-ripening crop, capable of providing a harvest in four months (WBSA, BRP (G) 1: 17 October 1794).

In western Bengal, *boro* rice land was "the lowest admitting of cultivation", which "requires no manure, produces a constant succession of rice *ad infinitum*, without any discernible decrease of vegetative power, requiring only [to be] annually sown with successive varieties of grain" (OIOC, Ms. Eur. F. 95, f. 30; emphasis original). In the largely flat alluvial plains of southern and south-eastern Bengal, the same land was used to procure multiple crops of rice in succession. Thus, in Midnapur, *jala* land of the "1st kind … produces two crops of rice at the same time, the first called ause … and the other aumeen" (IOR, BRC, P/51/15, 28 January 1787). In eastern Bengal:

> The aumun crop being cut in Aughun [November–December], the Reapers scatter Khassarie [vetch] amongst the stubble, while the soil is yet moist and soft from the inundation, which springs up without any trouble, and is gathered in Phagun [February–March]. The stubble and stalk of the khassarie are then set on fire and the ashes ploughed in with the soil. The boro dhan [paddy] mixed with aumun is then sown; this [*boro*] being of very quick growth is ripe in Jeyte or Assar [May to July]; it is then cut and the aumun which is of slower growth rises with the water [i.e.the seasonal inundation] and is cut in Aughun [November–December].
>
> (IOR, BRC, P/51/40, 15 July 1789)

Turning to the question of consumption, there is enough evidence now to refute notions of self-sufficiency even at the level of basic food grains. Consumption requirements were substantial, varied and ascended through a range of social and geographical spaces stretching from nucleated households in villages to the large and intermediate towns. Town demand had a clear effect on local trade in agricultural produce (Datta, 2015; cf. Mukherjee, T., 2013: ch. 2). Contemporary observers noted the increase in Calcutta's population throughout the century (Marshall, 1977: 24).

Dhaka had about 450,000 people living within its environs in 1765 (IOR, Home Miscellaneous 465, p. 146) and continued to be thickly peopled later on (Datta, 1986: 287). In 1757, Murshidabad was declared "one of the richest cities in the world" (OIOC, Francis Mss. Eur. E. 12, f. 250), and in 1764, Robert Clive described this city as "extensive, populous and rich as the city of London, with this difference that there are individuals in the first possessing infinitely greater property than in the last [named] city" (1764: 19).

The extent of urban consumption can be deduced from data on importations of rice into the city of Calcutta. In 1752, the annual importation of rice in the main markets of the city was 400,000 *maunds* (Holwell, 1764: 246), which, at 0.66 rupees per *maund* in 1752 (Long, 1868: no. 99 (1752), p. 47), gives a monetized value of traded rice at 264,000 rupees. In order to encourage the import of food into the city, the duties on rice and paddy were reduced to 4 per cent in 1759 (OIOC, Letters Received, E/4/24, letter of 29 December 1759). In 1773, duties collected on rice imports were 16,874 rupees, which, at the rate of 4 per cent duty, gives us a traded value of 416,850 rupees for that year (OIOC, BRC, P/49/48, 30 November 1774). In 1783, the city imported 2,031,534 *maunds* of rice (WBSA, BCP, 6 August–29 December 1783; 7 November 1783), which, at the prevailing price of 0.89 rupees per *maund* (*Asiatick Researches*, XII (1816): 560–1), gives us a monetized value of 1,808,065 rupees. In first four months of 1788, the city imported 312,532 *maunds* of rice (OIOC, BRC, P/51/19, 21 April 1788), which, at the prevailing rate of 1.5 rupees per *maund*, gives a monetary equivalent of 468,798 rupees (a hypothetical value of 1,875,192 rupees for the entire year).[5]

Calcutta's demand structure was extensive but not exceptional, compared to other places in the province. The demand for food generated by these towns exerted a crucial influence on the direction and movement of local trade. While the average monthly consumption of common quality rice in Calcutta was 250,000 *maunds* in the 1780s (OIOC, BRC, P/51/17, 4 March 1788), Murshidabad needed more than 130,000 *maunds* of rice and 57,000 *maunds* of paddy for its sustenance in the 1790s (ibid.: P/52/50, 19 October 1792). Towns lower down the scale needed proportionate amounts of food. Unfortunately, these needs cannot be worked out because of the scarcity of relevant information. Quantitative data of the amounts of money involved in the purchase of food and other items of consumption are equally scarce. However, the available evidence indicates that the amount of foodgrains available to merchants from different localities for the purpose of catering to town demand, and for exports outside the province (referred to as the "exportable surplus" in our sources) seldom fell below 20 per cent of the gross agricultural output under normal circumstances (Datta, 1986: 148).

It was rural demand for basic food items that militates most strongly against notions of rural self-sufficiency. It has been suggested that, based on the data provided by the decennial population censuses 1871 onwards, for 35–50 per cent of the rural population, consisting of very poor peasants, agricultural and non-agricultural labourers, artisans and service workers, access to food was related to "employment entitlements" (Ghose, 1982: 377). Interestingly, our evidence reveals a similarly high concentration of households with non-agricultural occupations in rural society in the eighteenth century, too. Pure artisans, that is, those who were completely separated from any form of agricultural production, accounted for 27 per cent of the households; petty administrative officials, literate and religious gentry comprised a sizeable 12.89 per cent. This suggests that an overwhelming number of households in rural society, at least 50 per cent, were directly involved in market-based transactions. The dependence of such people, particularly at least a quarter of them (the artisans), on the market for their basic sustenance was almost absolute (Datta, 2015: 357–8). It would take a subsistence crisis to bring this aspect out in the open with devastating consequences.

Further, there was a major change in the economic environment of consumption in early modern Bengal, brought about by phenomenal expansions of money use in rural areas and of Bengal's overseas exports in this period. A robust rural market for externally procured goods existed and can be seen from the voluminous records of non-agricultural (*sair jiha'at*) taxes kept by the state. *Shroffs* (bankers) percolated into villages, *cowri* shops exchanging the shell (imported largely from Maldives) began to be set up in the villages, and *cowri*–silver rupee exchange rates became matters of village-level importance (Datta, 2014: 95–6). Consumption was structurally linked to the market and household reproduction was inescapably linked to its vicissitudes. Notions of an idyllic and autarkic village environment are at odds with the brutal facts of households eating their seed reserves during dearth, barely able to support themselves, and reaching a point where "Musslemens [*sic*] and lower casts [*sic*] of Hindoos are glad to get persons to take [away] their children" (OIOC, BRC P/51/19, 17 April 1788).

Society was stratified, so were households, and consumption was thus naturally differentiated according to the position and rank of the household. This point was explicitly made by Francis Buchanan during his surveys of the district of Rangpur *c.*1807, where he divided households into seven ranks on the basis of their consumption profiles. His findings tell us that the higher the rank of the household, the higher was the per capita consumption of non-food, including the so-called luxury items. The lower the rank of a household, the higher would be the subsistence costs of household reproduction. Eighty per cent of household incomes of this latter rank was spent on purchasing food, compared to less than 20 per cent among the first two ranks (Buchanan, "Ronggoppur", OIOC, Ms. Eur. G.11, Table 39; Bhattacharya, 1982: 279–80).

Price movements and their implications

Scarcities began when harvests fell short. In other words, there was a decline in the gross availability of food grains which, depending on the extent of the damaged harvest, would constitute the critical difference between some starvation, serious starvation and famine starvation. Table 2.2 is indicative of these various stages.

At the broadest level, there were three economic symptoms of a subsistence crisis. These were: (1) severe food-availability decline at local levels; (2) enhancements in the spot-prices of rice and paddy; and (3) the inability of the people, especially the poor, to purchase their subsistence. The question, however, and one where the economic content of these crises becomes manifest, is how did such shortfalls convert themselves into crises of subsistence? The answer lies in the behaviour of agricultural prices, particularly the prices of paddy and rice, in the markets, both in towns as well as in the countryside. The degree, temporal duration and geographical spread of these rising prices were germane. The most distinctive feature of a price rise caused by a harvest contraction, and a sudden fall in market supplies, was its sharp and abnormal spike. Therefore, the steepness of the price line, and its deviation from what was considered "normal" determined the extent of the damage which would come about. In a study of famines in Bengal, W. W. Hunter pointed to the critically small dividing line between the "famine warning" and a "famine point" in the province, the central determinant of which was the price situation. For Hunter, the dividing line between the two could collapse "with the slightest rise in prices of agricultural produce" (1869: 16–17).

The important bearing that such sharp rise in prices had can be seen from the following complaints made by cultivators. Faced with a drought in 1774, the peasants of Burdwan complained:

> Our condition is most miserable; for though there is grain in the hands of the Merchants, ... they have leagued together to keep the price up and we are perishing with hunger. If we *cannot procure food even with money*, how is it possible for us to stay in the District?
>
> (OIOC, BRC, 30 August 1774; emphasis added)

Table 2.2 Harvest damage in dearth and famine

Year	Occurrence	Portion of crop destroyed (%)	Outcome
1769–70	Drought	50 to 28	Famine
1775	Drought	33.3 to 37.5	Dearth
1779	Drought	25	Dearth
1786–87	Flood	37.5 to 50	Famine
1791	Drought	33	Dearth

Source: Datta, 2000: 250.

Similarly, in 1791, it was found,

> The buzaars have hitherto been sufficiently well supplied to answer
> the immediate wants of the inhabitants; but the alarm of an approach-
> ing scarcity is now become so universal that *the poorer sort of people* will
> shortly experience considerable distress, as *the price of grain* and the
> difficulty of procuring it, *even for money*, is daily increasing.
>
> (Ibid.: P/52/27, 23 November 1791; emphasis added)

Figures 2.1 and 2.2 show the trends in the prices of four agricultural products during the severe famine of 1769–70 and the near-famine situation
in 1788.

Figure 2.3 shows the movement of monthly prices of ordinary rice
between October 1769 and September 1770 in Midnapur, a district which
had been severely hit by the famine.

My final data sets are given in Table 2.3, which contains prices of
ordinary rice (in rupees per *maund*) of the winter harvest in four areas of
the province which had been severely hit by the floods and had, in the
aftermath, experienced a near-famine situation.

Though the degree of excess mortality in 1788 was much lower than the
famine of 1769–70, there were some reports of deaths caused by unavailability
of food from eastern Bengal, whereas western Bengal remained relatively
unaffected. Both Figure 2.2 and Table 2.3 show that despite the degree of
the scarcity-induced spike in prices being less in 1788 than in 1769, the
sharpness in the rise was nevertheless significant. For instance, compared

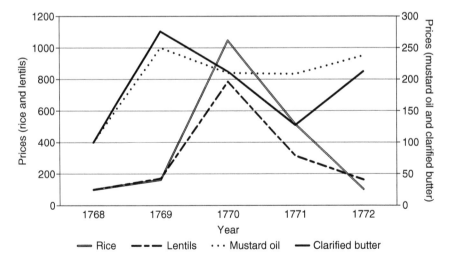

Figure 2.1 Agricultural prices, 1768–72 (1768 = 100).

Source: OIOC, Bengal General Ledgers and Journal, P/175/83 to P/176/29; and *Asiatick
Researches*, vol. XII, 1816, pp. 560–1.

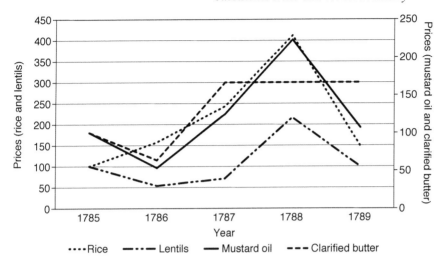

Figure 2.2 Agricultural prices, 1785–89 (rupees per *maund*).

Source: OIOC, Bengal General Ledgers and Journal, P/175/83 to P/176/29; and *Asiatick Researches*, vol. XII, 1816, pp. 560–1.

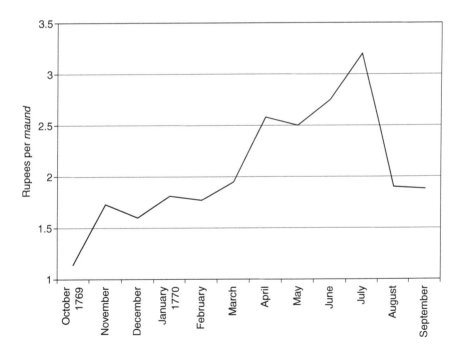

Figure 2.3 Monthly rice prices in Midnapur, October 1769 to September 1770 (rupees per *maund*).

Source: Price, 1876: 83.

Table 2.3 Prices of rice (winter harvest), in rupees per *maund*

Year	Calcutta	Chittagong	Dinajpur	Mymensing
1786	1.12	0.88	1.11	0.42
1787	1.12	0.57	1.09	0.40
1788	2.00	0.82	1.39	1.10
1789	1.69	0.78	1.38	0.92

Source: OIOC, BRC, P/51/12, 16, 17.34.

to 1787 the price of ordinary rice in Calcutta went up by nearly 179 per cent in 1788, whereas in the three other districts, prices increased between 143 and 275 per cent. Though this was undoubtedly much lower than the almost 900 per cent escalation in the price of common rice between 1769 and 1770, the increase was still enormous, and caused great distress. On the other hand, the sheer abnormality of the price rise in 1770, and its persistence for over six months, explains the corresponding enormity of the deaths which were reported, particularly from western Bengal in that one year (cf. Datta, 2000: chs. 5, 6).

One of the most harvest- and price-sensitive social groups in rural Bengal was the textile producer. Famine and dearth impacted upon them by hitting directly at their access to markets for their consumption requirements. The evidence from Malda and Purnea suggests that between half and one-third of those who died in the famine were spinners and weavers. The disruption caused by the drought to mulberry and cotton in 1769 and 1770 meant that those who reared silk-worms (*chassars*) and those who grew cotton (*kappas*) in these places were immediately affected. The cultivation of mulberry was an expensive enterprise: "under the most favourable circumstance mulberry will cost the Husbandman five or six, and often from ten to fifteen rupees per bigha", whereas the cultivation cost of rice was "not above one, two or at best three rupees a bigha" (WBSA, CCRM, vol. 6, 19 November 1771). This meant that once peasants entered this sector their survival depended on conducive precipitation and favourable food prices.

The situation in 1769–70 was precisely the opposite on both counts, and therefore proved disastrous for such producers. There was an "incredible mortality" among the *chassars* of Rajshahi during the famine (ibid.: vol. 6, 11 November 1771). This was for two reasons. First, the high costs involved in the culture of silk-cocoons meant that the *chassars* had no reserves to buy food at famine-point prices. Second, the *chassars* belonged to "only two casts [*sic*] of the Gentoos [Hindus]" who followed this vocation as a specialized occupation (ibid.). For these reasons, they were perhaps the most harvest-sensitive of all the affected social strata and, not having enough food reserves to fall back upon, they died in large numbers. Significantly, there appears to have been some mortality among the *chassars* even in Dhaka which was otherwise largely unaffected by the severity of the famine (WBSA, CCC 1: 15 October 1771; OIOC, BRC, P/49/52, from Richard Barwell to Council, 7 April 1775). Finally, there were the weavers, and it was reported that they also died in "large numbers" (Sinha, 1956: 1: 160–1), but these deaths were especially concentrated in areas like Purnea, Rajshahi, Malda and Murshidabad. The reports of such deaths suggest a higher concentration of excess mortality among the *chassars* followed by deaths among the "winders and weavers" who "suffered in proportion" to the *chassars* but not to the same extent (WBSA, CCC 1: 19 April 1771). This is corroborated by the following account from the famine of 1769–70.

[It] appears most probable that the mortality was mostly among the workmen, manufacturers, and people employed in the rivers, who were without the same means of laying by stores of grain as the husbandmen, so that the number of consumers who suffered by this calamity was greater, in proportion, than that of the cultivators of grain.

(Geddes, 1874: 421)

Conclusion

The intention of this chapter was to show how subsistence crises reveal the economic history of subsistence from the point of consumption. In other words, its two central arguments, namely, the market-oriented structure of consumption, and starvation-misery outcome of market forces, were tied to the movement of agricultural prices, and their deleterious impact on subsistence in an already shortage hit economy. I briefly return to these formulations in this concluding section.

As mentioned earlier, there existed a non-agricultural (*sair jiha'at*) tax collected by the state. My recent study of these *sair* taxes showed that the demand for goods in Bengal's countryside was of a differentiated nature. Most villages imported food grains. These imports could be as high as 68 per cent of the value of local trade conducted in the districts. Sugar, salt and tobacco constituted the other three main elements of primary consumption, followed closely by the consumption of betelnut and leaf (Datta, 2014). Francis Buchanan's survey of the district of Rangpur (*c*.1807) also showed that, in an aggregated sense, rice, various sorts of pulses, mustard oil, vegetables, chillies, spices, tobacco, molasses or sugar, salt, turmeric, betel nut and betel leaf were common items of food for all ranks. Clarified butter was usually an upper social rank indulgence, but since cows and other cattle were also maintained by the other social groups, it can be assumed that they had access to some milk products, though most of these were for sale (Buchanan, "Ronggoppur", OIOC, Ms. Eur. G.11). More importantly, the price of goods in the market (*nirkh bazar*) determined how much of what commodity a peasant household could consume beyond the stocks of rice or paddy available in their personal storehouses (*golahs*). The latter facility was not something which rural artisans possessed, which meant anything between a quarter and a half of the rural population did not keep food reserves beyond their daily requirements and were thus critically vulnerable to even the minutest dislocation in the food market.

Buchanan's survey of Rangpur also shows that per capita consumption in rural society was fundamentally linked to incomes and resources, and expenditures on food-related items varied inversely proportional to incomes. In other words, the lower the rank in terms of household income, the higher the subsistence costs. This was expected in a situation where the annual income differential between the first and the seventh ranks was an insurmountable 4070 rupees a year (Buchanan, "Ronggoppur", vol. 1, book 2, OIOC, MS. Eur. D.74, f.24). It is inconceivable that such disparities did not exist in other places, and this perhaps explains why, in April 1770, "the ryots [cultivators] in many villages, for want of rain" were "reduced to the necessity of selling their grain for seed and their cattle and utensils in order to support themselves"; and, as Campbell's records further observed,

> half of those who pay their revenues and cultivate the land will undoubtedly perish with hunger, whilst those remaining will be *obliged to purchase their subsistence* at least 500 percent dearer than usual [and] will be drained of that little stock which is the only resource for future revenue and cultivation.
>
> (1868: 20 April 1770, p. 115)

Therefore, subsistence crises provide information on the economic history of subsistence in three ways. First, they unravel the inner workings of commercial exchanges comprising the market and demand for increasingly scarce goods. Second, they reveal to us the exact way in which purchasing power in real terms becomes determined by price movements.[6] Third, they help us understand how starvation-induced debilitation or deaths were market-related. In other words, what they tell us is that these episodes were commercial phenomena, which had less to do with a temporary malfunction in traditionally sanctioned rights (entitlements) of subsistence. Cultural norms were important in determining social boundaries; but procuring food during such crises was also an economic matter fraught with grave consequences.

Notes

1 In Amartya Sen's view, entitlement signifies economic and legal rights: to food, access to food, or exchange of endowments for food. These can be identifiably economic (like money or property), socially sanctioned, or state-directed

interventions to ensure people's access to food. In this perspective, the market factor in subsistence crises may operate against certain groups by pulling away food to service the subsistence demands of groups with greater endowment powers: for instance, food being sucked out of the countryside to feed the towns because of higher prices in these places. Mohiuddin Alamgir argues that a famine is caused basically by a food availability decline, and is

> a general state of prolonged food grain intake deficiency per capita giving rise to a number of a company sub-states (symptoms) involving individuals and the community that ultimately lead, directly or indirectly, to excess deaths in the region or country as a whole.

2 Perhaps such constructs were not unique to traditional Bengali society alone. Did traditional European societies differ substantially in their conceptions of dearth and plenty? It would be difficult to argue that they did. Compare, for instance, Hoskins, 1968; Meuvret, 1988; Walter and Schofield, 1989; Mukherjee, A., 2015.

3 This section is based on Datta, 2000: ch. 1.

4 In the district of Rajshahi, it was cultivated "chiefly in beds of lakes and in the nullahs (small water courses)" (WBSA, CCRM, vol. 5, 30 April 1771).

5 In 1788 there was a severe food shortage caused by floods in eastern Bengal, and that perhaps explains the reduced imports of rice by the city.

6 It has also been suggested that in pre-industrial Europe, a seasonal price rise faster than usual could cause desperation among consumers, causing a further demand-induced pressure on the already rising prices (Ó Gráda, 2005: 162).

3 Climate signals, environment and livelihoods in the long seventeenth century in India

Vinita Damodaran, James Hamilton and Rob Allan

Climate history is an area of growing interest among environmental historians.[1] As John McNeill recently noted, historians working from textual sources – primarily in Europe and China where the records are good – have been moving into the terrain of scientists "who collect and analyze 'proxy' data on past climates; tree-ring series, fossilized pollen or ancient air bubbles trapped in ice" (2003). The historian Geoffrey Parker – amongst others – has drawn connections between historical climate change and periods of extreme weather which, he argues, were responsible not only for localised failure of harvest, price increases and human casualties, but also violence and rebellion on a global scale, stretching across Europe to India and China. Parker hypothesises that the widespread agrarian crisis of the seventeenth century, experienced in Europe and elsewhere, was related to spells of cold weather in the northern hemisphere caused by a variety of factors including atmospheric dust veils from multiple volcanic eruptions, the repercussions of which were felt on a continental scale across Europe, the Americas and Asia. Such history – which links climate to social upheavals – has many detractors, who criticise the implications of environmental determinism and denial of human and institutional agency. It is rightly argued that famine causation is complex and its effects are often linked to social and institutional factors rather than climate. This was particularly true of the 1770 famine, which can be attributed primarily to the extreme tax exactions of the East India Company (EIC), or, as Datta argues in Chapter 2, to market operations, and far less to the failure of the monsoon. Despite this, climate is increasingly entering into the equation as natural scientists and climate historians have begun to bridge the disciplinary gulf and to work in concord on both instrumental and textual data. There has been particular interest in the history of the El Niño, or more properly ENSO (El Niño Southern Oscillation), phenomenon, which, it has recently been established, affects patterns of drought and flood not only around the shores of the Pacific, but also in north-east Brazil, South Asia and much of Africa. Lately, historians have sought to link these phenomena to sustained famines around the world. The historian Richard Grove, for example, has persuasively argued that agrarian unrest associated with the French Revolution – which occurred during one of the greatest El Niños in modern times, 1789–93 (Grove, 1998) – was in part caused by the phenomena.[2] This chapter explores some of these debates on both a global and regional scale, with an evidential focus on the Indian subcontinent. In the process, it seeks to address the notion of the seventeenth-century crisis on the subcontinent, considering historiographic and scientific evidence as well as writings on famine and famine causality on eighteenth-century India, in the context of wider discussions in global environmental and climate history.

Historiography of the crisis

The seventeenth century crisis, and its climatic basis, has had significant impact on recent historiography. Using new research in climate history, historians such as Geoffrey Parker, Richard Grove, David Clingingsmith and Jeffrey Williamson have sought to assess the impact of climatic events on historical upheaval in the seventeenth and eighteenth centuries. Geoffrey Parker, in his magnum opus *Global Crisis, War, Climate Change and Catastrophe in the Seventeenth Century* (2013), and Sam White in *Climate of Rebellion in the Early Modern Ottoman Empire* (2011), present robust evidence that global cooling occurred in the seventeenth century, and that it had a dramatic effect on the events of the period. While the idea of a global crisis is highly contested, for these historians, at least, it is established, as is the fact that climate was at its heart. A central premise of these histories is that the synchronicity of many political disorders in mid-seventeenth-century Eurasia was no accident, but was a direct repercussion of climatic anomalies.

The term "seventeenth century crisis" was coined in a 1954 edition of *Past and Present* by the English Marxist historian Hobsbawm (33–53) and taken on in the first instance by Trevor-Roper (1967). More recently, climate – which was mentioned regularly by historians of the *Annales* school but rarely elsewhere – came to be seen as perhaps the most significant driving force behind those upheavals gathered under the term "crisis". How do we see the role of climate in history and how do we avoid crude environmental determinism? By exploring the arguments on the seventeenth century crisis in the context of Mughal India we hope to answer some of these questions.

The climate of the seventeenth century

For the seventeenth century, no meaningful instrumental weather or climate observations are available for India or the Indian Ocean region. Indeed, one of the earliest marine explorations on which a barometer and thermometer were taken on a vessel with the express interest of making scientific observations was by Edmund Halley on the sloop HMS *Paramore*

Pink from England to the South Shetland Islands and back in 1699–1700. It should be noted that at the time of Halley's voyage, the barometer was still in its infancy (invented by Torricelli in 1643), while his thermometer had a scale devised by Halley himself, and none of the now established scales – Réaumur, Celsius, Fahrenheit or Kelvin – had been invented.[3] As a consequence, documentary evidence has become a major source of information on weather and climate across the Indian Ocean and surrounding countries during the seventeenth century. With the ships, developing colonial land ports, settlements and factories of the trading companies of the Portuguese, Dutch and English being dominant in the Indian Ocean region at this time, their surviving registers, journals, gazettes, diaries, logbooks and the like are the prime sources of weather and climate information, impacts and extremes. The vast majority of seventeenth-century logbooks are in Portuguese, Spanish, Dutch and English repositories, with the great bulk held by the latter two countries. However, this material has not been recovered, scanned/imaged and digitised to the extent and in the systematic manner that later eighteenth- to twentieth-century holdings have been. Projects such as the Climatological Database for the World's Oceans (CLIWOC) 1750–1850, the International

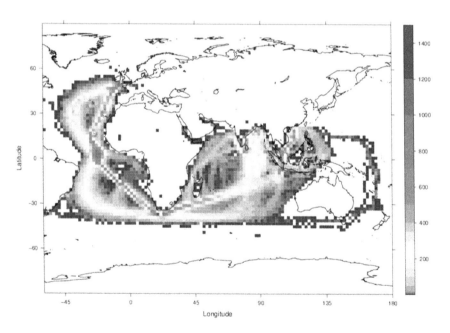

Figure 3.1 Geographical coverage of the tracks of English East India Company (EIC) ships in 900 ship logbooks from 1788–1834 which took instrumental weather observations (e.g. pressure, air temperature and sea surface temperature) and have been digitised under ACRE.

Source: Philip Brohan (Met Office).

Comprehensive Ocean Atmosphere Data Set (ICOADS) post-1854, the citizen-science-based Old Weather (English East India Company [EIC]: 1780s–1830s) and Weather Detective (1888–1903) provide examples of what might be achieved.[4]

In 2007/08, a UK Defra under-spend allowed the International Atmospheric Circulation Reconstructions over the Earth (ACRE) Initiative (www.met-acre.org) under the Met Office Hadley Centre climate programme to fund the scanning of some 900 EIC ship logbooks held in the British Library containing instrumental weather observations for the 1780s–1830s.[5] The historical weather data were subsequently digitised by the Climate Data Modernization Program (CDMP) in the USA and will be used in dynamical global 3D weather reconstructions – such as future extensions of the ACRE-facilitated Twentieth Century Reanalysis [20CR], currently covering the period 1850–2010 (www.esrl.noaa.gov/psd/data/20thC_Rean). Such an extension would entail further work under CLIWOC, the recovery of EIC logbooks stretching back to the beginning of the seventeenth century, and the extraction and digitisation of the

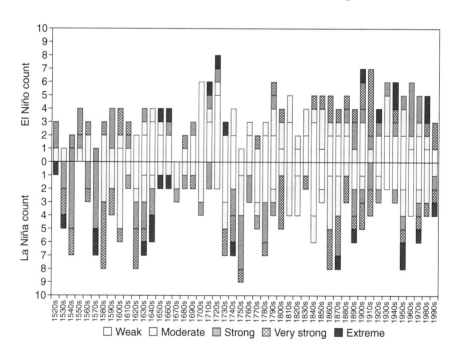

Figure 3.2 ENSO reconstructions: decadal trends in reconstructed El Niño and La Niña event magnitude characteristics, 1525–2000.

Note

Five percentile classes of the MQ time series were used to classify ENSO magnitude into extreme (>90th percentile), very strong (70th–90th percentile), strong (50th–70th percentile), moderate (50th–30th percentile) and weak events (<30th percentile).

Source: Gergis and Fowler (2009).

data – primarily wind direction and force estimates – contained therein. At present, wind data are not routinely assimilated into 20CR, but plans are in place to achieve this in the longer term and thus to extend reanalyses back into the seventeenth and eighteenth centuries – the incorporation of paleo/proxy data would also be a significant advance towards this goal.[6]

Long historical climatic indices using instrumental, documentary, proxy data and observations and records most relevant to the Indian Ocean region have tended to focus mainly on measures of the ENSO phenomena and the Indian/South Asian Monsoon. Recent examples of each of these reconstructions are shown in Figure 3.2 and Table 3.1.

Table 3.1 Protracted ENSO episodes

Episodes	Years	Episodes	Years
El Niño			
1964–69	6	1791–94	4
1957–59	3	1782–84	3
1937–42	6	1768–71	4
1924–26	3	1746–48	3
1918–20	3	1718–24	7
1911–15	7	**1659–61**	**3**
1876–78	3	**1650–52**	**3**
1864–66	3	**1618–21**	**4**
1856–58	3	**1607–09**	**3**
1844–48	5	1585–83	3
1814–17	4	1525–27	3
La Niña			
1988–90	3	1808–11	4
1984–86	3	1785–90	6
1970–75	6	1778–80	3
1955–60	6	1750–58	9
1921–23	3	1739–43	5
1916–18	3	1730–1733	4
1907–10	4	*1637–39*	*3*
1890–94	5	*1622–32*	*11*
1878–80	3	*1600–05*	*6*
1870–75	6	1576–81	6
1866–68	3	1571–73	3
1860–64	5	1540–42	3
1847–51	5	1531–33	3
Total			26

Source: Gergis and Fowler (2009).

Note
Protracted CEI ENSO events reconstructed since AD 1525. The seventeenth-century episodes are shown here: El Niño (bold) and La Niña (bold italics). Following Allan and D'Arrigo (1999), a protracted episode is defined as persisting for two years or more – only those of three years or more are shown.

The ENSO example details the resolution of both reconstructed El Niño and La Niña events and longer "protracted" El Niño and La Niña episodes. A protracted episode of either El Niño or La Niña "phase" is defined as a period of two years or more when measures of the phenomena (Southern Oscillation Index, the Pacific Niño 3 and 4 region sea surface temperature (SST) anomalies, and various precipitation extremes (drought or flood) in "ENSO sensitive" regions around the globe) persist.

Shi, Li and Wilson (2014) note that their reconstructed South Asian summer monsoon index (SASMI) captures 18 of 26 (69 per cent) reordered historical famine events in India over the last millennium; notably, 11 of 16 short events with durations of 1–3 years are accurately depicted in the reconstruction.[7] The long history of temperature anomalies from proxy sources, in Neukom *et al.* (2014), indicates that the seventeenth century embraced the peak of the so-called "Little Ice Age" (LIA).[8] It would appear then that any ability to reconstruct the climate for this period over the Indian Ocean domain would provide an informative picture of environmental conditions in this region during the coldest period in the last millennia.

As a step towards this goal, an investigation was made into the extent and nature of various palaeoenvironmental/proxy records relating to the Indian Ocean domain that have been published to date. Broad overviews around the turn of the twenty-first century show that proxy data are most readily available for terrestrial regions around the Indian Ocean, principally within Africa and Australia. Marine data are available via coral cores principally from the Pacific basin. Tree ring data is more readily available for north India and bordering regions. The drought maps for Asian droughts in Buckley *et al.* (2014) show the footprint of the historically important droughts in the period.[9] The above data appear to indicate that the mid-seventeenth century saw the weakest period of monsoons on record. The ENSO example details the resolution of both reconstructed El Niños and La Niñas plus longer protracted episodes of both. In the seventeenth century, ENSO events occurred every 2.5 years – half the five-year average. What impact did these climate events have on India in social and economic terms?

India, climate and the seventeenth-century crisis

For the longer part of its history and in the overwhelming majority of texts produced addressing the issue of the seventeenth-century "General Crisis", the focus has been on Europe. In 1974, Jonathan Israel began to extend the geographical boundaries of the debate in his work on Mexico (33–5). Further territorial expansion was slow to materialise – largely due, no doubt, to a general move away from structuralist thinking. Indeed, it was more than a decade before the Ming/Qing transition in China was first considered in this connection by Frederick Wakeman (1986), and not until 1990 that a special edition of *Modern Asian Studies*, presenting four articles – all economic histories – on "The General Crisis in East Asia", introduced to General Crisis theory the study of highly developed economies such as Japan, Indonesia and India. The contributions to this volume from Anthony Reid and William Atwell looked at South-East and East Asia respectively, John Richards considered the period in Mughal India, while Neils Steensgaard discussed "unity in Eurasian history" (cf. Parker and Smith, 1978). Two key commonalities can be drawn out of this phase of the historiography in which the debate moved into Asia. First, the notion of the Crisis as a fundamental transformation between epochs, era or *epistemes*, between old and new, which dominates the historiography of the crisis in Europe, faded as identification became more a matter of noting the coincidence of a sufficient number of negative incidents, encompassing a broad enough geography and sufficiently diverse areas of human life. Second, the downturn in global temperatures which became known as the LIA began to be seen – in the first instance by the *Annales* school – as a significant factor in bringing about the crisis.

The LIA is associated with two periods of unusually low sunspot activity, the Spörer Minimum (1450–1540) and the Maunder Minimum (1645–1715). Both solar minimums coincided with the coldest years of the LIA in parts of Europe. According to these climate-focussed histories, in the mid-fourteenth century, violent climate oscillations halved Europe's population and caused severe depopulation in Asia. A subsequent period of warming was followed by another dramatic cooling, peaking in the mid-seventeenth century. These cooler average temperatures prevailed from the end of the Medieval Warm Period up until the beginning of our contemporary era of global warming. Returning to Parker, we note that he does not engage in the wider debate and uses the LIA label to refer to climatic conditions between 1610 and the winter of 1708–09. He argues that three natural forces combine in this period to generate cooler temperatures and greater climatic variability, reduced solar energy being only one of them, increased volcanic activity and a greater frequency of El Niño being the other two (Parker, 2013).

According to Parker, the period is coincident with anomalies in ENSO currents which operate in two distinct phases alternating over a period of roughly 2–7 years. These phases are characterised by warming in the tropical Pacific and the Indian Ocean, often suppressing rainfall in the western Pacific in the case of El Niño – the converse being true in the case of La Niña. ENSO events vary widely in their manner of expression, centres of action, duration and magnitude, but are typically accompanied by extreme weather events. The link between ENSO and the Asian Monsoon is important here, as is that between SSTs in the Indian Ocean and those in the Pacific (Damodaran *et al.*, 2015). The mid-seventeenth century saw the weakest period of monsoons on record and in the seventeenth century ENSO events happened twice as often as on average. In fact, the period saw the weakest East Asian monsoons of the past two millennia. It has at times been suggested that ENSO events can also trigger volcanic eruptions and that the global footprint of ENSO events included three regions besides the land adjoining the Pacific, with the Caribbean suffering floods, Ethiopia and north-west India experiencing drought and Europe suffering hard winters.

We now come to the question of "Crisis" in India. The years of the LIA coincide well with those of the Mughal Empire, and Parker has argued that "although Europe and East Asia formed the heartland of the General Crisis, the Mughal Empire ... also experienced episodes of severe political disruption in the mid-seventeenth century" resulting in widespread violence. According to Parker, the Mughal Empire can be seen as having "come close to revolution ... in the 1650s, while the seventeenth century as a whole [was] ... a period in which wars were fought almost continuously". Droughts, floods and famines, particularly in the late 1620s and early 1630s, in Gujarat and the Deccan are also cited as examples of upheaval.[10]

The main event by which Parker attempts to bring Mughal India into the fold of the "General Crisis" is the 1658–62 war of succession. Coincidence of war and monsoon failure are seen to create particularly difficult

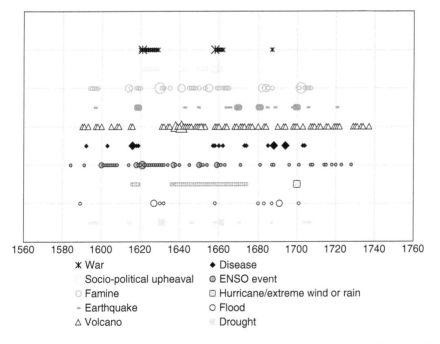

| 1560 | 1580 | 1600 | 1620 | 1640 | 1660 | 1680 | 1700 | 1720 | 1740 | 1760 |

✕ War   ◆ Disease

   Socio-political upheaval   ◎ ENSO event

○ Famine   ▢ Hurricane/extreme wind or rain

- Earthquake   ○ Flood

△ Volcano   ▨ Drought

Figure 3.3 Plot for India for the period 1560–1760 which allows identification of groupings and coincidences between various occurrences and events born of both natural and human causes.

conditions for the Indian population in the late 1650s and early 1660s; however, one should note that famine reports are mainly anecdotal and sometimes highly subjective: "people [are] dying daily ... the living hardly able to bury the dead" (in Parker, 2013).

The Mughal ruler Akbar's reign was dominated by major famines in Gujarat in 1556 and in 1595, lasting three years. Abul Fazl, the court historian, describing the horrors of this famine, noted that the mortality was great: "Man ate their own kin and the streets were blocked with corpses" (in Agarwal, 1983: 24). 'Abd al-Qādir Badā'ūnī, another contemporary historian, noted that the whole country was deserted and no husbandmen remained to till the ground (ibid.: 23). In 1595, when another famine caused by the failure of rains affected northern India, especially Kashmir and Lahore, Jesuit missionaries reported that the streets of Lahore were blocked with human corpses (Agarwal, 2006: 30). In 1618–19 there was famine in the Deccan and on the Coromandel coast (ibid.: 31). The traveller Methwold, who left the East coast in 1622, wrote of the ravages of the famine in Vijaynagara (1926: xiii). In the reign of Shah Jahan, during the protracted La Niña episode in 1630–31, a severe famine occurred which affected Golconda, Ahmednagar and parts of Malwa. In these years no rain fell in the Mughal territories of the Deccan or Gujarat and the drought was followed by severe floods (Lāhawrī, I, 1867: 362; Ray and Kuzhippalli Skaria, 2002: 132). The middle of the seventeenth century, as noted, had seen the weakest period of monsoons on record and the rains failed in 1646 and 1647. Heavy mortality was reported from Pulicat and Madras and it was recorded that half the people in the area of Nagapatnam were dead and the stench of the dead and dying bodies was terrifying (Foster, 1906: xxvii). The first year of Aurangzeb's reign was likewise marked by intense famine causing unspeakable suffering in Northern and Central India. Colonel Tod noted: "There was no longer distinction of caste, Sudra and Brahmin were indistinguishable. Men ate men" (in Agarwal, 2006: 36), cities were depopulated, and Bihar experienced severe famine in 1671 which encouraged the slave trade. In 1687 there was another severe famine in Golconda. The month of June 1687 saw floods and the city of Hyderabad was depopulated, houses, rivers and plains filled with corpses. In 1704–07 another great famine hit the Deccan but proved less severe (Agarwal, 2006: 36).

On the face of it, then, Parker's emphasis of climatic drivers in this period of Mughal history appears justified by contemporary descriptions. However, it should be pointed out that the usefulness of such descriptions, without supporting statistical or demographic data or at least estimates of numbers of people affected is questionable. Furthermore, the reliability of, in particular European descriptions, has been strongly questioned by work on the development of tropes in famine reporting of the period (Agarwal, 1983: 21–78). Lack of comparative and contextual data on monsoon failure also leaves Parker's argument somewhat open to criticism

– details of how common these were, their geographic extent, how long they lasted, what traditional coping mechanisms existed, what social and administrative contingencies were in place, are needed in order to form any accurate idea of the meaning and significance of monsoon failure in general, and of specific droughts for Indian society. Parker's claim of "exceptional violence" in the seventeenth century as a whole sits in some contrast to the historiography. For example, John F. Richards, Irfan Habib, and others, have described the seventeenth century as a period of relative calm and stability. That Parker can point to near continuous warfare is not in itself proof of exceptionalism in a rapidly expanding and militaristic early modern empire, which, throughout its existence, failed to define solid boundaries and was always involved either in expansion or suppression of rebellion somewhere in its vast territory (Edwards and Garrett, 1974; Gommans, 2002; Balabanlilar, 2012).

John F. Richards saw no evidence of a seventeenth-century crisis in India, identifying, instead, continuity and prosperity which endured well into the following century when the region experienced a distinct and unrelated eighteenth-century crisis as Mughal emperors lost power to local lords and, later, the EIC. Richards' conclusions are not very different from those reached some 30 years earlier by the distinguished economic historian of early modern India, Irfan Habib, in his work *The Agrarian System of Mughal India*. For Habib, it was the strength of the Mughal Empire as an administrative unit which was its most remarkable feature; the revolt of 1580 and the Rajput revolt a century later being practically the only points at which the elite or the theocracy made any play of contesting the power of the semi-divine monarch. Moreover, Habib holds – contrary to Parker – that in the light of the refusal of contesting parties to ever discuss or consider partition, the wars of succession beginning in 1628, 1658 and 1707, should be viewed not as moments of weakness or near collapse, but as markers of the remarkable durability and cohesion of the empire (Habib, 1963).

According to Habib, Mughal military supremacy afforded security and stability – albeit accompanied by violent suppression and coercion of the masses of peasants and workers – and the extreme, if impermanent, power afforded to the emperor via the *Jagirdari* system of delegated revenue collection. This system rendered the *Mansabdars* "completely dependent on the will of the Emperor" (317), and allowed for the collection of taxes which reduced the populace to bare subsistence, producing enormous and highly concentrated wealth for a small elite (320). The system was, however, fundamentally flawed. Multiple layers of delegation in tax collection, the regular relocation of regional administrators, and a lack of central control over these *zamindārs*, who were seen as the primary threat to order in the empire, left the system open to exploitation whereby the masses suffered enormously at the expense of the various layers of the elite (320–2). In time, some local lords – particularly in Hindustan – began to rebel against centralised power, refusing to pass on revenue. Poor and sub-jugated elements were drawn to rebellious regions by more tolerable and equitable conditions, and thus the power of rebellious elements grew (366). By the mid–late seventeenth century the Jat, and later the Maratha, revolts had become a significant threat to imperial order – they would eventually be its undoing (346) – yet these were slowly developing and evolving states of confrontation, which spread gradually, slowly eroding centralised power, rather than a well-defined crisis prompting its collapse (346–99).

For David Clingingsmith and Jeffery Williamson (2008), it was again the eighteenth century which witnessed the most significant upheavals in India's economic and political structure. Herein, it was seen that the turmoil accompanying the dissolution of the Mughal Empire, into a con-stellation of smaller states and their forced regrouping under the EIC, frustrated commerce and industry, leading to economic decline. Even here, however, the notion of crisis, and even of economic decline itself, remains controversial and is far from settled as an historic fact. Work by Chris Bayly (1993), Muzaffar Alam (1998) and Peter Marshall (1982) lays emphasis on continuity rather than disruption, with Mughal administra-tive units seen to remain largely intact, pre-existing growth trajectories are maintained (Clingingsmith and Williamson, 2008: 211), and the only major change is in the amount of money passed on by local powers to central Mughal administration. It was, furthermore, in the latter part of this era – the years 1700 to 1760 – that India peaked as a manufacturing centre (ibid.: 223).

In light of the apparent historiographical consensus that the seven-teenth century was a time of relative calm in the Mughal Empire and that major upheaval did not occur until the early–mid-eighteenth century, Parker's attempt to extend the crisis into the subcontinent are considered, at present, somewhat tenuous and, at the very least, in need of a more solid evidential basis. Parker's arguments in the case of India appear to be open to exactly the same criticisms as those levelled at the arguments of Hobsbawm, Trevor-Roper, and others beyond the 1960s: that levels of upheaval were simply not that exceptional and continuity in systems of power was more marked than transformation. What makes these weather anomalies different from those a century earlier or a century later? Parker asserts that "the seventeenth century experienced extremes of weather seldom witnessed before … and never so far since" (2013: 112). In his ana-lysis the LIA is decisive, intervening in historical processes, influencing the outcome of battles and destroying empires. The claim requires com-parative and quantitative evidence and more detailed work on documen-tary and paleo sources. Furthermore, in terms of climate, it is important to note that impacts are always asymmetric; simplistic notions such as weak or strong monsoons or intense ENSO episodes take no account of the possib-ilities of variation in mode of expression and centres of action of these climate events. A more useful approach, then, is one that focuses on regional and national differences and the resilience of agricultural production in the face of population pressure, exogenous shocks and environmental change. Famine causation is complex and links between drought and famine in the early modern period need to be reassessed. There is a clear incentive to develop a database that will help improve famine, climate, disease, wage and price series for South Asia and the Indian Ocean world for 1500–1900, which are currently woefully inadequate.

Drought, famine and causality in eighteenth-century India

The following section discusses famines in eighteenth-century India, the study of which – through contemporary and near contemporary reports – is disruptive of simplistic, climate-led causalities, often assumed in the work of Parker and other historians looking to establish links between anomalous climatic conditions and societal upheaval.

Between 1765, when the British EIC took over Bengal, and 1858, the region experienced 12 famines and 4 severe scarcities. From the late eighteenth century, many Indian communities were disturbed by the interventions of the EIC and their revenue and agricultural regimes, which increased taxation, encouraged sedentarisation and attempted to restrict raids, hunting and nomadism. One commentator wrote that

> the oppressions of India … under the rapine and cruelties of the servants of the company have now reached England and there is a clamour here … to such monopolies were imputed the late famine in Bengal and the loss of 3 million inhabitants.
>
> (Walpole, I, 1910: 72; cf. Damodaran, 2007: 149; 2015)

Knowledge of the ecological basis of various peasant economies is critical to the understanding of the capacity of certain communities to withstand drought and famine. The famine of 1770 was one such, where – whilst weather played a role – the actions of the company, particularly in relation to taxation, turned localised scarcity into full-blown crisis. The famine of 1770 was preceded by a partial failure of the monsoon in Bengal and Bihar in 1768, 1769–70 was a year of dearth, commentators noted that the fields of rice had become like fields of straw, mortality and beggary exceeded all expectation, and many surviving peasants migrated to Nepal where the state was less confiscatory. More revenue was collected in 1770–71 than in 1769–70 and no remissions were granted by the EIC. Rain in September 1770 brought some relief, but came too late to avert depopulation; the crisis was further compounded by the outbreak of smallpox which became epidemic, killing millions. By May 1770, one-third of the population was calculated to have disappeared; in June, the deaths were returned as six out of every sixteen, and it was predicted that half of the cultivators and payers of revenue had perished. Final mortality estimates by some commentators reached 10 million.

The failure of a single crop, following one year of dearth, had wiped out millions. The monsoon was on time in the next few years but the economy of Bengal had been dramatically transformed and agricultural classes decimated. Amongst lime workers in Birbhum, mortality was especially high, with only 5/150 surviving. Mortality was also high among the non-agricultural workers such as weavers, spinners, and boatmen. As many as 1500 communities out of 6000 in the Birbhum region were destroyed, and Birbhum itself reverted to jungle inhabited by wild beasts. In the years subsequent to the famine, starving peasants with no seed or implements, burnt, pillaged and plundered in bands of 50–1000 men, provoking the Sanyasi rebellion led by fakirs and mendicants. To summarise: it is the cultural, societal, political and economic factors which loom large in this causality – while the winter of 1772 was perhaps unusually severe, climate appears to have played a relatively insignificant role in the development of what remains one of India's most disastrous and costly famines.

Two late-eighteenth-century EIC reports reveal further issues relating to famine reporting and causality. The first, Danvers' *A Century of Famine*, is interesting not merely as a source on meteorology and famine chronology in India, but also contains much which allows us to place climate and particularly rainfall variation within a larger causal framework. Danvers stated that

> famines in India have arisen from several different causes … the most general cause has been the failure of rains. Distress has also, however, been caused by hostile invasions; by swarms of rats or locusts [or ants in the case of the 1790–91 famine in Kach], by storms and floods; and not infrequently by the immigration of starving people from distant distressed parts, into districts otherwise well provided with food supplies; and excessive exports of grain into famine stricken districts, or by combination of two or more of the above named circumstances.
>
> (Danvers, 1877: 1)

However, Danvers' key, but perhaps counter-intuitive, observation (predicting Amartya Sen) is that most deaths in times of famine were not caused by actual shortage of food: "It is an important fact", he states, "that famines in India are more generally famines of work than of actual absence of food throughout any large extent of the country" (ibid.: 2). Danvers' point then is that the causal link between lack of rains and famine is more complex than might be assumed. The problem is often not that insufficient rains lead to poor local harvests and subsequent shortage of food. It is more that lack of rain disrupts agricultural employment patterns and leaves poorer workers without sufficient money to purchase food. Danvers continues on this topic to describe how "from a study of the history of past famines it appears that these visitations are almost as liable to be caused by unseasonable rains, or by their unequal distribution, as by deficient amount of rainfall during the year". He concludes by stating that "there are altogether so many circumstances connected with rainfall and its influence on the crops that it is difficult to arrive at any definite conclusion as to the actual proportionate deficiency of rain that would constitute a famine drought" (ibid.). A glance at Danvers' map of areas affected by famine (here reduced in Figure 3.4 from its original coverage to the period 1770–1825 only) shows the asymmetry of famine distribution. Even this half-century of frequent famines displays vast areas that remained completely immune. Danvers' map then, much like his report, points to a markedly complex relationship between deficient rains and significant social impact.

The second of the two major sources here considered, George Campbell's *Extracts from Records in the India Office Relating to Famines in India 1769–1788* (IOR, V/27/830/14), was published in 1868 and gives details of the famine around Madras in 1782, primarily driven by warfare in the area: "when the enemy was at their walls, and by his ravage, in every part of the adjacent country, had destroyed the cattle and reduced the inhabitants to the most pressing difficulty to obtain the common necessaries of life." A note from Bengal in the 1783–84 famine is particularly interesting for the light it shines on the experience and cultural construction of drought, famine and scarcity in the region and the period. A letter describes how the "shocking experience" of the 1770 famine "still fresh in the memories of most people" combined with the shipment of vast quantities of grain to Madras in the preceding seasons left Bengal vulnerable to artificial shortages (Campbell, 1868: 114–15).

Figure 3.4 Map of famine areas in India, 1770–1825.

Perhaps the most valuable section of this collection is the one containing details of the famine and general upheaval caused by a series of storms in 1787. Several sources reported on this event: an article in *The Nautical Magazine* recorded that "Captain Huddart describes one [storm] which destroyed ten thousand persons in the neighbourhood of Coringa, in May, 1787, and penetrated twenty miles over the country" (1832: 293). William Roxburgh noted a major loss of his papers, including those on various plant species in his collection, as a result of this event:

> I had made and noted down many observations on its uses, when in large practice in the General Hospital at Madras in 1776, 77 and 78, but lost them, with all my other papers, by the storm and inundation at and near Coringa in May 1787.
>
> (1832: 34)

The Madras typhoon of May 1787 was one of a series of very severe storms which occurred that year in Bengal. Reports of floods from the *General Letter from India* of 15 December 1787, describe a "violent inundation" of which the author states that

> no memory can recollect any preceding instance of similar inundations [...] the distress occasioned by the inundation was aggravated by a storm which happened on the 2nd ultimo, [i.e. November] and which, wherever it prevailed, destroyed much of the existing crops.
>
> (Campbell, 1868: 142)

An important point here with regard to the meteorological record is that the second storm (along with others described below), which occurred in November, exacerbated the already difficult situation caused by the typhoon in May. This second disaster made the problems associated with the first much more difficult to recover from. The governor general, Lord Cornwallis, was suspicious of false claims, warning that "it will be the duty of the board of revenue to make the most scrupulous investigations, and to reject every ill-founded claim for deductions". Again an embargo on export was put in place, now for six months (ibid.: 141). More disparities emerged in the aftermath of the flood and storms. Grain prices were very high in Murshidabad and Dhaka, in particular, "where sufferings of the poor inhabitants were the greater", but much more normal in Benares and Bihar "where the crops had been abundant"; thus exports from these regions to the affected areas were encouraged. In addition to the Madras event in 1787–88, other reports recorded early and abnormally heavy rains in Bengal and Bihar. Through "the latter part of March to the latter half of July, they had continued with such violence as almost to render cultivation impossible." A government-imposed ban on grain exports was credited with resolving the situation by June 1788 (ibid.: 21).[11]

By 1 June 1788, the *General Letter* could state "that the distresses which have been suffered by the scarcity of grain, in different parts of the country and particularly in Dacca, have been of late much relieved". The proceedings of the revenue board reveal the internal conflict over the continuation of collections through times of scarcity. As shown above, Cornwallis was resigned to the fact that remission would be necessary, but aimed to scrupulously investigate any suspected false claims. W. Hindman, an acting collector, wrote on 20 July 1787 that since the 11th:

> ... rains have continued with a violence hitherto unknown, and, it grieves me to inform you, that by the advice I have received from the Mofussil [rural areas], I am apprehensive of a total depopulation of all the *pergunnahs* [subdistricts], if the weather does not soon moderate ... about two thirds of the *ryots* [peasants] have retired for safety with their families to the hills and others are following daily, whole villages have been swept away.
>
> (Campbell, 1868: 152)

He continued:

> ... it is impossible for language to convey the distressful situation of this province; where ever you go you see nothing but a sheet of water, with here or there the tops of houses and trees. Whole crops have been levelled and villages, cattle, grain, and implements of husbandry swept away. Many of the inhabitants have been drowned and whole *pergunnahs* deserted ... the small islands before the city of Dacca are entirely overflowed, and only a few of the tops of the houses are to be seen, the oldest inhabitants remember nothing like it ... The overflowing [of the] banks of the Berhamputer [Brahmaputra], a circumstance never known before, has certainly occasioned this dreadful inundation.
>
> (Ibid.)

The collector of Chittagong reported that "the deluge of rain which has recently fallen in these parts exceeds, I am given to understand, the memory of the oldest inhabitants" (ibid.: 147–53). Campbell's collection shows how very severe weather difficulties – again and again made worse by repeated storms, and very likely combined with administrative determination to continue tax collection to the greatest possible extent – left great want and dislocation amongst the poor. The collector of Nuddea wrote in September 1787 that:

> The rivers which run through this district have risen to so alarming a height that I should consider myself deficient in my duty did I omit to communicate the intelligence to you; the Jellingy in particular, which

passes by this place has swelled to such a degree that there are few parts where its banks are not overflowed on both sides and to judge from my own observation and the opinion of people here, it must be at least two feet higher than it was in the rains of 1785, and then it was higher than the oldest inhabitants had ever remembered it.

(Campbell, 1868: 175–7)

At the end of that month "vast torrents" were recorded in Midnapore by which "those poor creatures that survived the calamity have lost everything in the world" (ibid.). Similar reports came from Burdwan, Sarun in the west to Sylhet, and Rungapore in the east (ibid.: 185). Numerous collectors wrote to the Board of Revenue warning that the population could not support regular tax collections. In some cases, the Board permitted collectors to exercise discretion, but in other cases remittance was refused.

Danvers' and Campbell's collections of famine reports appear to show a significant increase in climate-related societal difficulties during the 1780s–1790s. Although the 1770 famine was extremely severe, no other famines are described for the remainder of the 1770s, whereas a total of six notable famines are described between 1780 and 1791 (including the Doji Bara and Chalisa famines), none in the remainder of the 1790s, two in the 1800s and two in the 1810s. All of the 1780s famines were in part born of climatic irregularities, although as described above, through notably complex causal links. The most frequent climatic contribution was lack of rain, but disruptions to the expected timing of rain, excessive rain, and a notable season of extreme storms, floods, and intense winds in 1787 also contributed to famine when they occurred. Campbell's collection of reports on the storms of 1787 add much detail to previous knowledge of the May typhoon and suggest that areas of Bengal were struck repeatedly by dramatic storms and floods of an extent not known in living memory. Such reports appear to support Allan *et al.*'s (2003) and Gergis and Fowler's (2009) identification of a more extended La Niña episode beginning in mid-decade.

Although statistical data are absent, Danvers' qualitative assessment of the 1790–92 famines suggests they were the most severe of the period. However, it would be impossible from the information contained here to assess their impact in relation to the 1770 famine, which Campbell in 1868 – with the benefit of hindsight – referred to as "the Great Famine of 1770". Significant evidence not found elsewhere indicates that at least in some regions the 1790–92 famine was remarkable in its impact, thus supporting Grove's identification of intense ENSO activity at this time (Grove, 1998). These include: reports of direct governmental famine relief through the distribution of rice, the institution of employment programmes through public works, subjective judgements of its extreme severity, descriptions of the failure of rains, and of resort to suicide and eating of children.

Conclusion

This chapter has argued that the idea of a climate-induced seventeenth-century crisis for India requires more detailed mining of documentary and paleo sources – both in terms of time and space – for comparative and quantitative evidence. The establishment of true exceptionalism, both in terms of climate anomalies and societal, cultural, political and economic transformation, needs more evidence. Furthermore, it has underlined that famine causation is complex, and that whilst climate is often an important factor, its impact is always geographically and demographically asymmetric. Simplistic notions such as weak or strong monsoons or intense ENSO episodes take no account of possible variation in mode of expression and centres of action of these climate events, or of the determining role played by governmental action such as tax relief, grain embargoes and employment programmes. A more useful approach, then, is one that focuses on regional and national differences and the resilience of agricultural production in the face of population pressure, exogenous shocks and environmental changes, a project which calls for – in the first instance – the establishment of a comprehensive database of sources that will help us construct clear famine, climate, disease, wage and price series for South Asia.

Notes

1 See Le Roy Ladurie, 1971; Atwell, 2001. A window into recent developments in Chinese climate history is Marks, 1998; see also Zhang and Lin, 1992, which includes abundant historical information.
2 The seventeenth-century crisis was perhaps also linked to strong El Niños that produced withering droughts and famines in much of south and south-east Asia in 1614–16, 1623–24, 1629–32, 1660–62 and 1685–88. The last was one of the most pronounced El Niños in recorded history. See also Grove, 2002.
3 Cited by Rob Allan of the MET office, Hadley Centre, who worked jointly with the authors of the paper on a McGill University, Montreal, funded project on the seventeenth-century crisis. See also his initiative, International Atmospheric Circulation Reconstructions over the Earth (ACRE) Initiative (www.met-acre.org).
4 Climatological Database for the World's Oceans (CLIWOC) 1750–1850 (http://webs.ucm.es/info/cliwoc/intro.htm). A European Union-funded project which ran from 2001to 2003. See also www.weatherdetective.net.au/about.
5 This climate data is provided by Rob Allan. Some of the EIC sources he consulted include: Edward Terry (Chaplain to Sir Thomas Roe), *A Relation of Sir Thomas Roe's voyage into the East Indies* (1665); Foster Rhea Dulles, *Eastward Ho! The First English Adventurers to the Orient. Richard Chancellor – Anthony Jenkinson – James Lancaster – William Adams – Sir Thomas Roe, etc. [With Plates, Including Portraits.]* (London: John Lane, 1931); Thomas Roe, *Sir Thomas Roe's Journal of His Voyage to the East Indies and Observations There During His Residence at the Mogul's Court as Embassador from King James the First of England* (1732).
6 For a version of Figure 3.1 in colour, see Damodaran, Allan, and Hamilton (2015), unpublished paper, Food Security and the Environment in India and Britain Workshop (http://foodsecurity.exeter.ac.uk/wp-content/uploads/2015/09/17th-century.pdf).

 7 See figure 3 in Shi *et al.* (2014), where the grey periods indicate the 26 famine events identified in India over the past millennium (www.nature.com/articles/srep06739).
 8 See figure 3 in Neukom *et al.* (2014), "Extreme periods" (www.nature.com/articles/nclimate2174).
 9 See figure 4 in Buckley *et al.* (2014) www.sciencedirect.com/science/article/pii/S0277379114001462?via%3Dihub.
10 The 1630s Gujarat famine is discussed by Mukherjee in Chapter 4 of this book.
11 In Chapter 5, Bhattacharya reconstructs in detail the effect of the 1788 disasters on local ecologies and economies.

Part II
Roads and rivers

4 Famine chorography

Peter Mundy and the Gujarat famine, 1630–32

Ayesha Mukherjee

In 1556, a famine inaugurated the reign of the Mughal emperor Akbar (Fazl, 2015–19, 3: 105–7) – part of a series of subsistence crises that occurred in India during the sixteenth and seventeenth centuries, whose chronology runs uncannily parallel to that of similar crises in Britain from the 1550s onwards (Hoskins, 1964, 1968; Walter and Schofield, 1989; Habib, 1963, 1999; Moosvi, 1987, 2008; Datta, 2000; Grove and Chapell, 2000). As the previous chapter has argued, global climatic conditions offer a possible explanation for this chronological correspondence.[1] Literature of complaint, in the English context, referred constantly to climatic anomalies, presenting them as *flagella Dei*, afflictions sent by God, which produced famine and dearth (Walter and Wrightson, 1976; Walsham, 1999). Similarly, in India, official Persian chronicles and popular vernacular literature, such as the Bengali *Mangalkavya*, expressed climatic anxieties (Parker 2013; Dasgupta, 2000). In Britain and India, there developed local and state-guided discourses of famine, incorporating concerns about climate, place, and mobility, whose strategies of representation, this chapter argues, had a spatial basis. Potential interactions between these discourses need investigation. During a difficult phase of English famine, marked by four disastrous harvests from 1594 to 1597, the average wheat price rose 83 per cent above the norm, and the nation saw increased levels of vagrancy, destitution, and food riots, especially in the uplands of the north and west, which suffered owing to the inaccessibility of markets. Anonymous parish register entries show that bodies of the displaced rural poor migrating south and east were found under hedges, in barns, or on the roadside. There was a substantial increase in deaths, arguably, from starvation and inferior diet (Walter, 1989; Mukherjee, A., 2015). This context may seem remote from that of East India Company traders travelling through famine-affected Mughal provinces; but this chapter aims to show that perceptions of Indian topography, economy, and ecology among early Company employees were not driven by ecologically naive expectations of finding infinite resources elsewhere to displace environmental anxieties stirred by the experience of dearth or famine in their own land. Their experience of the Indian environment was more complex, shaped by travelling through the land, and by interaction with local economies, communities, and knowledge networks, to which they would have brought their own local understanding and experience of dearth.

A wider aim of this book is to examine the emergence of early notions of food security, and this chapter will focus on perceptions of space and place as driving factors for early modern British understandings of alternating dearth and plenty in India. East India Company employees, like the Cornishman Peter Mundy, were constantly on the move, whether by sea or on land, and experienced mobility as an endemic condition (Fumerton, 2006: 1–11).[2] Their narratives of travel and economic crisis in India adapted developing modes of representing domestic mobility in Britain, and constructed what I will call "famine chorographies". The chapter thus begins by tracing key elements of the discourse of space, place, and mobility in early modern Britain and Mughal India, drawing attention to their potential intersections as well as radical differences. It will then examine how local English discourses of space, mobility, and dearth were reapplied to describe travel in India, using Mundy's text and narration during the notorious Gujarat famine of 1630–32 as a case study. This famine is also described in the Mughal courtly chronicles, the *Pādshāh nāma*s, using very different representational strategies, which are here placed in dialogue with Mundy's account, in an attempt to understand the cross-culturally informed socio-economic discourses that shaped the construction of famine narrative and remedy.

Discourses of space, place, and mobility

The political model of social and spatial organisation that assumed the English nation was divided into stable, self-sufficient communities was reinforced by the monarch and legal statutes and structures like the Statute of Artificers and the Poor Laws. These regulated domestic mobility by rhetorically encoding the assumption that England had a settled population, each labourer had his superior, and each pauper an identifiable place of residence so that neighbours could take responsibility for their relief (Appleby, 1978: 29; Hindle, 2001: 45–6; Slack, 1988, 1992). James I's well-known formulation saw this static sense of place, surveyed and governed by the monarch, as a reflection of order in the natural world – "as every fish lives in his owne place, some in the fresh, some in salt, some in the mud, so let every one live in his owne place, some at Court, some in the Citie, some in the Country" (James VI and I, in Somerville, ed., 1994: 227). Such formulations raise the question of what travelling may have meant in this context, legally and theoretically. Was it regarded as a variety of vagrancy or migration? Vagrancy legislation could be brutal to the displaced, aiming to resettle vagrants in the parish where they were born. John Taylor the Water Poet, in his *Pennyles Pilgrimage* (1618), describing a journey on foot from London to Edinburgh, carefully distinguished himself from beggars and vagrants, defining himself as a "travailer on foot". Conscious of the problems of sustaining this distinction, he also published a pamphlet defending beggars (1621).

In practice, keeping everyone "in his owne place" proved unenforceable. Statutory definitions of settlement were subject to local debate as distinctions between "vagrants" and "migrants" remained elusive. As Steve Hindle argues, legal ambivalences and variations in local rural practice meant that cases ultimately relied on the discretion of parish officials, who, in the first half of the seventeenth century, were not entitled to remove the poor simply because they were destitute or chargeable; but by 1662, settlement laws allowed officers to pre-emptively remove indigents who *might* become chargeable to the parish (Hindle, 2004: 306–10; Fumerton, 2006: 12–33; cf. Dyer, 2007). If the momentum of the legislation from 1589 onwards ensured the replacement of traditional practices of undifferentiated charity with parish-bound support, attempted to create classifications for defining "rogues, vagabonds, and sturdy beggars", reinforced "parochial xenophobia", and turned placelessness itself into a crime (McRae, 1996: 95; Slack, 1988: 25; Hindle, 2004: 319), there were many counter-pressures upon this system – not least from the plying of trades that were crucial to mercantile exchange on which the economy's nascent capitalism relied.

Watermen (like Taylor), tinkers, pedlars, carriers, chapmen, and other workers whose trade demanded mobility, and who were regarded with continuous suspicion, nevertheless constituted a range of "petty traders" who were beginning to extend markets beyond localised boundaries and arguably creating the basis for a consumer society.[3] They were also, I would argue, creating mechanisms for coping with dearth. In this milieu, Taylor's attempts to distinguish between beggars and travellers, or pedlars and carriers, and his efforts to map the movements of the latter suggest a parallel cultural impetus to realign the place of mobile traders within the geographical and socio-economic landscape of England. Taylor's work in the 1620s and 1630s challenged traditional perceptions of markets as regulated spaces, and the authorities' concerns about idle beggary and the "undeserving" poor. *The Carriers Cosmographie* (1637) provided the first guide to private carriers operating on standard routes between London and the provinces. In his preface, Taylor claimed his information was gathered with "Toyle" by interviewing (often hostile) carriers, hostellers, and porters. The verbal mapping of routes was a standard feature of his work, and *The Pennyles Pilgrimage* had, through this process, realigned traditional codes of hospitality as facilitators of mobility (McRae, 2009). Taylor's beggars, traders, and travellers were dynamic entities and, inverting contemporary diatribes against vagrants, "enemie to Idlenesse". Travel and industry were aligned, as McRae argues, especially in relation to his own quotidian travel as a waterman, in his address to the river Thames: "Thou the true rules of Justice doth observe,/To feed the lab'rer, let the idle sterve" (1630: 75). English domestic travel literature, in other words, could ascribe positive value to travel or travail, operating in conjunction with practical manuals – like Hugh Platt's *Remedies against Famine* (1596) and food and drink for mariners (1607) – which created itineraries for labour specific to conditions of dearth (Mukherjee, A., 2015: 39–42).

The seventeenth-century Mughal state, meanwhile, had its own means of creating the myth that places (and people) could be made obedient to the emperor's will. The peripatetic mobility embedded in Mughal court culture (Lal, 2005: 70; Gronke, 1992: 18–22; Balabanlilar, 2012: 71–84) reflected, paradoxically, a desire for static order, and reinforced the unchanging centrality of the emperor's authority. No place was ultimately more authoritative than the emperor in person: as long as he and his court moved, everyone else kept their place. Reliance on peripateticism to consolidate imperial identity, power, and stability was partly a dynastic inheritance from the nomadic mobility of the displaced royal courts of Timur and his successors (Balabanlilar, 2012; Gronke, 1992). Indeed, the first Mughal emperor Babur described his life of constant warfare and exile as a state of "vagabondage" (*qazāqliqlārda*) and continuous "interregnum" (*fatratlārda*),[4] while the court of his son Humayun became a mobile imperial "camp" (*urdū-i mu 'allā*), which fostered nomadic trade to support itself (Balabanlilar, 2012: 73; Bābur, 1995: 16 and 1996: 21; Bernier, 1934: 365; Monserrate, 1922: 108). Traces of this survived during the reigns of later Mughal princes, quick to recognise political advantages of mobility. However, their massively scaled, grand migrations across the land, similar to the progress and pageantry of English monarchs, starkly contrasted with the train of caravans and its mixed social groups that characterised famine migrations of the kind described by Mundy, who, nevertheless, observed and even sketched such a progress of the "great Mogul" Shahjahan (Bodleian Library, MS. Rawlinson A.315, inserted f.68v–69r). Imperial peripateticism in seventeenth-century India afforded opportunities to modify land and construct obedient manipulated landscapes to reinforce the Mughal monarch's Turko-Mongol legitimacy (Subtelny, 1995: 20; Lentz, 1996: 39). Mobility itself was thus shrewdly used to create static patterns of authority. For example, James I's contemporary Jahangir boasted in his memoirs how he came upon a stream flowing from the ferry and ordered it to be diverted so that he could build a garden "such that in beauty and sweetness there should not be in the inhabited world another like it. I gave it the name of *Jahān-āra* [world-adorning]" (*Jahāngīr*, Persian, 2006: 62–3; English, 1909–14: 106).

Such acts recalled similar past acts. Jahangir's ancestor Timur had constructed a garden in Samarkand by appropriating the course of a river, so that "highland and lowland, steppe and plain, were/Turned into ... Paradise", and "Forage herbs became tulips, stones became/Rubies and pearls, grass became elixir, and the/Ground became gold", said Yazdi's *Zafarnāma*, in its hyperbolic recording of this transformation of terrain

(Persian, 1957; English, 1989: 91). The construction of *Jahān-āra* took place during Jahangir's tour of Kabul, re-enacting his great-grandfather Babur's survey of the gardens of Herat in 1506, and recalling the latter's attempts to then tame the "harsh and unwelcoming" (*karāhat wa nākhoshluk*) north Indian landscape, with its heat, wind, and dust, into the classic *bāgh*s or gardens of Transoxiana. This "imperialism of landscape architecture" (Balabablilar, 2012: 81; Dale, 2012: 186) controlling "free" spaces continued throughout subsequent reigns of Mughal emperors. Imperial travel itself became an act of memory and memorialisation, both emulative and competitive. The garden in Kabul *Shahr-āra* ("city-adorning", and alluding to the name of its creator Shahr Banu,[5] "lady of the city/land") was bettered by Jahangir's *Jahān-āra* ("world-adorning"). The new name of the modified, compliant landscape synchronised, unsurprisingly, with the emperor's own name, *Jahān-gīr* (world-seizer). Notwithstanding the erasure of local topography, land ownership, and possibly the practical needs of the ferry connecting to the stream which was diverted; by his son Shahjahan's reign, the tradition of creating obedient landscapes by manipulating courses of rivers and canals had stimulated the development of satellite settlements of craftsmen and labourers employed for the upkeep of gardens. As in the English context, the counter-pressures upon imperial definitions of place, I would argue, came from the mobility of trade and labour that was created partly in response to Mughal manipulations of landscape.

Their spatial and technical management of gardens and small scale public water systems were imbued with political and economic meanings (Wescoat, 2007; Eaton, 1993; Habib, 1999: 24–36; cf. Wittfogel, 1958; Welch, 1996). Mughal emperors were in turn emulated by the Indian nobility. The consequent proliferation of gardens meant such places could only grow by interaction with activities outside their walls of enclosure. Waterworks linked gardens with cities and countryside (Wescoat, 2011a). The word "*bāgh*" (garden) could apply equally to the independent "*chār-bāgh*s", and to groves, orchards, or mixed gardens growing fruit and flowers. By the seventeenth century, even independent courtly gardens performed economic functions, being, as Habib notes, "not simply sources of aesthetic pleasure", but sites for horticultural experiments based on imports, transplanting, and grafting to augment fruit supplies (1996: 128). Flower gardens stimulated distillation experiments, initially in aristocratic households, leading to improved production techniques, expanded cultivation, and economical pricing. Surplus production created commercial objectives, and gardens began to be annually rented to market the produce. By the latter half of the century, smaller privately owned gardens were being bought and sold. Gardens sold off by heirs were ploughed and turned into fields or wastes. Gardens were thus also sites of investment, where expenses had to be recovered. Habib tables calculations found in a contemporary manuscript (*c.*1642) of the labour, cattle, and implements used in four gardens in and near Agra. The largest of these, Bagh Dahra, covered 429 bighas and employed 236 gardeners, 162 oxen, and 46 rope and bucket chains (ibid.: 133). Apart from their function as aestheticised symbols of power, and sites of imperial recreation and deliberation, the continued existence of these transformed spaces depended on their ability to adapt to pragmatic concerns and incorporate networks of exchange and labour, operating beyond their defined spatial remit.

Famine chorography

While EIC factors like Mundy encountered pressures of defining place from both the available English political model and from political and administrative structures of the Mughal empire, they were also aware of fundamental challenges to traditional, seemingly stable, conceptions of place. In both contexts, vagrancy and/or migration for subsistence or improvement, the operations of markets and trades, and travel within and beyond national boundaries created "abstract spaces" of "networks", shaped by processes of mobility and exchange (Lefèbvre, 1991: 2). Mughal transformations of spaces and Taylor's local travels are illustrations of these processes and challenges, which took specific forms in India and Britain, but were comparable and potentially interactive, especially when we consider their effect on verbal and visual demonstration of space in contexts of famine and dearth. In a text like Mundy's *Travels*, this representation itself occurred in a state of mobility – he wrote journal notes and made sketches of scenes on the move (Bodleian Library, MS. Rawlinson A315). As a result, the text was informed by direct, immediate, fluctuating experiences of dearth and plenty, later revised and organised. This led to the construction of a "famine chorography": a dynamic kind of spatial representation categorising places as a locus of plenty or want, and appearing as a mode in genres of writing that depicted mobility – a journal, journey poem, or vagrancy literature. Places of fluctuating plenty or want were identified along or near routes with an established political or economic significance, pre-defined by traditional, national, or imperial conceptions of space, which the famine chorography of literature representing mobility from below might question or challenge.

I use the term "chorography" in the Renaissance sense of written description of regions, often combined with visual elements, including maps, and considered distinct from chronicle history in its prioritising of place above time (Schwyzer, 2009; McRae, 2009, 2015; Klein, 2001). Mundy's description of travel through famine-affected areas contained elements common to British domestic travel writing, which utilised and modified chorographic traditions. In seventeenth-century Britain, as McRae notes, the empirical exercise of gathering data for the benefit of gentlemen and the commonwealth was applied in domestic travel, which was a cheap alternative or supplement to foreign tours, making England an equal object of scientific enquiry (2009: 7–18). Spatial knowledge acquired through travel became a means of manipulating space. Consequently, domestic travel writing used the mode of cornucopoeia, a figure of plenty, applying it to natural resources, information, and objects of curiosity. Travel allowed access to abundant findings, turning the itinerary form into a crucial tool – specifics of date, place, coordinates, geographical features needed codified presentation (McRae, 2009: especially 67–90). Categorising places as pleasant/unpleasant, I suggest, became part of the itinerary: the distinction was often determined by economic factors, like poverty and poor sanitation described by the eighteenth-century traveller Celia Fiennes (1682–1712; Fiennes, 1984), or concerns with local hazards, hospitality, and commerce in the poetry of Richard Corbett (1582–1635), Richard James (1592–1638), or John Taylor (1580–1654). While Corbett, uncomfortable with the propensity of alehouses and inns to contest the status quo of every fish and human being knowing their place, complained that ostlers could rise to be innkeepers, tapsters could bully priests into paying higher prices for bread and beer (1807: 161–84); in James' journey poem, an old fisherman offered more subtle criticism of travelling "gentlemen" whose mobility, a product of affordable leisure, contrasted radically with the localised labour of communities which ensured food availability. James' fisherman thus itemised his labour which rationed time: "making, mending nett,/Preparing hooks and baits, wherewith to gett/Cod, whiting, place.... Where with to feede ye markett and our selvs" (James, 1845: ll. 126–36).

The issues Taylor raised were closer to the circumstances of Peter Mundy's travels in India. Locating labour in the persona of a penniless pilgrim, Taylor focussed on finding food and categorising places as representative of want or plenty as he "travailed on foot" from London to Edinburgh, reversing his Water Poet's norm ("My legs I made my oars, and rowed by land") and encountering "strange (yet English) fashions" (1618: 1). In the itinerary mode, he ticked off provisions and practical hazards: hunger, disease, and their remedies. He filled his "knapsack, (to pay hunger's fees)" with "good bacon, biscuit, neat's-tongue, cheese/With roses, barberries, of each conserves,/And mithridate, that vigorous health preserves" (2), making a conscious choice, as his title page claimed, to undertake this journey "not carrying any Money to or fro, neither Begging, Borrowing, or Asking Meate, drinke or Lodging". He conducted a regional survey of the survival of hospitality in an economic context that had placed under strain values of stewardship and communality. The penniless "pilgrim" survived on the hospitality of ale houses, and the lack thereof was, as Taylor called it, "drought" (6). In a comic, inverted famine chorography, the drought was allied to parts of the route. Alternating, unpredictable dearth and plenty not only defined spaces and places but propelled Taylor's narrative forward. Intermittently, the landscape yielded free food for the penniless pilgrim and his starving horse:

My nag made shift to mump green pulse and peas.
Thus we our hungry stomachs did supply,
And drank the water of a brook hard by.

(6)

At other times, he breakfasted on "material Sunshine" in the absence of
an actual meal (14), observing that the "wit" to utilise the materials of
nature was quickly stimulated by "want":[6]

Wit's whetstone, Want, there made us quickly learn,
With knives to cut down rushes, and green fern,
Of which we made a field-bed in the field,
Which sleep, and rest, and much content did yield.

(Ibid.)

Unlike nature's provisions, not all hospitality encountered by the pilgrim
was free, let alone unproblematic. At Daventry, he found a strange hunger
for his travel tales at the inn, not unconditional hospitality. To the locals,
the traveller was a curiosity, identified with exotic imports – "some
monster sent from the Mogul", "some elephant from Africa", or "some
strange beast from the Amazonian Queen" (8–9). With comic exaggeration, Taylor's similes emphasised that the very condition of travel and continuous displacement made even the domestic traveller "foreign".

Taylor's deft ironic modulation of plenty and dearth connects his work
with earlier authors such as Thomas Nashe and Robert Greene, who
observed similar ambivalences during the 1590s dearth and famine in
England (Hutson, 1987: 199; Mukherjee, A., 2015: 55–9). But in Taylor,
the previous decade's discourse of dearth appears to merge with a spatial
and travel-oriented discourse. While discussions of food, traffic, or trade
featured in domestic travel writing partly for pragmatic reasons – travellers
needed to find provisions – travel also brought to light food substitutes
and strategies for survival used across the country, and beyond. Travellers'
specialised knowledge of survival on the move, with perpetually limited
resources, was re-adapted to fit local or domestic contexts of dearth and
famine. Hugh Platt's widely circulated *Remedies against Famine*, for
example, published food experiments based on his interactions with
sailors and soldiers, who were familiar peripatetic types in early modern
Britain. His experiments demonstrated the development of a local
economy of crisis foods through interaction with consumption practices
originating beyond local or national boundaries (Platt, 1607; Mukherjee,
A., 2015: 40). This kind of dynamic exchange made it harder to keep a
particular type of food in its particular place, geographically or morally;
while the heightened awareness of trade and traffic pushed against the
impetus to contain markets within models of space committed to values of
place and settlement.

Representing the Gujarat famine

A sailor from the age of 14, and the son of a Cornish pilchard merchant, Mundy belonged to itinerant communities motivated by the need to find innovative ways of stretching limited resources,[7] possessing a literary, pragmatic, and political discourse of their own, that adapted modes and debates in domestic travel writing. When these modes of writing were displaced, so to speak, and entered accounts of travel in India, complex tensions and new mixed modes were created. We see this, for example, in Mundy's attempts to use figures of plenty, repeatedly frustrated by the sheer scale of Indian famines. The Gujarat and Deccan crisis he narrates began with a drought in 1630, attacks on crops by mice and locusts in the following year, and then excessive rain.[8] Famine and water-borne diseases created high mortality: 3 million died in Gujarat in 1631, and a further million in Ahmadnagar.[9] People migrated towards less affected areas, many died on the way, and dead bodies blocked the roads. Persian and European sources provide a subverted cornucopoeia of grotesque consumption patterns: cattle-hide was eaten, dead men's bones were ground with flour, cannibalism was frequent, and people fed on corpses. Carts belonging to *banjaras* transporting grain from more productive regions of Malwa were intercepted, and supplies diverted to the royal army in Burhanpur (Mundy, 1907–36, II: 56; Foster, 1630–33: 165). The pre-famine price of wheat was approximately 1 *mahmudi* per *man*; in September 1631 it had risen to 16 *mahmudis* (van Twist, 1937: 68; Foster, 1630–33: 165, 196). Imperial charitable practices of opening free kitchens and offering revenue remission had limited effect. Gujarat was one of the main production centres for calico cloth, and trade was badly affected by the death and migration of weavers (Mundy, 1907–36, II: 276; Foster, 1630–33: 180).

Official chronicle histories, such as the *Pādshāh nāma*s of Md. Amīn Qazwīnī and ʿAbd Al-Ḥamīd Lāhawrī, closely defined the spatial and temporal range of the famine. Lāhawrī began with a comparison of the present year (1631) and the previous.[10]

سال گذشته در محال بالا گهات خصوصا نواحی دولت آباد باران نباریده بود

[*sāl-i guzashtah dar maḥāl-i Bālāghāt khoṣuṣan nawāḥi-i Daulatābād bārān nabārideh bud*]

In the previous year, at places in Balaghat, specially in the vicinity of Daulatabad, it had not rained.

(Lāhawrī, I: 362)

He continued,

و درین سال اگرچه در اطراف و اکناف نیز کمی کرد امّا از ملک دکن و گجرات بالکل منقطع گشت و سگان آن دیار از انقطاع مواد اکل و فقدان مایهٔ قوت به اضطرار افتادند

[*wa darin sāl agarche dar aṭrāf-o aknāf niz kami krad amma az mulk-i Daccan wa Gujrāt bilkul munqaṭe'a gasht wa sukkān-i ān deyār az inqeṭā'e mawād-i akl wa fuqdān-i māyah-i qut be iẓterār uftādand*]

This year, although rain was less in the surrounding region, in Gujrat and Daccan, it did not rain at all and the inhabitants of that place were under great distress due to paucity of edibles and dearth of nourishment.

(Ibid.)

It is clear that Lāhawrī draws on his predecessor Qazwīnī's account of the regional impact:

و از قضایای آسمانی که درین سال رویداد امساک باران وقوع قحط و غلا در کل ولایت دکن و ملک خاندیس و گجرات است. سال پیش در اکثر محال بالای خصوص نواحی دولت آباد امساک باران شد امّا درین سال عام گردیدهٔ بحدّی رسید که پیران کهن سال مدّة العمر مثل آن ندیده و نشنیده اند

[*wa az qazẕayāi āsmāni ke darin sāl ruy dād imsāk-i- bārān, waqu'e qaḥṭ wa ghala dar kull-i vilāyat-i Deccan wa mulk-i khāndis wa Gujrāt ast. Sāl-i pish dar aksạr-i mahāl-i bālāyi khuṣuṣ nawāhi-i Daulatābād imsāk-i bārān shud ammā darin sāl ām gardeedah bahaddi raseed ke pirān-i kohan sāl muddat-ul'umr misl-i ān nadeedah wa nashuneedah and*]

And among the misfortunes brought about by the destiny that year [1631] was scarcity of rain and occurrence of famine and drought in the entire region of Daccan, Khandesh, and Gujrat. In the previous year, too, there was scarcity of rain, particularly in the vicinity of Daulatabad, but this year, it was more common, and reached the extent that has never been witnessed and heard of earlier by the elders in all their lives.

(Qazwīnī, British Library, MS. Add. 20734: ff. 218r–219v)

It was formulaic in Mughal chronicles to use spatial and temporal precision, as well as exact details of weather and climate,[11] to frame the more lurid narration of how the famine was experienced. This is where subtle variations between accounts tended to occur. Narrative style could shift to emphasise local suffering, blurring lines between factual reportage and emotive effect, as we see in Qazwīnī's insistence on the unprecedented and exceptional nature of the calamity, neither seen nor heard by elders in all their lives. While Qazwīnī continued with a snatch of verse to underline the physical conditions of drought (f. 218v), Lāhawrī adopted a different literary tactic.

جانی به نانی می‌دادند و کس نمی‌خرید و شریفی به رغیفی می‌فروختند و نمی‌ارزید

[*jāni be nāni mi dādand wa kas nami khareed wa sharifi be raghifi mi farokhtand wa nami arzid*]

Life was offered for bread, and no one was buying it; nobility was
being sold for one flat bread, but no one was valuing it [in exchange].

(Lāhawrī, I: 362)

The balanced syntax ironically conveyed how daily patterns of exchange
and reciprocity were disrupted by famine – the price of bread was life
itself, while the virtue of nobility had no value. As regular economic relationships were overturned, the charitable giver turned beggar and classic
dearth-time consumption and adulteration practices confounded the
economy further: dog's flesh was sold as goat's flesh, and dead men's
bones were ground with flour, as both chroniclers noted (Qazwīnī, f. 218v;
Lāhawrī, I: 362). Eventually, when cannibalism became the final resort,
closest kinship ties fell apart:

گوشت فرزند را شیرین تر از مهر او می‌دانستند

[*gosht-i farzand rā shirīn tar az mehr-i ou midānistand*]

The flesh of a son was considered sweeter than his love.

(Lāhawrī, I: 362)

There is nothing like the macabre brilliance of this line in Qazwīnī's
description. Lāhawrī pushed the narrative of suffering, extreme want, and
socio-economic dislocation to its climax, perhaps more adeptly than
others. Famine migration and deterioration of land formed the extreme
points in this story of decline from past plenty to total want in the present:

و درین ولایات که به آبادی مشهور و معروف بود اثر معموری نماند و این بلای شدید وباهای گذشته و
غلاهای رفته را که در تواریخ سالفه به رسم تعجّب نوشته اند در نظر بی‌اعتبار گردانید و در مولفات لاحقه
چون مثل مضروب و سمر مکتوب مرقوم خواهد گشت.

[*wa darin velāyat ke be abādi mashhur wa maaruf bud aṣar-i ma'amuri
namānd wa ein balāye shdeed wabāhaye guzashtah wa ghalāhaye rafteh ra ke
dar tawārikh-i sālifah be rasm-i ta'ajjub nawishtah wa dar naẓar be'itebar
gardānid wa dar moallifāt-i lāḥeqeh chun maṣal-i maẓrub wa samr-i maktub
marqum khwahad gasht*]

No trace of population was left in this region which was known for its
habitation. After this great calamity, which will later be cited as the
ultimate example and will be noted as legendary, all accounts of
previous epidemics and famines of the past which have been narrated
with wonder, shall become insignificant.

(Lāhawrī, I: 363)

The official chronicle's purpose was to represent the emperor as the
singular provider of famine remedy; thus Mughal chronicles rarely missed

a chance to lay claim to "the worst famine of all time", which the emperor could be seen to address.

Lāhawrī concluded his description of famine with a cornucopoeia of charitable measures proceeding from the emperor, marking a return to specificities of place. Shahjahan, we are told, with "treasure-scattering hand and ocean-like heart [دست گنج افشان و دل دریا/*dast-i ganj afshān wa dil-e darya*]" (ibid.), instructed his officials at Burhanpur (the headquarters of the imperial army fighting the Deccan wars), Ahmedabad (the centre of power in Gujarat), and Surat (the main port in Gujarat) to set up *langar*s, or soup kitchens, in localities under their administration. As long as the emperor remained in Burhanpur, Rs 5000 were distributed to the poor every Monday, the day of the week when Shahjahan had ascended the throne. Lāhawrī noted that in 20 Mondays, 1 *lakh* (100,000) rupees were distributed in the vicinity of Burhanpur (363–4). It was thus ensured that charity *visibly* flowed from the person of the emperor, reaching those who were geographically close enough to the current centre of imperial

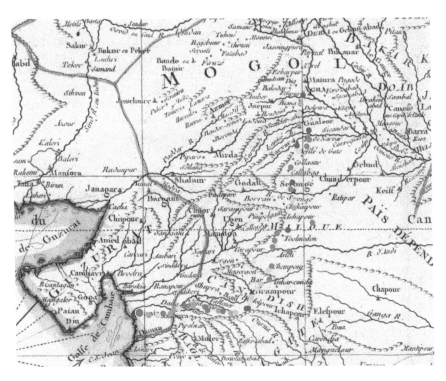

Figure 4.1 Peter Mundy's route from Surat to Agra 1630–31, showing his categoris- ing of places on a scale of plenty to famine.

Source: the colour map, which designates plenty in green and famine in red, may be found on the Famine and Dearth project web database: http://famineanddearth.exeter.ac.uk/ index.html.

activity. This centre, as we have seen, shifted frequently, and famines allowed the opportunity to demonstrate more starkly to his subjects that the emperor was the only true source of sustenance. Highlighting the spatial organisation of charity was therefore a concerted strategy in the official chronicle's account of famine. The *Pādshāh nāma*s made the point that networks of charity beyond the imperial seat in Burhanpur were also within Shahjahan's control. Lāhawrī claimed that Rs 50,000 were distributed to relieve the poor in Ahmedabad; while tax remission amounting to 70 *lakh*s of rupees (apparently, one-eleventh of the whole revenue) was offered in other regions. Lāhawrī commented, if this was the extent of remissions from the imperial exchequer, one could accordingly imagine how great the reductions made by noblemen holding *jāgir*s and *mansab*s may have been. The emperor gauged, in other words, the extent and severity of famine-related suffering and determined the extent and nature of official support across the realm. The chronicle's narration of local specificities in this regard was more nebulous.

Mundy's itinerary shows how English travellers and traders negotiated this environment, conflicted with ecological, socio-economic, and political disparities and anxieties. The itinerary format in British domestic travel writing emphasised that the nation depended on the circulation of people, commodities, and information across local communities, not just within communities bound by designated spatial limits of a piece of land. Mundy's journal constructed his itinerary acutely aware of the dynamics of local mobility in his new setting.[12]

He started from Surat on 11 November 1630 and his narrative, filled with local topographical detail, merged the journal form with a famine chorography different from the imperial *Pādshāh nāma*s. His landscape description suggested a practiced sensitivity to local engagement with shortage, complicated the contrast between the fertile Malwa region and deprived localities below the Narbada river, and identified tensions between localities. There was a concentration of food supplies in Viara, "fortefied with a good Castle and accommodated with a very prettie pond or Talao stored with fish and fowle", and market towns such as Chopda, Navi, and Bahadurpur (Mundy, 1907–36, II.40; f. 32r–v). Between Viara and Chopda, Mundy itemised places badly affected by famine. Just 14 miles from Viara was a poor town, "halfe burnt upp and almost voyd of Inhabitants, the most part fledd, the rest dead, lyeing in the Streets and on the Tombes" (II.40–1; f. 32v). In Daita, people sold their children (II.42; f. 32v). Mundy's party had difficulty pitching their tent at Nandurbar because the town was congested with dead bodies. They bought food at "unreasonable rates", and were overwhelmed by the smell "from a great pitt, wherein were throwne 30 or 40 persons, men, woemen, and children, old and young confusedly tumbled in together without order or Coveringe" and the sight of "poore people scrapeinge on the dunghills for food … in the very excrements of beasts belonging to Travellers, for graine that perchaunce might come undigested from them". People looked like "anatomies, with life, but scarce strength enough to remove themselves from under mens feet" (II.43–4; f. 33r–v). For Mundy, the dead and starving constituted part of the landscape from Surat onwards, lying along highways and near towns, piled outside city gates where bodies were dragged and left. His analogies and images highlighted the way control over the landscape was frustrated by famine which challenged the fixity of quantification and the regulation of boundaries demarcating spaces such as markets, towns, cities, estates, roads, rivers. The land was intractable and rhetorically marked out as an inversion of any constructed "*Jahān-āra*".

The rhetoric itself demands attention, because when describing unpleasant places, moral or aesthetic disgust was complicated by empathy in Mundy's language. His perception was shaped by the communal conditions of travel. His *kāfila* (caravan) had started at Surat with 150 people, 15 carts and some camels. Joined daily by people escaping famine, it consisted, by Nimgul, of 1800 people, 300 carts, and cattle (II.45; ff. 34v–35r). The flow of people – the rhythm of movement is vital to Mundy's representation of landscape – progressed towards Burhanpur, the prosperous city centred on Shahjahan's castle and estate. If Burhanpur was an imagined locus of plenty, the market towns leading to it brought into view palpable contradictions between the "plentifull Bazaar" and starved bodies in streets, obstructing trade and travel. Burhanpur was a site of imported and tentative plenty:

> The Bazare … which joins to the Castle is very faire and spacious, and now, by reason of the Kinges being here, plentifully stored with all provisions, beinge supplied with all things from all parts, farr and neere, which otherwise, it may bee believed, would feele the same Calamitie with her Neighbour Townes, for theire is litle or nothinge growes neere it for many miles.
>
> (II.50–1; f. 35r–v)

Mundy's narrative of his journey through the fertile Malwa region was countervailed by the practice of looking back at this politics of dearth. Despite green fields, villages stored with grain, and plentiful rivers, the sinister flow of this plenty towards Burhanpur army camps haunted Mundy's description throughout. Just as Hugh Platt's or John Taylor's local engagement with communities coping with contradictions of dearth and travail allowed them to query famine remedies and definitions of place imposed from above, Mundy's chorography questioned royal estate-centred discourses which, as noted earlier, described charity flowing from this centre, reinforcing the emperor's benevolence, divinely constituted political authority, and control over the environment, land, and resources.

Mundy felt removed from the resources consumed by imperial landmarks he ambiguously admired and undermined. His own perspective was the diffused migratory one of travellers and tradesmen, local and foreign. He camped with the local trader Mirza, learning from his resourcefulness and the local knowledge of *banjāra*s, local carriers or drovers, whose trade served and depended on mobility (Habib, 1999: 69–70, 1990: 371–99; cf. Kothiyal, 2016). Mundy's famine chorography was thus informed by the mixing en route of racial and social groups with different agendas, making cooperative and competitive demands on resources, a characteristic ambivalence in chorographic works in his own national context. Mundy thus saw *kāfila*s as practical demonstrations of local cooperation: the mixing of people, lengthening of the caravan, and shaping of mutual dependence, as the *kāfila* wended its way through the land, demonstrated to him survival strategies and knowledge of land organised from below. Like Taylor, he located positive industry in travel itself. More than a train of carts, the *kāfila* was a temporary mobile household travelling across, and coping daily with, the shortage-driven landscape, exchanging information about the availability of resources with seasoned local traders for whom mobility was also an endemic condition. In Mughal Sarai, Mundy's *kāfila* met a group of *banjāra*s carrying provisions:

> It was at least 1½ miles in length, and as many more returning emptie to bee reladen, and all the face of the earth, as farr and distant as wee could descerne, covered with greene Corne. But of all this aboundance poore Guzeratt was never the neere, where there was most neede, it being all to Brampore to supplie the kings Laskarrie (or Armie) lyeing there against Decan.
>
> (Mundy, 1907–36, II.55–6; f. 37r)

This crossing of routes and witnessing movements of provisions reinforced anxieties surrounding the finitude of resources and local problems caused by displacement.

Mundy explicitly made cross-cultural connections between this group of nomadic traders in north-west India and English carriers ("Their course of life is somewhat like Carriers, continually driveing from place to place"), observing that mobility was their condition of life. They travelled, as Mundy rightly noted, in a *tanda* (local term for a caravan of *banjāra*s and their cattle) and "carrie[d] all their howsehold along with them". He estimated the *tanda* consisted of 600–700 men, women, and children, and 14,000 oxen "all layden with graine, as wheat, rice, etts.; each Oxe, one with another, carryeinge 4 great Maunds, each Maund neere 16 Gallons is 112,000 bushells London measure" (II.95–6; f. 45r–v). The groups travelled slowly and "dispersedly", journeying no more than 6 or 7 miles a day. Mundy constantly converted local measures of volume or distance to English measures familiar to him, and simultaneously tried to make sense of the *banjāra*s trading networks. He astutely commented on their ownership of mobile capital, such as cattle, and the flexibility of their exchange mechanisms.

> They are sometimes hired by Merchants, but most commonly they are the Merchants themselves, buyinge of graine where it is Cheape to be had, and carryinge it to places where it is dearer, and from thence again relade themselves with anythinge that will yield benefitt in other places as Salt, Sugar, Butter, etts.
>
> (Ibid.)

In other words, Mundy was aware that their trade was flexibly governed by changing local space and demand, instead of being attached to static traditions of production and exchange. The *banjāras'* position may have seemed closer to EIC factors like Mundy, who served and depended on the Company's centrally authorised operations but, at the same time, had to rely on mobility to meet their trading needs.

Placing famine: the "Deccan"

Mundy's observations about the Deccan wars crucially uncovered economic considerations determining movements of Mughal army camps, whose equally endemic mobility compounded matters, for the army had its own particular approach to space, provision, and travel, guided by local ecology and imperial geopolitics. First, the army focused its movements along the Arid Zone where alluvial agricultural areas intersected with dry marchlands which often constituted a famine tract, where inhabitants undertook survival strategies, such as cattle tending, weaving, peddling, and temporary military employment. The empire relied heavily on seasonal peasant labour supplies from arid areas for its growing military labour market, and on the pastoral economy for supply of war horses and dromedaries. Armies moved most efficiently when marching along the frontier between settled agricultural societies providing food supplies and the pastoral marchlands providing fodder and space (Gommans, 2002: 7–37; Kolff, 1990: 1–31). Second, as Stuart Gordon shows, a main force army was like a "moving city"; typically comprising three horses for every two riders, a groom and servant for each mounted warrior, often over 100 oxen to pull each piece of artillery, elephants for commanders, an infantry, a full bazaar to supply the army, and treasure for soldiers to buy provisions in the bazaar. It could not move more than 10 miles a day, with two stationary days per week (1993: 37–8). Smaller armies or sub-units, however, could move faster, as Lāhawrī's account of army movements discussed below will show. Mughal armies with better organisation of cantonments, officer corps, supply lines, and core professional soldiers, moved faster, coordinating a host of satellite missions related to the objectives of the main force.

Third, imperial highways constructed along frontier zones utilised their connecting capacity. The south-eastern Dakshinapath followed extensions of the Arid Zone to connect Madhyadesh through Malwa and the Deccan plateau to the Carnatic coast of the Bay of Bengal (Gommans, 2002: 18–19; cf. Gole, 1989: 91–3). Since roads allowed control of "nuclear zones of power", areas combining agricultural surplus, marchland, and trade routes, army routes frequently traversed spaces *between* the abundant and arid, plenty and dearth. The intersection of Malwa, Khandesh, and Gujarat along the Dakshinapath, just above the Deccan border, was such a space. Heaviest "imperial traffic" occurred along the line from Kabul to Burhanpur (Gommans, 2002: 103), the southern end of the route, to which Mundy saw the supplies from Malwa being directed. Shahjahan's southern campaigns, through Rajasthan and Malwa, involved zigzagging across the main highways in search of pasture rather than clearly following the main route. As Jos Gommans notes, the royal camp "steadily ate its way round the empire" (104). But this was achieved by relying on various criss-crossing networks of *banjāras* bringing food and fodder, merchants, accountants, and bankers ensuring ready availability of money, and *qasba-tis* providing military labour supplies (Kolff, 1990: 5–6). Arguably, the empire's nomadic character was more evident along its peripheries and, during the Gujarat famine, along the unstable, ever-shifting southern border.

When Mundy alludes to the King's army lying in Burhanpur against the Deccan, he seems aware of the relational status of this geographical term – what constituted the Deccan depended on where the southern border lay at a point in time. The geopolitics of regions above the current border, along his route from Surat to Burhanpur, was closely connected to that of regions immediately below. Not only Gujarat, but northern Maharashtra suffered acute famine at this time. The region the Mughal army sought to conquer depended on regional trade between ecologically complementary areas of the Konkan (fertile, rice-growing) and the Desh (pulse-growing) separated by the mountainous Western Ghats, a retreat for rebels who raided productive areas on either side (Gordon, 1993: 12–13; Lāhawrī I: 360). Produce was transported between the Konkan and Desh by bullock caravans travelling over the Ghats. This region also participated in the cotton trade centred on Surat and Burhanpur, and the coastal trade in the west. On the whole, it was thinly populated, showed low monetisation levels, and rain shadow areas below the Ghats faced a regular cycle of depopulation and recolonisation (Gordon, 1993: 22–3). In 1630–32, the Mahadurga famine, as it was locally known, devastated countryside of northern Maharashtra, along the contemporary Deccan border, with three successive failed monsoons and large-scale depopulation – a crisis com-pounded by Mughal political ambitions. Following the deaths of the Ahmadnagar rulers, Malik Amber in 1626, and Bijapur's Adil Shah in 1627, the Mughals focused on the vulnerable Ahmadnagar state as a point of entry to secure the south. This aim governed the army's activities described in the *Pādshāh nāma* throughout the latter years of the 1620s, culminating in Shahjahan's 1630 campaign to gain control of the northern Deccan.

If approached from a spatial perspective, Lāhawrī's account, from the start of Shahjahan's reign in February 1628, of complex movements of the imperial army in the Deccan, emerges as a meticulous chorographic exercise, describing precise geographical movements of sections of the imperial army in 1628–31 over a particular frontier zone (Lāhawrī, I: 316–433). Lāhawrī's famine chorography thus begins much before the description of the famine itself. The army's movements were closely concentrated in the regions of Gujarat, Malwa, Khandesh, Baglana, Berar, and Daulatabad, corresponding to modern Gujarat, Punjab, and Maharashtra. Armies descended from Agra or Burhanpur towards the Deccan to quell frequent rebellion or gain control of territories belonging to Nizam-ul Mulk (Burhan Nizam Shah III), the current leader of the Nizam Shahi dynasty which ruled the Ahmadnagar Sultanate. The *Pādshāh nāma*s record the management of mobility in these regions as the complex conflicts and alliances which shaped the Deccan wars were conducted. Simultaneous military expeditions, from 1628, were led by Abul Hasan, Abdulla Khan, Mahabat Khan, and Azam Khan, generals entrusted with the task of controlling rebellious princes like Jajhar Singh, treacherous courtiers like Khan Jahan Lodi, or decaying sultanates like Nizam-ul Mulk's. In 1629–31, these expeditions involved continuous movement and presence of the army, especially along areas south of the Narbada and Tapti rivers. In 1628, soon after Shahjahan ascended the throne, Abul Hasan set out from Agra in pursuit of Khan Jahan Lodi, chasing him down to Dholpur and across the Chambal river, but Lodi appears to have escaped into the Bundela forests, taking advantage of the army's difficulties with following him through this terrain, making his way through Gondwana and Berar, aiming for Ahmadnagar. Next year, Hasan was sent from Agra again to conquer Nasik, Trimbak, and Sangamnir. He stopped at Burhanpur, and made his way to Dhuliya (half-way between Burhanpur and Nasik) where he waited till the monsoon rains had passed. He was joined by Sher Khan with reinforcements from Gujarat, whom he despatched to attack the Batora fort in Chandor, close to Nasik and Trimbak. Sher Khan returned with the proceeds of this attack, and Abul Hasan moved from his resting point at Alang Fort (near Dhuliya) and passed through Baglana going towards Nasik and Trimbak. On this route, his forces found deserted villages near Jarahi *ghāt*, whose inhabitants had fled to the hills. He sent his men to seek out their settlements and to the still inhabited villages, which were plundered to obtain resources to support the army. When the Nizam's forces intervened, Shahnawaz Khan travelled 20 *kosh* (approximately 45 miles) to make a counterattack. Meanwhile, Khan-zaman was sent to attack the enemy camp at Sangamnir.

While Abul Hasan's forces focussed on these conquests, Azam Khan's army fought the rebel Afghans, moving on from Dewalgaon (60 miles south of Burhanpur) where they had rested during the rains, in pursuit of the rebels Mukarrab Khan and Khan Jahan Lodi to Pipalnir, Bir, and Siugaon, where they were joined by Bhonsla, defecting Hindu commander of the Nizam's army. Lāhawrī notes, the scarcity of provisions in Daulatabad, owing to the presence of rebel armies, prevented Azam Khan from proceeding there. Instead, the imperial army planned a strategic attack on Dharur fort. Azam Khan proceeded from Siugaon to Damangaon (20 *kosh*/45 miles from Ahmadnagar) to Jamkhair (in the Nizam's territory, 30 miles south-east of Aurangabad) and left a force there. He then went further south-east to the banks of the Manjira river (12 *kosh*/24–5 miles from Dharur fort) and backed up to Partur on river Dudhna, thus closing in on Dharur, and camped 3 *kosh*/7–8 miles from the fort. By 1630, the imperial army had made significant inroads into the Nizam's territory. Azam Khan attacked Dharur and seized its ammunition; while Abdulla Khan and Muzaffar Khan, traversing a complicated route from Malwa, crossed the Narbada river, pursued the rebels under Khan Jahan Lodi who were plundering Ujjain, and eventually chased them to Sironj, passing through Dharampur, Lonihara, Depaulpur, Nulahi, and Khilichpur. As Lodi fled from Sironj towards Kalpi, the army caught up with him in the village of Nimi, at Bhander (north-east of Jhansi). He was eventually caught and killed in Seundah, north of the Kalinjar fort, where another commander of the army was stationed (Lāhawrī, I: 316–62).

The *Pādshāh nāma*'s narration was about progressive mastery over spaces and provisions. As the imperial army increased its reach into Deccan regions, its pursuit and punishment of rebel leaders, and its capture of key military bases, were carefully coordinated. This coordination utilised and created access to local knowledge of the regions, increasing imperial visibility and power. Climate was presented as an impediment to this process – monsoon rains forced armies to halt for long periods of time, or drought altered the spatial dynamics of habitation, impeding access to local provisions. Depictions of landscapes, from a military perspective, were guided by the gaining of vantage points and self-provisioning through local raids and sieges. Lāhawrī described the siege of Parenda, 60 miles south-west of Dharur, near the Sina river, on Azam Khan's route from Ahmadnagar to Sholapur (360). He sent his ally Jai Singh to first plunder the town – typically, the target was the market located 1 *kosh* (2 miles) from the fort. As Singh raided the market, Khan arrived and placed a month-long siege on the town. But, says Lāhawrī, there was no provender or grass within 20 *kosh*, so Khan was obliged to raise the siege and continue to Dharur. He managed to fend off the Adil Khani supporters of the Nizam and camped on the banks of the Manjira. The next day, he captured and plundered the town and fort of Balni, before marching to Dharur. Just as the imperial army relied on local raids for provisions, so did rebel armies. Lāhawrī noted, with an air of distaste, that Khan Jahan Lodi and his men had begun collecting revenues from the dependencies of Bir, and raiding merchants' provisions in the towns of Kehun and Kiorai, when they heard rumours of the impending arrival of the imperial army. Regions covered by constant movements of armies were thus not only affected by drought; better provisioned markets and towns in these localities were also the site of competitive raiding by imperial and rebel armies.

It is therefore unsurprising that, when Mundy returned to Surat in 1633, out of the 21 Company men living at the time of his departure, 4 were alive. Gujarat itself had "scarce 1 left of 10" (Mundy, 1907–36, II.275–6). No factories remained, and Mundy gloomily estimated the region would not recover for the next 20 years. Seventeenth-century English travel journals such as Mundy's offer an alternate perspective to Mughal courtly discourses of space, mobility, and resource management, drawing upon chorographic debates and representational modes in their own national context. Attending to similar narrative processes, among the Company's papers and correspondence, can highlight the anxiety among Company men that plenty was temporary, deceptive, and ill-distributed. These texts created tension with relatively static constructions of food availability, ecological control, and place in official discourses, and began the process of constructing mobility itself as a repository of positive values of enterprise, cooperation, and exchange. In this regard, they were part of a rapidly emerging discourse of global networks of knowledge and trade operating across cultural zones or national boundaries; but they also viewed spaces beyond Britain through the lens of domestic mobility, which had its own persistent, indigenous insecurities. If we are to recover an early modern "global" understanding of food security in its own terms, this chapter suggests looking more closely at overlapping modes of representing place and processes of mobility in a famine context, not only extrapolating facts about places from such accounts and related sources.

Notes

1 On the "seventeenth-century crisis" and global climatic events in the *longue durée*, see especially Parker (2013), Grove (2002), Grove and Chappell (2000). A critical examination of these ideas, with further evidence, is undertaken by Damodaran, Allan, and Hamilton in Chapter 3 of this book.

2 Later figures like Edward Barlow, analysed by Fumerton in her account of "unsettled subjectivities", were drawing on decades of seafaring experience, traditions of mobility, and identity formation in travel accounts.

3 There are differently nuanced arguments about this: Westerfield (1915, 1968) for types of petty traders; McKendrick *et al.* (1982: 86–8) on the development of a consumer society; Spufford (1984: 5–20) on the increasing circulation of consumer goods; McRae from the viewpoint of domestic travel (2009: 102). Woodbridge (2004: 151) argues pedlars were suppressed because they

threatened commercial interests of (traditional) fairs, weekly markets, guilds, and pawn shops.

4 *Qazāq/qazāqliq* had a specific usage in post-Mongol central Eurasia where it described a state of political vagabondage (Lee, 2015: 23–5; Dale, 2004: 98–9; Subtelny, 2007: 29). *Fatrat* had the more focused meaning of an interregnum, highlighting the anxiety of being in a state of eternally seeking political stability.

5 Daughter of Mirza Abu Said, great-grandson of Timur and Babur's paternal grandfather.

6 The idea that wit proceeds from want was a common motif in 1590s literature of dearth (e.g. Weever, 1599: I.21, II.4).

7 On the decline of the Cornish pilchard trade which probably led Mundy to seek employment with the EIC, see Carew (1602: 52–3); Pritchard (2011).

8 Accounts of the famine in Gujarat and the Deccan in the 1630s are found in the following sources, from which the details here have been drawn: Qazwīnī, MS. Add. 20734: 218r–219v, Or. 173: 220v–221r; Khān, Or. 174: 29r–32r, Or. 1671: 17r–18v; Lāhawrī, I: 362–3; Foster, 1630–33: 73, 134–96, 203–68; 1634–36: 40; Mundy, 1907–36, II: 38–70, 276; Van Twist, 1937: 63–77. For a wider chronology of Mughal Indian famines, see Habib, 1999: 112–22.

9 Reported by the Portuguese Viceroy at Goa in 1631 (Foster, 1630–33: xxi). Lāhawrī reported that Gujarat suffered most (I: 363).

10 Translations from Persian by Azarmi Dukht Safavi (with my occasional amendments); transcription and transliteration by Md. Ehteshamuddin, in *Famine and Dearth*, http://famineanddearth.exeter.ac.uk/index.html.

11 Sadiq Khan, however, reported excessive rain spoiling crops in 1630, drought in 1631, and attack on crops by mice and locusts in 1632 (OIOC, Or. 174: 29r–32r, Or. 1671: 17r–18v). Habib, 1999 (115, n. 19) suggests this reflects the different ways the famine was experienced in different regions – thus Khan is possibly focussing here on the Deccan experience where excessive rain was the initial cause.

12 Textual references to Temple and Anstey edition (1914, 1936) and Bod., Rawlinson MS. A315.

5 Rivers, inundations, and grain scarcity in early colonial Bengal

Ujjayan Bhattacharya

River water movements and price inflation closely resemble each other in their impacts on the agricultural economy. A moderate inflation is arguably beneficial to the economy just as a continuous and moderate flow of water enhances productive possibilities. But immoderate increase in prices have a corrosive effect on the economy, just as excessive flow of water wreaks destruction and havoc on the crops. Such similarities in the nature of the two phenomena prompt us to investigate further how rivers and inundation might directly affect prices and the economy in times of dearth and famine. Floods, droughts, or other physical disruptions of normal life bring about price rise in the core regions affected by such events, and have a ripple effect on wider regions. This can produce famine-like situations, if not an actual famine. In 1787 and 1788, many districts of Bengal experienced excessive, repeated, and violent flow of water on the crops, caused, as Damodaran, Hamilton, and Allan demonstrated, by a series of severe storms. This immediately increased the price of grain in the market. Flood waters, by reducing the scope of producing food for the future, continued to impact on the price rise till 1790, when restrictions on the movement of food were removed. While it has been claimed that inundations are generally beneficial for an agricultural economy, excessive and destructive water currents reduce the scope of producing food and preserving food-stock, and lead to economic degeneration. This chapter shifts our focus to take a closer look at the socio-economic impact of exogenous climatic shocks, such as that delivered by the Madras Typhoon of 1787. The periodicity of rains and frequency of inundation were responsible for high prices in core affected regions as much as human manipulations of food-stock, and prices were liable to be affected even in the region beyond the core. In this context, one should distinguish between annual inundations that are the regular and characteristic ("normal") feature of floods in deltaic Bengal, and the exceptional flooding that had severe destructive effects on food production. I aim to show, through this detailed case study of the effects of a specific disaster, how severe climatic events could disrupt local ecologies and affect the micropolitics of exchange and relief in local economies. The high price of grain, total destruction of habitations, and change in the courses of rivers, severally or singularly, could change the nature of local economies and thus have long-term effect on a region. Such eventualities could be accompanied by famine and depopulation.

David Clingingsmith and Jeffrey Williamson have shown that India experienced a historically low rate of drought during the period 1650–1735. Till 1640, the average rate of drought was one drought every three years. The rate fell precipitously to the average of one drought every six years after 1650, and remained at that level till 1725. It then fell to an even lower level, i.e. one drought every ten years from 1735 to 1775, when it rose again (Clingingsmith and Williamson, 2005). However, nine instances of drought between 1767 and 1793 have been recorded by Rajat Datta. Barring the drought of 1769–70, which caused a great famine in many districts of Bengal, the other droughts of high intensity, causing "famine panic" and "public scarcity" occurred in 1779 and 1783 (Datta, 2000: 243). Floods, during the eighteenth century, in the absence of prevention measures, did cause heavy destruction and had the potential to cause famine. They could be the cause behind scarcity, dearth, and near-famine whenever river inundation was accompanied by excessive rainfall (ten instances between 1737 and 1787) (ibid.: 240, 243). The only major exception perhaps was the drought of 1769–70 in Bengal, when the misery was caused, as Damodaran argues, primarily by unprecedented level of revenue collection (Damodaran, 2007).

The climatic event

As introduced in Chapter 3, the major climatic event which brought about a near-famine situation in 1787–88 in east and north Bengal were the typhoon and storms leading to flooding of the rivers of that region. Though in terms of the intensity of impact, floods in Bengal rivers at other times were as turbulent and destructive – such as the flooding of the river Damodar in 1773 – the climatic disruption of 1787–88 was marked by its prolonged effects. It caused devastation in the rural economy as it impeded the process of regeneration of cultivation, and encroached on the resources that were saved for the future. Such aggravations prompted people to flee their habitations in search of food. Further problems were caused by the rise of water to great levels (Proceedings of the Board of Revenue (Miscellaneous) (BRP (M)) 25: 28 September 1787, from Nadia to Board of Revenue), and this was identified in the Board of Revenue Proceedings as the primary cause behind loss of habitation especially where the flow of water was turbulent (BRP (M) 25: 21 September 1787, Tipperah). Geographically, the floods were widespread. The climatic disturbances which were responsible for heavy rainfall and swelling of the river continued throughout the year – from March till November. The floods spread over the provinces of Dinajpur, Rangpur, Mymensingh, Tipperah, Sylhet, Jessore, Nadia, Burdwan, Birbhum, and Midnapur.

There were, however, some variations in the movement of flood waters. The greater intensity of impact on habitation and food-availability in north and east Bengal was due to the fact that rivers in these regions were beyond the deltaic zone, originating from mountains and hills, and came down with great turbulence and force. This was uncharacteristic of the rivers of the Gangetic delta.

The combination of environmental change and economic events that generated the impact on human lives involved the duration of flood and breach of the cycle of agricultural activity in the rural economy. The greater the duration and repetition of inundation, the greater the possibility of famine. The destruction of the crop sown in one season could be compensated by abundant growth of another, by taking advantage of the alluvium added to the soil (Mukherjee, 1938: 160–79). Similarly, difficulties with the payment of revenue by *ryots* (peasant cultivators) after one season of flood could be obviated if collection was made in the subsequent season. However, if inundations were prolonged, and aggravated by the cascading effect of repeated floods, there was no possibility of growing much crop to compensate for previous losses or pay up the arrears of revenue. Moreover, the labour necessary for constructing embankments could be diverted elsewhere for agricultural work – within the same locale or outside – rendering the prevention of further inundation difficult (Proceedings of the Provincial Council of Revenue (PCR) at Murshidabad 1: 3 January 1774, Lashkarpur to PCR). These instances illustrate that the rhythm of nature tended to break into "ecological disaster points" (Datta, 2000: 238), particularly when flood waters acted with the physical force that could cause destruction, and it was not merely an excess flow. What could follow was an "ecological dislocation" (ibid.) with impact not only on the existing availability of food and possibility of cultivation but also on the future prospect of growing crops in the succeeding season. The peasants faced starvation, and lost their dwellings and their wherewithal for renewal of agriculture.

The floods of the year 1787 were unprecedented in contemporary memory. The oldest inhabitants of the district of Mymensingh and Tipperah remembered nothing like it (BRP (M) 21: 31 July 1787, from Mymensingh; 26: 9 October 1787, from Mymensingh; 21: 31 July 1787, from Resident Tipperah to Chittagong); in Sylhet, though people shuddered at the thought of the distresses of 1784, the water levels in the year 1787 were "considerably higher than they were ever at any period that year and the damage infinitely greater" (BRP (M) 21: 31 July 1787, from Sylhet). In Nadia, the flood was two feet higher than in 1785, and it was reported that the oldest inhabitant had no recollection of such a deluge (BRP (M) 25: 28 September 1787, from Nadia). Most of these districts had abundantly fertile lands, so it could be expected that enough stores of grain – from the *aus* (spring) harvest of the previous year or the *boro* (intermediate) harvest of the spring season – would provide relief, directly or through the market, in the season of floods in July and August. But that was not to be, as the rains had begun in March and the stores of grain or *golas* located in the *ganjes* (localities) had been destroyed.[1] The immediate effect of it was the rise in prices of grain.[2] The landowners and overseers (*zamindars*, *chaudhuries*, and *talukdars*) of the *zillah* (district) of Mymensingh informed that rice in parts of the country were selling at 16 or 17 *seers* per rupee (BRP (M) 21: July 1787, from Mymensingh); and the collector of Mymensingh reported that grain of a very coarse kind was available at 20 *seers* per rupee (BRP (M) 21, 31 July 1787, from Mymensingh). About the situation in Tipperah, the Resident wrote that "the price of grain rose and still continues to rise" (BRP (M) 21: 31 July 1787, from Resident Tipperah to Chittagong). The next casualty was the *aus* crop, and almost every collector wrote that the crops were destroyed leading to the suspension of *kists* (installment payments of monthly revenue). The only exception was the district of Nadia from where the collector reported that the *aus* crop had been saved, despite the deluge, and he would be able to fulfill the revenue obligations of the district (BRP (M) 25: 28 September 1787, from Nadia). Jessore too was saved from much damage despite the rise of rivers due to timely repair of embankments (BRP (M) 24: 4 September 1787, from Jessore). Finally, possibly the most important cause behind the famine was the impact of inundation on the *kharif* (autumn) harvest which affected *aman* (winter crop), or the largest harvest in Bengal. From the accounts of the district officers and their superiors in Calcutta, we know that in most districts the *ryots* and *zamindars* sought the installments of revenue to be postponed till the *aman* harvested, hoping that it would mature. Their hopes were belied by continuous rainfall, flooding of the rivers, and other climatic anomalies.

Prolonged effects

In 1787, the possibility of famine was increased by repeated inundations and climatic distresses. Hopes of revival were raised by moderation of weather at certain intervals, but extreme forms of climatic disturbances leading to inundations brought about further misery for the cultivators. In July 1787, it was reported from Sylhet that by "the great fall of rain … since the month of March last" all the "low parganas [sub-districts] were entirely overflown, the inhabitants driven from their houses and obliged to take shelter on boats" and the greatest part of the cattle drowned. The villages had lost not only the rising crops (that is *boro*) but also the seed "which is the greater loss". The price of rice was greatly enhanced as a result of "many *Gholas* [grain stores] having been swept away" (BRP (M) 20: 31 July 1787, from Sylhet). The damage was sought to be salvaged by cultivating in higher lands which had not experienced inundation till then. But "the circumstance instead of being an alleviation has proved the source of greater misfortunes", said the reports. During "the interval of fair weather which never exceeded a week many more were induced to attempt to sow their lands". Some of the *ryots* did so three times and "instead of reaping the fruits thereof have had the misfortune to find that they have not only lost their rising crops but also the seed which is greater loss" (ibid.). *Zamindars* were called to raise another crop but their hopes "vanished" – the Collector reported – as "after three repeated attempts the crops have been drowned by succeeding inundation and the season is gone" (BRP (M) 25: 21 September 1787, from Sylhet).

As a consequence, the *ryots* did not have resources to engage for the next year's revenues. At Dinajpur, in the early stages of the floods, "the *rubby* [i.e. rabi, winter-sown] crop was entirely destroyed" and the *ryots* refused to come to any settlement unless heavy remissions were granted or the demand for revenue was altogether postponed and "thrown upon the *kurieff* [kharif] and *assasheen* [ashwin, autumn] crops" (BRP (M) 24, 7 September 1787, from Dinajpur). Soon after this communication, the inundation was reported as calamitous, "water having risen at different periods and the crop transplanted in the interval when the water apparently was subsiding". Due to the subsequent sudden rise of the river waters, crops "decayed in the ground". The local officials apprehended that the effect on the *kharif* harvest would be ruinous, and particularly "upon the damage done to the Ruby crop", as the *zamindars* depended on it. The loss of cattle was another result of prolonged and repeated flooding. This not only prevented the possibility of cultivation but also did "materially retard the bringing to the market the crop which may be reaped, as without cattle the grain cannot be cleaned" (ibid; BRP (M) 21: 31 July 1787, from Dinajpur). Thus, the initial vulnerability caused by the extended rains was evident when the *rabi* crop was destroyed and the *ryots* could not engage for the new year's revenue in May and June with the *zamindars* or the government's collectors. This was further aggravated by the continuing rain and river flooding till the month of August. On the instruction of the Board of Revenue to report on the effects of inundation and state of floods in eighteen *parganas*, on 14 August 1787, the Collector reported that the *parganas* where the *ryots* were in economic distress were laid waste by rain and river water, and the principal casualty were the *rabi* crops which had been sown in October of the previous year. These crops consisted of the *boro* rice and spring crops consisting of peas, pulses, oilseeds, and miscellaneous greens (Hunter, 1869: xii).[3]

Detailed reflection on the nature of calamity caused by rains and river water suggests that, apart from the long drawn-out impact on the food producing fields, which broke the cycle or the rhythm of agricultural economy, it was the violence of river waters breaching through the mountainous passes and falling on the plains which had caused enormous destruction to the process of cultivation. At Mymensingh, the *zamindars* and *ryots* had signed the revenue settlements "in the month of *Jeet* [Jyesth; May–June]" hoping that they would be able to pay the rents regularly. Unfortunately, from the beginning of *Assar* (June–July) the waters rose to an extraordinary height and destroyed all possibility of undertaking cultivation. The rains continued for fifteen days at a stretch, and the floods drowned lands in eight *parganas* causing scarcity of food and bringing agriculture to a halt ("Petition of the Zemindars of the parganas Sreesory, Surriel, Jamshy and Lutluffpore to Mymensingh", BRP (M) 20: 31 July 1787).

Geographical impact

The floods and extreme weather conditions affected the grain prices within a wider ambit, including places beyond the inundated regions. Except in Chittagong, in the month of October, 1787, every district recorded lesser availability of rice in the rice harvesting months of 1787, compared to 1786. Table 5.1 shows the variation in grain prices between October 1786 and December 1787 in six districts of Bengal.

Rice prices in December 1787 at Dinajpur, a district within the core region affected by floods, were better than at Rangpur, the adjacent district most affected by the floods. At Rangpur, the prices were 18 *seer*/rupee in the countryside, and 23–5 *seer*/rupee in Rangpur town.

Transportation through the flooded rivers could not have been easy, but there is no evidence to suggest this was hindered by the floods to cause scarcity in different districts of Bengal. Yet, scarcity in the core famine region had a cascading effect, as authorities laid embargo on the exportation of grain through river channels and prevented the transfer of grain

Table 5.1 Comparative prices of paddy and four sorts of rice in six districts of Bengal in 1786 and 1787

Districts	Months	Rice prices in seer/rupee		Paddy prices in seer/rupee	
		1786	*1787*	*1786*	*1787*
Midnapore	*October*	30.25	22.12	–	–
	November	35.62	27.37	–	–
	December	36.64	28.26	–	–
Chittagong	*October*	39.56	43.76	40	76.25
	November	56.42	46.82	113.37	94.56
	December	68.06	51.31	110	95
Boglepore	*October*	47.29	33.14	–	–
	November	44.42	33.81	–	–
	December	43.59	32.62	–	–
Purnea	*October*	61.87	47.54	122.58	86.55
	November	77.81	53.46	141.62	89
	December	82.81	45.68	169.37	58.06
Houghly	*October*	39.24	34.54	65	50
	November	40.59	29.71	65	57
Dinajpur	*December*	36.31	28.87	–	–

Source: WBSA, BRP, 25 January 1788.

Table 5.2 Per rupee food prices at Dinajpur in 1786 and 1787

	Wheat 1st sort	Wheat 2nd sort	Boot	Buree	Cally moog	Boot doll	Moog doll	Musoory doll	Motor doll
1786	1 md, 12 sr, 8 cht	1 md, 32 sr, 8 cht	1 md, 5 sr	1 md	1 md	27 sr, 8 cht	28 sr	1 md, 5 sr	1 md, 15 sr
1787	35 sr	1 md, 5 sr	25 sr	23 sr	23 sr	24 sr	17 sr	29 sr	1 md, 15 sr

Source: WBSA, BRP, 25 January, 1788.

Key
md = *maund*; sr = *seer*; cht = *chhatak*.
1 md = 40 sr; 1 sr = 16 cht.
In modern measures, 1 *maund* = 37.32 kilograms; 1 *seer* = 0.93 kilograms; 1 *chhatak* = 58 grams.

from one region to another. In fact, evidence suggests there was not much grain to be transferred, as what was in store, from the previous harvests, was held back to provide relief. Thus, floods and the consequent scarcity in northern Bengal affected grain trade all over the country, and the zone of scarcity was extended to central and eastern Bengal, thereby giving the impression of near-famine in the wider province of Bengal. The floods in eastern Bengal were no less grim, and the possibility of depending on their own supplies was as remote as in the northern districts ("A translation of the *Arzee* of Seid Aly Cawn enclosed in the letter from His Highness the Nawab Mobarick ud Dowlah to Mr. Pott Collector Government Customs at Murshidabad", BRP (M) 21: 31 July 1787; and, 31 July 1787, from Chittagong reporting about Comilla; BRP (M) 25: 28 September 1787, from Rangpur). While Rangpur, and the adjoining district Dinajpur, were epicentres of famine conditions, regions beyond it like Murshidabad, Dhaka, and Rajshahi were also affected. The Murshidabad district, an agricultural region feeding its own people, was also a major grain trading centre of eighteenth-century Bengal, where grain merchants resided. The district was linked to the grain-producing areas of northern and eastern Bengal through water channels, and was dependent on those regions for supply. It was apprehended that there would be a grain scarcity in Murshidabad because the price of rice was raised considerably and the grain merchants "continue daily increasing it" (BRP (M) 21: 31 July 1787, and "enclosures from the Collector of Government Customs at Moorshedabad"). This happened in consequence of information received of grain scarcity "in the districts of Rungpore, Dinagepore, Dacca and Rajeshahy". The authorities feared that the "dreadful consequences" of a real scarcity caused due to natural factors would be increased if the grain merchants of Murshidabad, by trick and artifice, exported grain out of Murshidabad to more profitable destinations like Calcutta. The collector thus proposed an embargo out of Murshidabad (BRP (M) 21: 31 July 1787; "Private letter from Mr. McDowal of Rungpore to Mr. Pott Collector Government

Customs at Moorshedbad", 6 July 1787; BRP (M) 26: 12 October 1787, from Collector Govt. Customs).

The grain merchants in turn told the authorities that "from a great length of time" they had constantly purchased at "Dubba in the district of Rungpore, grain and other articles of merchandise" which was "kept in store there". In the rainy season, according to their annual custom, they brought grain and foods to Murshidabad. This year, the collector of that district prevented them from transporting the grain and told them to sell it at Rangpur instead of Murshidabad ("Translation of a petition from the 11 dealers in grain to the Collector Government Customs at Moorshedabad", BRP (M) 21: 31 July 1787). The collector reported that the people of Rangpur had been "threatened with a famine" and it was necessary to lay an embargo on rice exportation out of the district. The merchants were asked to send stored grain to Rangpur and sell it at one *maund* per rupee, which they refused. At Dhaka, a situation similar to Murshidabad prevailed. Consignments of grain were expected from Bhagalpur, Rangpur, and Dinajpur, and the grain dealers were asked to receive those at river junctions like Sooty and Jellingy. Because of the lack of availability, grain became exceedingly dear in Dhaka and its neighbourhoods, and it was not possible to supply grain to areas of insufficiency, which was a customary practice in times of dearth ("A translation of the *Arzee* of Seid Aly Cawn", BRP (M) 21: 31 July 1787).

The famine

By September 1787, there was widespread scarcity of grain and famine prevailed all over the inundation affected areas. Even if there was hope that some amount of crop could be grown "when the violence of weather" abated, it was frustrated by an acute scarcity of cattle and fodder. On 13 September 1787, the first piece of local level information received suggested that Rangpur was visited by a full blown famine (BRP 25 (M): 28 September 1787, from Collector of Rangpur, dated 13 September 1787). The Collector of Rangpur not only reported a scarcity but also wrote to his superiors that people were in need of relief or state charity, and could not live without it. This was the point at which scarcity turned into famine, for administrative purposes (Hunter, 1869: 7). The Collector could not provide relief locally, and requested the assistance of the government for provision of food. He reported that grain was selling for 23–5 *seers* per rupee at Rangpur, and 18 *seer* per rupee in the countryside.[4] In the early stages of the scarcity, the Collector was hopeful that those "unhappy creatures who by repeated inundations have been expelled from their places of abode have resorted to this station and they have been relieved from all the miseries of Famine, to which they otherwise have fallen a certain sacrifice". But soon after, the numbers of these hapless people increased so much that within a few days

> 3–4000 of them assembled at this place and they still continue to flock from all quarters many of them not having tasted food for eight or ten days, and dying in the streets before the necessary relief can be afforded.

People were driven to the town of Govindganj in mid-September 1787, when the season for cultivation was over. They had to be supplied with food for two or three months until the new rice could be brought to the market. In the Collector's estimation, the per capita requirement per day being one-third of a *seer*, a supply of 2124 *maunds* of coarse rice was required to afford subsistence to 5000 people for 75 days (BRP (M) 25: 28 September 1787, from Collector of Rangpur, dated 13 September 1787). The Collector wanted to know whether it was possible to purchase rice from neighbouring districts, and the authorities in Calcutta responded he could do so only if he could make the disbursements on the spot in order to avoid "risk, delay and disappointment" (BRP (M) 25: 28 September 1787, from BR to Governor-General in Council). The famine continued till the *kharif* season. On 20 November 1787, which in normal times would have been the season of harvest and plenty, there were in Rangpur town "upwards of six thousand people who are daily supplied with Rice". In that month, following another tragic climatic disruption – a storm, no less than forty "of these poor wretches" died. A meagre *kharif* harvest, promoted with "great pains" by the Collector himself, was "now just getting into the ear" but was likely to be "injured" by depopulation and the effects of the storm (BRP (M) 28: 20 November 1787, from Rangpur).

In the lower *parganas* of the Sylhet district, "the principal and only crop" of the season (*aus*) was destroyed, leading to depopulation of the area. The Collector went to inspect the *parganas* located on relatively higher plains. He reported that even in those areas

> there is scarce a village but has suffered some loss either in cattle or desertion of the riots who have retired to the hills for safety; the few surviving cattle are subsisted by the roots of grass drawn up by bamboos; nothing but ocular demonstration can form an idea of the unhappy state.

The human cost was now beyond description, it seems. The Collector, however, assured that he would continue to provide relief, but did not request assistance from the central authority (BRP (M) 25: 21 September 1787, from Sylhet).

Government response

The effect of the floods of 1787 on government decisions was visible not so much in the effort to organize distribution of food, which was severely in want even many months after the beginning of inundations, but rather in seeking to redeem a situation in which normal revenue collection was not possible. Remissions were demanded and allowed, but in many instances the revenue collectors were impeded, if not completely obstructed, by the physical dislocation of normal life in villages (BRP (M) 24: 7 September 1787, from Dinajpur). Possibly due to the fear of food riots taking place in the countryside, the officers asked for *sepoys* from Calcutta (BRP (M) 21: 31 July 1787, from Dinajpur). In the threshold years of the permanent settlement, government revenue policies were premised on "uniform rate of taxation" and "obtaining accurate knowledge" before an assessment could be made. Faced with a terrible crisis as that of 1787–88, when a deduction amounting to two-thirds of the estimated assessment was demanded by the *zamindars*, the knee-jerk reaction of the central government was to declare the lands *khas* [fallow], or bringing the lands under direct government supervision by appointing *sezawals* [government officers] and suspending the authority of the *zamindars* (Orders from BR to Rungpore, communicated to Governor-General in Council, BRP 24: 11 September 1787; Governor-General in Council's instructions to Board of Revenue on Rungpore and Purneah, BRP (M) 25: 25 September 1787). In the absence of accurate knowledge, perhaps, the government felt obliged "to suspend the demands for the rents where Inundation renders it necessary" (BRP (M) 26: 2 October 1787, from Governor-General in Council to BR); but this always carried the proviso that the "indulgence" was not to be abused by the *zamindars* and other categories of revenue payers.

There was hardly any system of providing relief to the displaced population. As Hunter noted about eighty years later, people knew that the December rice harvest (*aman*) was the great crop of the year, but few adequately appreciated the impossibility of making up for its loss by the produce of the preceding September harvest (*aus*), or of the green crops (*rabi*) in the following spring, or by the early rice crop (Hunter, 1869: 1). Thus, in a situation, as in 1787–88, when both *aus* and *aman* had been destroyed, the stored grains of previous year had been inundated, and the seeds for next year's *boro* crop had been destroyed, the matter was even graver. The famine-point, defined by Hunter as the point at which government relief operations became necessary, was reached in 1787 when the Rangpur Collector appealed for state charity. However, given the distance and isolation of the north and east Bengal districts, it was not possible to arrange relief from Calcutta, the central administrative location. Reliance had to be placed on the availability of food in neighbouring areas which were not affected by floods, and the ability of the Collector to co-ordinate (BRP (M) 25: 28 September 1787, from BR to Governor-General in Council).

Climate, famine, and riot

The extraordinary year of 1787 saw the climatic aberrations continue till the end of the year. Storms and rains struck even those places which were not affected by the floods at the beginning of the year. These districts were beyond the central deltaic zone of Bengal, towards the west of the province. The incidents caused further damage to crops and raised the prices. The rivers in the western part of the province, and also in north Bengal, are of a different nature. These rivers descend from hills and small mountains located in the west and flow towards plains in the east. In October 1787, "vast torrents that rushed down from the westward" overflowed the bank of the river near Midnapur town, carrying down cattle, men, women, and children. The remarkable feature of this deluge was its rapidity, noticeable in other instances of flooding in western Bengal. The "violent storms of rain and wind" destroyed the stores of grain and straw and the necessary implements for agriculture, causing acute scarcity of food in twelve *parganas* and Midnapur town (BRP (M) 26: 9 October 1787, from Midnapur, dated 3 October; BRP (M) 28.2: 13 November 1787, from Midnapur). *Parganas* in Bissenpur (Bishnupur) were also struck by a similar torrent destroying crops and cattle, resulting in scarcity of grain and suspension of revenue collection (BRP (M) 26: 12 October 1787, from Birbhum, dated 6 October; BRP (M) 28.2: 9 November 1787, from Birbhum). More importantly, the grain district of southern Bengal, thirteen *parganas* of the district of Burdwan, suffered heavy and violent floods of the rivers Damodar, Ajay, and five other rivers of the plains. The flooding of Damodar was particularly destructive as it breached the embankments and flooded Burdwan town (BRP (M) 26: 12 October 1787, from Burdwan, dated 9 October). The events of the month of October rounded off the calamities that began early in the year of 1787 and prolonged the food crisis.

The impact of the floods on the economy, and its subsequent impact on revenue, brought to the fore tensions embedded in society, even after a year had lapsed. In the Carjeehaut *zamindari* division of Rangpur district, the area most affected by flood, there was depopulation and serious damage to the crop. The administration's attempt to collect more than half of the *jama* [assessed amount of collection] from Soobaumgunje *pargana*, which had remained in arrears due to the floods, in the month of April (the onset of summer months) through a new settlement, was violently resisted by the *ryots*. The administration was not able to collect even half of the arrears, and *zamindars* who attempted to do so were attacked, and their *karamcharis* [employees] at the *Cutcherry* of Soobaumgunje insulted and held hostage (BRP (M) 36: 9 May 1788, from Rangpur, dated 2 May).

In this resistance, the role of the head *ryot* or the *bumiah* became prominent. Seven or eight head *ryots* who had influence over the mass of *ryots* gathered a large body of them at Soobaumgunje. They were not satisfied with the deductions that had been granted to them. Their targets were *zamindars* and their men, who collected revenues according to a settlement they made with the government. The *zamindars* of Carjeehaut, being vulnerable, reported the matter to the Collector, who in turn resorted to severe measures to put down the "rebellion".

The government's response to the incident brings out the fractures within a society under the impact of a natural calamity. While the resistance was led by the head-*ryots* or *bumiahs* in the *mofussil* [rural division], targeting the *zamindars*, the government at the *sadar* [town] insisted on an increase in the *jama* or assessment in 1788 to compensate for the losses of the previous year, though the collector admitted the district had suffered severely by inundations and famine. Here, the government faced resistance from those *zamindars* whose estates had suffered heavy damages. The reason was, after conducting the collections with "utmost moderation" as stated by the collector, the government used the opportunity to assess the productive capacity of the estates afresh by declaring the lands *khas*. Carjeehaut, which paid for 90 per cent of the revenue of this region held by four *zamindars*, refused to engage for revenue (BRP (M) 57.2: 30 December 1788, from Rangpur). Their refusal did not spare them from the attacks and hostilities of the *ryots* and *bumiahs* on whom the burden of taxation fell, and who had borne the consequences of the environmental disaster.

The conflict between government and *zamindars*, on whom "every justifiable coercion" was applied, was again witnessed when they refused to erect flood-preventing dams on the instruction of the government. The government responded harshly by selling off the lands of those who refused to engage in such work (BRP (M) 36: 6 May 1788, from Rangpur to BR, and BR to Rangpur). The crisis was thus compounded, as ties of kinship, obligations of stewardship, and structures of hierarchical authority were simultaneously strained to a breaking point.

Food markets

The food, particularly grain, crisis, occasioned by the floods of 1787, had serious impact on the markets in 1788. Throughout that year, the grain crisis continued unabated, and even in December 1788, the government considered it unadvisable to lift the embargo due to uncertainties about what could be "produced for export" after procuring for internal consumption. In January, the price of grain had "risen to a scandalous degree" in Murshidabad. The machinations of the grain merchants led to exorbitant prices, complicating already straitened circumstances caused by flooding. Rice was selling at a high price of 23 or 24 *seers* to a Sicca Rupee (BRP (M) 30.2: 18–29 January 1788). The Collector of Customs reported that suspension of duty on grain trade "has only been an additional profit to the merchants, and no relief as was intended to the poor". The Board of Revenue, the coordinating agency, in advising the government on strategies to be adopted on the apprehension of a scarcity before the "crops of the next season" may be expected to ripen, said, "there exists at this moment a scarcity of grain in most of the interior districts of Bengal, particularly in those that have suffered most from the inundation and storm". They feared this scarcity would probably increase

> as the great crop of the current year is now in the market without having removed the evil, and as the first crop of the ensuing season being the smallest of the two will not be in the market before August.
> (BRP (M) 30.2: Cons. 25 January 1788, from BR to
> Governor-General in Council)

The Calcutta grain markets, which had the advantage of procuring grain from areas in the Gangetic plain, where floods were not so disastrous, did not register a favourable trend in terms of 1787 prices compared to the previous year, as shown in Table 5.3.

However, by the end of 1788, eastern districts seemed to have recovered from the severe effects of the inundation. Officers of the Dhaka district wrote to their authorities that they were happy to inform, "from the favourable prospects the crops now have", there was every reason to hope the inhabitants would meet with relief from resources of the district, and that orders may be issued to officers at Patna to stop any further dispatches of grain for the relief of Dhaka (BRP (M) 57.1: 4 December 1788, from Messrs Day and Bebb, dated 17 November). The government at Calcutta began to take stock of the general state of the crops in the interiors of the district and began to think of exploring the possibility of exports (BRP (M) 56: 2 December 1788, from BR to Governor-General in Council).

Table 5.3 Bazar prices of grain for three years in the markets of Calcutta

	Medium 1785		Medium 1786		Medium 1787	
	Seer	Chatak	Seer	Chatak	Seer	Chatak
Wheat	23	5	32	13	34	9
Table Patna Rice	17	9	20	14	21	10
Table Country Rice	25	13	30	–	27	10
Middling	30	8	35	–	30	9
Coarse	33	13	40	–	34	9
Chatta Balam	36	12	41	–	36	8
Donny Balam	41	14	50	–	45	2
Chatta Lottee	47	4	55	6	48	–
Donny Lottee	52	12	60	6	52	13
Piarry	37	10	50	–	43	2
Moongy	31	10	39	8	36	–
Buddy	$15\frac{1}{2}$ baty	–	$18\frac{1}{11}$ baty	–	7 baty	–
Calley Gram	30	–	37	–	37	4
Boot Gram	23	10	39	2	44	–

Source: BRP, 30.2: 25 January 1788.

However, the government, cautiously, did not call off the embargo till 1790. The effects on market operations and responses of the authorities illustrate that the still nascent regulatory and relief mechanisms were put under considerable pressure by the network of climatic, ecological, economic, and social causes of the 1787 crisis of food.

Rivers and famine

Historical debates about floods in Bengal, and their effects on the economy, have contended with a paradox. Floods are supposed to be both a blessing and a curse, and geographical comparisons between the flooding of the Nile valley and the inundations in Bengal have led environmentalists to assert this more forcefully. As Beinart and Hughes show, monsoon and associated floods could be considered as crucial to Bengal's agriculture as the annual flooding of the Nile is to Egypt (2007: 140). Thus, floods on an appropriate scale are traditionally supposed to bring prosperity to agriculture due to the deposition of silt on alluvial soil. Radhakamal Mukherjee (1938: 160–79), James Rennell (1793), and Henry Thomas Colebrook (1794) shared this view, making distinctions between deltaic Bengal and those regions which were to the north and west of it. The distinctions entailed further differences in the nature of inundations by the rivers of the two geographical zones. Rennell and Colebrook had written about annual inundation on the plains, which assumed a sort of regularity in its timing.[5] But the monsoon and the rise in water level in major rivers and their tributaries could vary from one year to another, and the rivers' potential to cause damage was expressed in the frequently apocalyptic rhetoric of local officials managing the crises.

Almost a year after the calamities of 1787, the Collector of Rangpur wrote about the "sudden and violent breaking in of Teestah during the latter rains" and stated that:

> In many parts of the district the River has in a most extraordinary manner has forced its way through the cultivated grounds to a very considerable distance from its channel and from thence has overflowed the whole of the adjacent country ... the destructive effect of which I was an eye witness to.
>
> (BRP (M) 36: 6 May 1788, from Rangpur)

Accounts of Mymensingh floods relate that the overflowing of the banks of the river caused dreadful inundation, carving out dramatic alterations of terrain. In mid-June of 1787 "a pass in the Golessive Mountains was forced by the waters which rushed in with such violence as to sweep down whole villages and carry away inhabitants, cattle, grain and everything" (Representation of the *zamindar* of Sreesory *pargana*, Mymensingh, BRP (M) 21: 31 July 1787). In other neighbouring *parganas*:

From the beginning of *assar* the waters from the Rogonandan and Roshanabad Mountains forced themselves a passage and rushed with such velocity as to breakdown the Banks of Magha and River Kavie which at once overflowed the whole pergunnah and totally destroyed the crop that were coming on.

> (Representation of the *zamindar* of Surriel, Mymensingh,
> BRP (M) 21: 31 July 1788)

We never saw or heard of such constant and severe rains and storms as we have had since the beginning of *assar*, this greatly hurt the country – the passes Rogonundun and Noorah Mountains breaking at the same time rushed with such velocity as to overflow the banks of Burrumpoter, Kaird, Burack etc. rivers and made an inundation into these Mehauls at once in such a manner as to carry away whole villages.

> (Representation of the *zamindar* of Jamshy and Lutluffpore,
> BRP (M) 21: 31 July 1788)

This picture is in contrast to that depicted by Rennell and Colebrook about the Gangetic delta. In the delta, even extensive floods could have regenerative potential, and did not disrupt the entire cycle of cultivation. They were not the unprecedented apocalyptic deluge described in accounts of the 1787 famine.

The climatic and economic crisis of 1787 thus offers a clearer perspective on how local ecological conditions and economic patterns could interact to create a famine. The effects of an ecological dislocation caused by nature, within a core region of cultivation in eastern and northern Bengal, could thus ripple across a large part of the province because of the destruction of grain crop, consequent scarcity, and high grain prices. This, in turn, shaped official responses and policies, leading to the development of an official stance on when a threat of scarcity might be termed a famine, and when and in what form state relief or charity might be offered. Unlike the better-known famine of 1769–70, this crisis was more explicitly influenced by climate events which had, as this chapter demonstrates, a significant impact on local communities, ecologies, and official administration.

Notes

1 Reports from Sylhet (July 1787) indicated that Azmerygunj and many *golas* were swept away. Reports from Tipperah (July 1787) noted that at Sujahgunje, the market with all its produce was carried away; while Jerwargunje in Comilla could not be reached. In Mymensingh (July 1787), there was a representation from the zamindar of Sussong pargana, stating that water rushed with violence to "sweep down whole villages and carry away inhabitants, cattle, grain".

2 Measures of weight used were: 1 *maund* (md) = 40 seer (sr); 1 sr = 16 chhatak (cht). In metric measures, 1 md = 37.32 kg; 1 sr = 0.93 kg; 1 cht = 58 g.

3 The spring crop of Bengal, or *rabi* crop, would also have included the *boro* seed sown in October and reaped in March.

4 According to calculations by W. W. Hunter in 1866, the famine warning price was 2 rupees, 10 *ana*s per *maund*. The prices in 1787 at Rangpur were very close. See Hunter, 1869: 9.

5 As Rennell explained, in his *Memoir of a Map of Hindoostan or the Mogul Empire* (1793: 270):

> The rice I speak of is of a particular kind; for the growth of its stalk keeps pace with the increase of the flood at ordinary times, but is destroyed by too sudden a rise of the water. The harvest is often reaped in boats. There is also a kind of grass which overtops the flood in the fame manner, and at a small distance has the appearance of a field of the richest verdure.

Part III

Politics of climate and relief

6 Chaotic interruptions in the economy

Droughts, hurricanes and monsoons in Harriet Martineau's *Illustrations of Political Economy*

Lesa Scholl

Harriet Martineau's career as one of the nineteenth century's most prolific public intellectuals spanned almost 60 years. As a journalist, political commentator, travel writer, novelist, reviewer and historian, her literary impact was unsurpassed; yet it was her economic series *Illustrations of Political Economy* (1832–34) that made her a household name and gave her national and international access to politicians and other people of influence from a range of political persuasions. Influenced by the early political economists such as Adam Smith, David Ricardo, Thomas Malthus and James Smith, Martineau intervened in this male dominated field at a crucial moment in economic thought, when statistical analysis and mathematical modelling were beginning to gain precedence. Martineau's tales deliberately resisted the idealism of such models, and refused to ignore the complications of political economy as practised in human society. As her series progressed, both Whig and Tory Members of Parliament sent her Blue Books, asking her to focus on particular aspects of policy, while internationally her work was translated into French, German, Dutch, Spanish and Russian, with the intention of disseminating the series through school systems. However, when she initially sought a publisher for the series in 1832, the fraught social condition of Britain – the initial rejection of the Reform Bill in 1831 led to riots throughout most major cities and towns, while London was under threat from cholera – caused publishers to hesitate, including key London publishers from Baldwin and Craddock, Whittaker, Treacher and Arnot, and the Fox brothers, the latter eventually taking on the project, although it was Martineau herself who had to gain subscriptions. Martineau's determination to see the project through arose from her conviction in the importance of the work, as well as the public demand for it. She told William Fox, "the people want this book, and they *shall* have it" (Martineau 2007, first published 1877: 144).

By making political economy accessible to a popular readership, Martineau enabled readers to critique the established economic and political systems. In this chapter, I argue that she encouraged critique through her portrayal of uncontrollable variables that disrupt economic theory: that is, the effect of environmental disasters on food security. In this way, she complicates the idealism of supply and demand and the invisible hand of early political economy, anticipating post-Malthusian paradigms of food access, such as Amartya Sen's understanding of the individual's or community's relationship to a commodity, legitimacy and structures of ownership: "Starvation is the characteristic of some people not *having* enough food to eat. It is not the characteristic of there *being* not enough to eat" (Sen 1981: 1). In Martineau's illustrations, supply and demand do not reconcile because of structures of social and economic privilege that are revealed, often through environmental devastation. The juxtaposition of political concerns with a waterborne disease in the publishers' hesitancy is particularly telling, for Martineau contends not just with the potential disruption of visceral human responses to inequality and want, which could arguably be controlled or moderated, but with climatic interventions over which humans have no control. In his introduction to *Principles of Political Economy* (1836, first published 1820), Thomas Malthus observes that the "desire to simplify" in political economy "has occasioned an unwillingness to acknowledge the operation of more causes than one in the production of particular effects" (5); yet even in Malthus's own work, there is a fascinating absence of climatic events in discussions of supply and demand. Famine is related simply to increased population, rather than facing uncontrollable, sudden natural disturbances. Further, when Malthus speaks of the "study of natural laws", rather than considering the environment, the uncontrollable factors he discusses are political, such as the inability of one nation-state to control the prosperity of an adjacent nation-state (10). In his earlier *Essay on the Principle of Population* (1798) Malthus references earthquakes and volcanos briefly, but refuses to accept the immediate devastating effect that such events can have on a region. Indeed, he suggests that these kinds of events are essentially rare, trivial and ineffectual:

> The most tremendous convulsions of nature, such as volcanic eruptions and earthquakes, if they do not happen so frequently as to drive away the inhabitants, or to destroy their spirit of industry, have but a trifling effect on the average population of any state.
>
> (42–3)

One of the flaws of political economy that Martineau's work reveals is the myth of continual progress, which does not sufficiently account for environmental disasters. Political economists clung to Malthus's famous claim of population increasing geometrically and subsistence arithmetically (1836: 7), and the "season of distress" he references (11) is based purely on excessive population growth, not, for instance, on the destruction of crops by storms. At no point does Malthus seriously try to contend with environmental disasters. In this way, Malthus falls into line with other economists, for whom the environment is inconveniently uncontrollable: it disturbs the order of their theory. When there is an excessive focus on statistically based economics, it is easier to focus on what can be controlled through human intervention. Indeed, Malthus attempts to place emphasis on the *consistency* of the laws of nature; however, as much as economic theory can be imposed on policy, it has no jurisdiction over environmental disasters.

While Martineau was influenced by key economists like Smith, Ricardo and Mill alongside Malthus, in contemporary reviews she was most often criticised for being Malthusian in her approach. In her *Autobiography* she defends the "pure, benevolent, and scientific spirit of Malthus" (2007: 164) and goes on to defend both his moral and mathematical methods:

> All that I know is that a more simple-minded, virtuous man, full of domestic affections, than Mr. Malthus, could not be found in all England; and that the desire of his heart and the aim of his work were the domestic virtue and happiness should be placed within the reach of all, as Nature intended them to be.... Such is the moral aspect of Malthus's work. As to its mathematical basis, there is no one ... who could question it that might not as well dispute the multiplication table.
>
> (169–70)

However, as much as Martineau professes this line, and as much as she was both celebrated and vilified as a proponent of political economy,[1] her counter-narratives of climatic extremes exacerbating hunger and desperation overturn classical economic theory. In *The Physiology of Common Life* (1859), George Henry Lewes would go on to describe hunger as "the very fire of life, underlying all impulses to labour, and moving man to noble activities by its imperious demands.... But when its progress is unchecked, it becomes a devouring flame, destroying all that is noble in man" (1–2). This observation, almost three decades after Martineau's series, resonates with Malthus's depiction of the French Revolution "which, like a blazing comet, seems destined either to inspire with fresh life and vigour, or to scorch up and destroy the sinking inhabitants of the earth", and humanity's "perpetual oscillation between happiness and misery, and after every effort remain still at an immeasurable distance from the wished-for goal" (1836: 1). In both Lewes and Malthus hunger is seasonal, but it is still perpetual: the people are always hungry. Hunger is the catalyst for momentum, with physical hunger feeding the social hunger for inequalities and injustices to be addressed. What Martineau's tales reveal, though, is the chaotic nature of such hungers in dialogue with each other at moments of environmental crisis. As she works to show what economic theory would look like *in practice*, the characters who espouse political economy's ideals become increasingly problematic, marginalised and silenced in the face of environmental disasters that have an immediate and sudden impact on the local economy.

While people have *enough*, they have little impetus for change; but when one is hungry, there arises an acute awareness of lack, and a desire to be satisfied. Historically, uprisings and revolutions can almost always be tied to seasons of dearth and starvation, and a recognition that some people are affected more than others by the lack. This visceral response is exacerbated when supply is suddenly taken away through environmental interventions. At the same time, though, extreme longstanding hunger can lead to debilitating hopelessness; and it is in this kind of state of inaction that climatic events necessarily move people to act. I will examine three of Martineau's tales in which extreme weather functions to compel communities to react against economic strictures. *Sowers Not Reapers* (2004, first published 1833) opens with an alienated local community succumbing to drought during England's 1830 Swing Riots.[2] *French Wines and Politics* (1833b), set in France during the 1788 lead-up to the French Revolution, is haunted by the hurricane that devastated crops and caused the famous price rises in bread in October of that year, which were considered instrumental in the immediate inspiration of the revolution.[3] Martineau, while commenting on France, also emphasises Britain's economic investment in the French Revolution, refusing to allow her British readership to distance themselves from the unrest. The third tale, *Cinnamon and Pearls* (1833a), is set in Ceylon under the regime of the East India Company; and alongside the implications of imperialism and colonisation on the lives of the Cingalese, the figure of the monsoon season operates to destabilise the economic and cultural expectations of the community. Problems of scarcity and starvation are exacerbated in each of these texts, while access to particular foods – as well as food in general – becomes crucial to characters' perception of their social and political agency. The weather events operate both literally to disrupt economic supply – crops are destroyed in each of the tales – but they are also metaphorical representations of the hunger of the people, and catalytically work to overturn political economy's myths of stability and order. The political merges with the environmental, creating a dialogue akin to that between physical and social hunger.

The debilitation of drought

The effect of the Corn Laws[4] on food security in *Sowers Not Reapers* is complicated by the natural elements through the prolonged and difficult to frame event of a drought. Unlike hurricanes, or even the monsoon season, which I will discuss in relation to the other two texts, it is difficult to determine the beginning and end of a drought. Whereas a storm generally has a clear definition as a weather cell, and distant lightning can warn of its onset, the blurred edges of drought make it challenging for such an event to motivate people to act: once the drought is recognised, the people are already thirsty and crops have failed. Furthermore, even a brief shower cannot determine the end of a period of drought, and so there is also the possibility of repeated false hope that results in despair.[5] After dealing with the nature and power of hunger in *The Physiology of Common Life*, Lewes goes on to discuss thirst as "a disturbance far more terrible than that of starvation" (1859: 31). He argues that "the sensation of Thirst is never agreeable, no matter how slight it may be, and in this respect is unlike Hunger, which, in its incipient state of Appetite, is decidedly agreeable" (40). In this sense, thirst takes on a character of an extreme greater than hunger, with no redeeming qualities. In terms of physiological need, hunger and thirst can be envisaged within the same spectrum, with thirst exceeding hunger in terms of its debilitating power. Once one feels thirst, one is already dehydrated; but with hunger, the initial stirring in the stomach does not signal starvation. This physiological understanding mirrors the onset of drought, although famine is also difficult to frame. Even so, as Lewes observes, the human body can survive much longer hungry than it can thirsty, and the implication is that it is more possible to relieve hunger than it is to relieve thirst; once thirst has come, the situation is more bleak.

It is within the despairing context of "the more urgent evil of thirst" that Martineau sets her tale (Martineau 2004: 297). The Swing Riots of 1830 developed in a similar way to thirst, initially seeming innocuous, but developing from machine breaking into the destruction of any objects of perceived oppression, including workhouses, then destroying food sources by burning barns full of grain and rick-burning, to the macabre maiming of cattle. Protests over the price of corn turned into political protest, but descended into cruelty and self-destruction. Peter Jones comments that protesters "rarely, if ever, requested higher wages or set out to destroy threshing machines alone. Instead, they expressed a series of interrelated demands which can only be properly understood when taken together" (2007: 275). The complexity of demands reflects the chaotic response of the people, who were responding not just to hunger, but to thirst and, within that response, a desperate fear and hopelessness in not knowing when the drought would break. In *Sowers Not Reapers*, the opening scene is one of a dislocated and fragmented community, fraught by its inability to contend with either nature or human government:

> Others were also abroad, with the view of relieving their hardships instead of seeking to avenge them. The dwellers on high grounds were so far worse off than the inhabitants of the valleys, that they could not quench their thirst, and lost in sleep their weariness and their apprehensions of hunger.
>
> (2004: 297)

The tale centres on the misfortunes of the Kay family, with Mrs Kay, who is present in the opening scene, ironically succumbing to alcoholism. The devastation of drought is intensified by Mrs Kay's memories of abundance, which she reminisces over with her sister-in-law, Mary, as they trespass on the property of Mr Warden, the miller, in order to smuggle water from his spring: "When I used to have my fill of meat every day, I little thought that the bread I ate with it would grow scarce among us" (299). In this time of extended drought, lines of criminality, like property borders, are broken down in the community. Yet rather than condemning the women for tres-passing and theft, Mr Warden sympathises with the women's plight; after all, whereas they look for water, he looks for wind to power his mill. Neither they nor he have the ability to control the elements in order to produce what they need. The sympathetic response in this community is what prevents its ultimate devastation.

The tragedy of Mrs Kay's situation is exacerbated by her alcoholism. It is telling that while there is no water to drink, let alone to replenish the fields, there is access to relatively cheap alcohol. Mrs Kay confesses to her husband that she drinks to dull the pain of hunger, but her addiction overtakes her: even when food is offered, when times seem to be improving, she is unable to eat. She succumbs to her addiction in the end; and her hopeless *ennui* reflects the desolation of unquenchable thirst. After her husband and family have helped her to stop drinking alcohol, and she is "taking nothing stronger than tea" (361), it remains that food is still in poor supply: "poppies coming up instead of wheat, and stones strewed where lambs should have been browsing" (370). In her last cold moments, Mrs Skipper, the baker, who was sitting with her, recounts that Mrs Kay "kept stretching [her hand] out as if she thought to reach something; and I supposed she was thirsty" (377), yet this action is an impulse of her habit of drinking alcohol. Although Mary pleads with her, "it was hunger that did all that! Don't dwell upon that!" (377), Mrs Kay cannot forgive herself, and dies, in a fading manner, voicing her self-recriminations. The drought of *Sowers Not Reapers* portrays the most lethargic, hopeless state of society along the lines of Lewes's view of thirst. Mrs Kay gives up hope, much in the same way as the men who raid towns in the depth of night, causing devastating criminal damage. The loss of com-munity boundaries in this way – the inability or refusal to respect the prop-erty or boundaries of others in a seemingly unhuman quest for destruction (or self-destruction in Mrs Kay's case) – is evidence of having lost hope of ever being able to regain an investment in the land and community.

Mrs Kay's destruction is an individual, human representation of the effects of natural crop failure on the community. Nature is more central to the community's concerns than political interference or selfish neglect because it is more immediately present; yet the event of food destruction, which was prevalent throughout the Swing Riots, provides evidence of their social hunger and desperation. Martineau describes this response in terms of economic panic:

There had been enormous importations of corn during the winter, – importations which in the end proved as ruinous to the corn-dealer as the farmer at home. The bargain with the foreign corn-growers having been made in a panic was agreed upon at a panic price. The foreigners had naturally laid heavy duties on corn, both because it was known how much the English wanted food, and because what they bought was not a surplus regularly grown for sale, but a part of the stock of the countries they bought of. In the midst of a panic, and in entire uncertainty how long the ports might be open, the corn importers could not possibly calculate how much would be wanted, any more than the people ascertain how much was brought in.

(357)

This account reveals the way in which political economy's obsession with statistics and mathematical formulae falls down in the face of human, affective response to scarcity. All figures are operating on panic rather than rationality because numbers cannot be known. Economic politics clearly comes into play on an international scale, with foreign traders not invested in the plight of the starving British; rather they see an opportunity to take advantage of the situation, perhaps justifying their actions to themselves on a moral economic level through the fact that they are reselling what they have themselves imported. However, as seen in *French Wines and Politics*, this kind of exchange invariably leads to the prosperity of the seller, for whom maintaining the profit margin is the most essential aspect, and for that margin to diminish would be considered an irrecoverable loss.

Britain's investment in revolutionary France

French Wines and Politics parallels *Sowers Not Reapers* in the way they both engage with food destruction by violent mobs. The setting of revolutionary France buys into the continuing fear of the Terror within Britain, which persisted well into the Victorian period, and breathes through the chaos of Martineau's other economic tales.[6] Martineau uses the French setting to speak to British concerns by emphasising Britain's economic and social investment in France. This tie is reinforced by geographical proximity: just as there was widespread fear of the Terror seeping across the Channel into Britain, it is possible that weather cells that devastate France could also move across Britain's shores. Beyond the possibility of sharing weather events, though, the close economic ties of the nations through trade agreements meant that any sudden loss of crops in one nation would affect the prosperity of the other. In this sense, Martineau makes Malthus's "laws of nature" even more related to the natural environment, than to political behaviours. The real hurricane that Martineau references in her tale may not have meteorologically crossed the English Channel, but its impact was felt throughout Britain and Europe in the months and years to come due to the force of destruction on crops.

At the beginning of *French Wines*, two episodes of crop destruction are juxtaposed, deliberately tying the political world to the pangs of the natural environment. In the first, the Marquis de Thou, with a party of boar hunters, chase a wild boar through crops and vineyards. The response of the people is one of apathy. When Steele, an English businessman, questions the vineyard owner, Antoine, about his inaction, Antoine responds:

> It is the only way to keep what we have left.... There is no use, but much peril, in complaint. Redress there is none; and ill-will towards the lord's pleasure is resented more deeply and lastingly than injury to his property.
>
> (Martineau 1833b: 9)

Antoine's slippage into the term for the English aristocracy – "lord" instead of "marquis" – linguistically ties the two businessmen together, alongside their business transactions. Antoine's passive acceptance, though, also suggests that he will be able to recoup his costs in a way that characters who do not at this stage have a voice would not be able to; Antoine, like his brother Charles the winemaker, has enough wealth to endure the marquis' destructive pleasure.

In contrast to Antoine's acceptance, however, the devastating hurricane of the next day gives voice to the broader community. It rouses within the people the resilience and outcry necessary for revolutionary determination. The preternatural noise of the hurricane becomes inseparable from the hungry uprising of the people, operating as a deliberate motif of the volatile, self-destructive power of hunger, and as a persistent response of the natural world to the trauma of the nation. The storm returns throughout the narrative, sometimes as thunder, sometimes as rain, to undergird the violence of political unrest with the violence of the natural world. The climactic scenes at the Bastille, and then with the guillotine, take place in the rain, blood mixing with water; while the eye of the storm creates a pregnant, ominous moment in the text, with the king fortressed in the Tuileries, and soldiers and revolutionaries outside huddled around fires. Yet, as much as Martineau uses the hurricane as a metaphor and a dramatic literary device, it is crucial to her economic illustration that this hurricane was a real, historical event that caused material damage to the land and produce:

> Throughout Guienne, the Orleannois, and other provinces, not a score of revolutions could efface the recollections and traditions of the hurricane of July, 1788. Perhaps it may still be a subject of dispute a century hence whether it was charged, in addition to the natural agents of destruction, with a special message to warn the French nation of their approaching social convulsion.
>
> (1833b: 18)

Martineau adopts the long-standing myth of climatic violence as divine judgement upon an unjust society (Walter and Wrightson, 1976; Walsham, 1999; Mukherjee, A., 2015). Crucially, though, she recognises that the storm had more than a prophetic role in bringing about the revolution. She catalogues the crop-destruction caused by the hurricane in much more detail than that of the boar hunters the day before; and it is evident that the more significant devastation by nature led to the notably bad harvest of 1788:

> The corn-fields were one vast morass. The almond groves were level with the ground; and of the chestnut woods nothing remained but an assemblage of bare poles. The more exposed vineyards were so many quagmires, and many dwellings were mere heaps of ruins. All who witnessed were horror-struck at the conviction of general, immediate, pressing want; and the more thoughtful glanced forwards in idea to the number of seasons that must pass away before all this damage could be repaired.
>
> (1833b: 12–13)

Indeed, the devastation caused by this hurricane has been closely linked to the French Revolution. Historian George Rudé notes its effects on bread prices, which was particularly dire given that bread made up approximately 50 per cent of the French diet:

> In September 1788, when Parisians were celebrating the *parlement*'s second return, a sharp increase in the price of bread transformed the scope and nature of the riots. In the following April, the Réveillon riots in the Faubourg St. Antoine were probably due as much to the high price of bread as to the manufacturers' attacks on wages: in fact, food shops (but no others) were broken into, and the lieutenant of police himself believed that the insurgents had the twofold aim of settling accounts with Réveillon and of compelling authorities to reduce the price of bread.
>
> (Rudé 1964: 108)

It is important, then, that Martineau does not focus only on the immediate destruction of food by nature, but also on the irrational food destruction by angry crowds, and the long-lasting effects of both on the economy: she is able to emphasise the economic inequalities that contribute to social unrest. Unlike the political economists that Malthus references, through literary representation Martineau is able to explore the causal complexities of economic instability and political unrest; and in doing so, she challenges political economy's narrative of barely fazed progress in light of environmental disaster.

Although Martineau's tales were understood to be promoting political economy, it is evident that only a few characters in each tale can afford to hold to its tenets. Her own claim of the complexity of her presentation can be inferred from her response to her readers in her *Autobiography*: "but it certainly seems to me that this course of imputation originated some obscure dread of me and my works among timid and superficial readers" (Martineau 2007: 169). In *French Wines*, Antoine's brother, Charles, espouses the ideals of rational political economy; yet on closer observance he is shown to be able to hold to this philosophy because, first, he comes from a position of luxury and, second, he himself profits economically by the hurricane, and is able to justify his progress to himself morally in spite of the plight of the poor. His wealth and his investment in foreign markets enable him to diversify his economic role: when the French cannot afford to buy his wine, Charles is able to exchange his surplus wine for fruit from Italy and the Levant. He also purchases large quantities of grapes from Steele, his brother's English colleague, to sell as fruit instead of wine, and in turn sells Steele his surplus second-grade wine for England, for

> the demand for fruit in London being at present insignificant in comparison with that for claret, and the direct reverse being the case at Paris, it was Steele's interest to transmit more wine and less fruit, and Charles's to take fruit in exchange for his wine. It was therefore settled that, in addition to their standing bargain for first-rate wine, Steele should have a large choice of second-rate claret, in payment for chestnuts from Spain, oranges and citrons from the Madeiras, olives from the Levant, and almonds from Italy.
>
> (1833b: 31)

Like the utilitarians Jeremy Bentham and Robert Owen, Martineau bought into the idea of a free market. However, this conviction was not unqualified. The network of foodstuffs throughout Europe is central to Martineau's vision of free trade, but it also reveals the way in which trade takes advantage of lack, and promotes self-interest as a moral good over the interest of the community. In this way, Charles and Steele both represent what Regenia Gagnier refers to as the "manifold irony" of Adam Smith's political economy, "that selfish individuals could make an altruistic society; that the pursuit of profit could be an ethical failing in an individual but lead to the wealth of all" (Gagnier 2000a: 316). The resolute blindness towards the real suffering caused by such economic and social visions remains problematic in terms of human concerns. Martineau thus challenges the ideals of utilitarianism that would enable and give traction to the 1834 New Poor Laws.

When Charles "eagerly" tells his wife, Marguerite, of the great progress being made in society through the character-building nature of starvation and hardship, he evokes Malthus, saying: "I see every day, not only splendid instances of intellectual effort ... but moral struggles and self-sacrifices which dispose me more than ever to bow the knee to human nature" (Martineau 1833b: 41). Malthus claims in the *Principle of Population* that

The sorrows and distresses of life form another class of excitements which seem to be necessary, by a peculiar train of impressions, to soften and humanize the heart, to awaken social sympathy, to generate all the Christian virtues, and to afford scope for the ample exertion of benevolence.

(2007, first published1798: 144)

Yet this view affords room for Charles's justification of self-interest in a way that Marguerite does not allow:

But why should the corn-owners be enriched by the scarcity of bread, and you by the destruction of vineyards? You tell me that your gains by this storm will nearly compensate the losses it has cost you. Is this fair?

(Martineau 1833b: 36–7)

Marguerite draws attention to corn-growers – those who produce bread. The growers are profiting by the starvation of their customers, who can no longer afford even the bare staples. Britain is implicated in this unjust prosperity through Steele's participation and success in the French market following the hurricane, and Steele, Charles and Antoine all participate in the self-interest that Malthus warns against:

The advocate for the present order of things is apt to treat the sect of speculative philosophers either as a set of artful and designing knaves, who preach up ardent benevolence and draw captivating pictures of a happier state of society, only the better to enable them to destroy the present establishments and to forward their own deep-laid schemes of ambition.... The advocate for the perfectibility of man ... brands him as the slave of the most miserable and narrow prejudices, or as the defender of the abuses of civil society, only because he profits by them.... In this unamicable contest the cause of truth cannot but suffer.

(2007: 2)

Marguerite, in fact, represents the moral truth of the matter, although "the best and safest means of removing abuses" (Malthus 2007: 3) remain elusive. It is because of this elusiveness that political economy avoids these questions; yet it remains that these three men represent a class that ironically, and even perversely, profits through the advent of the storm.

The taste of dispossession, food security and imperialism

Britain's foreign investment is taken further in *Cinnamon and Pearls*, for where *French Wines* essentially deals with two imperial nations in trade agreement, *Cinnamon and Pearls* portrays the effects of imperial dispossession. The narrative focuses on Marana and Rayo, a Cingalese couple who represent the dispossession of their nation, both culturally and economically, by the East India Company. Like the rest of their community, they are impoverished and unable to make a living sufficient to buy food; but even worse, because of the imperial company's dominance, they are also not permitted to grow their own food. While *Sowers Not Reapers* ends in a tone of continued devastation, with "the pressure of want, – the main spring of the vast machinery of moral evil by which society is harrowed and torn", and the desolate repetition of "How long? … How long?" (Martineau 1833c: 378), *Cinnamon and Pearls* ends with an idealised sense of community restoration. However, the devastation leading up to the moment of restoration persistently haunts the text's conclusion. It is important to recognise the different types of weather events that cause devastation in the three texts: the drought, as I have already noted, is a very different kind of event that is difficult to define; the hurricane of *French Wines* is more definite, while the monsoon in *Cinnamon and Pearls*, while still destructive, is a seasonal event: as such, while it cannot actually be controlled, it can be predicted, which creates a sense of order. Martineau disrupts this order, however, by having the monsoon arrive late. It is left to the superstitions and witchcraft of the locals to try to find some sense of order and control in the face of this delay, calling into question any kind of economic agency.

The lack of control over weather systems in *Cinnamon and Pearls* functions as an extension of the dispossession of the Cingalese. Like the hurricane in *French Wines* being situated as an omen of revolution (as well as a cause), the lateness of the monsoon rains, which causes the rice-fields to languish and the mountain-tops to "crave … the light clouds which floated around" (Martineau 1833a: 65), is seen as a punishment to Marana and Rayo, who have had to move inland after Rayo was tempted to steal pearls when given the opportunity to be a pearl-diver for the imperial company. Marana is particularly preoccupied with the myth of the sea-hag, her "troubled spirit" interpreting the "moaning of the rising wind … and the dull roar of the distant sea" as "hags riding the blast, and curses cradled in the clouds" (66). When Marana sells a charm in order to get money for food, Rayo jokingly asks "[d]oes it not taint your fingers with leprosy" (67); yet within this jest there is an accepted rhetoric of superstition that provides an explanation for disease and starvation – the material effects of dispossession. Within her tale, though, Martineau refuses to deny or diminish the material causes: Mr Carr, the East India Company's overseer, observes that the prevalence of elephantiasis and leprosy in the Cingalese population would be lessened if they had "flesh to eat, or good bread, or even the seasoning … necessary to make their vegetable food [agreeable]" (45).

Cinnamon and Pearls suggests a significant difference from *French Wines* and *Sowers Not Reapers* in that it seems to deal with luxury, auxiliary items rather than staples: cinnamon, cardamom and salt are spices and seasoning, considered exotic to a European readership, whereas the bread of the other two texts speaks of the necessaries of life. However, spices are also used for food preservation, and Martineau also emphasises the economic importance of these crops in terms of supply and demand as well as ownership. As Mr Carr observes, too, the agreeability of food is important: what seems exotic in Europe has actually been central to the diet of the Cingalese. The implications of the devastation of these crops, then, are as serious as that of corn or wheat for the European. The situation is further complicated, however, by the fact that the Cingalese still cannot access these foods, even if the crops are good, because they are sold by the East India Company to a foreign market. Access to taste is crucial to cultural and social agency; therefore, the fact that the Cingalese are denied access to their traditional flavours speaks to their social and political dispossession as much as it does to their economic impoverishment.

The starvation of the Cingalese is related to their denial of tastes, which is akin to hunger, illuminating absence in a way that sparks recognition of inequality and injustice. Sensory historian Mark M. Smith argues that "[h]unger threaten[s] to catapult man back in space and time, rendering him more animal than human", and further that "[s]carcity of food peel[s] back civilized man's exterior and reveal[s] an animal that would eat anything to survive" (Smith 2015: 90–1). In this sense, not having the capacity to distinguish tastes is equated with dehumanisation, in a way that relates keenly to imperial justifications for dispossession. It is evident throughout Martineau's text that the Cingalese are read in animalistic terms, without a recognition that they have been rendered such through the actions of empire. Smith argues that "taste bestow[s] status, interlacing consumption with aesthetic worth" (89), while David Hume remarked on the othering nature of taste – that we call barbarous whatever departs from our tastes (1757: 203). Therefore the response to tastes in *Cinnamon and Pearls* determines a character's social agency in relation to empire as much as it has very real implications for survival. Hunger is visceral, while taste is acculturated; but in Martineau's text they become entwined, as she reveals that being denied tastes had deep ramifications not just for ideas of civilisation, ownership and belonging, but for food security in a context in which certain foods or tastes are culturally inappropriate, or certain preparations are deemed necessary.[7]

The way Martineau uses the language of taste access to express dispossession is heightened by the complex interaction of the natural world, and the brutality of the monsoon season, first by its delay, and then by the way it silences the dispossessed further. The silencing reaches its climax in a scene of crop destruction. Like characters in *French Wines* and *Sowers Not Reapers*, and indeed in the same vein as the historical 1775 Flour Wars throughout France, other European food riots, and the destruction of grains during the time of England's Corn Laws, Rayo seeks to destroy the cinnamon plantations with fire as an act of protest. His act is one of desperation, as one who has no legal access to the produce, but is forced to work in the fields to help profit the Company. Although preceding Marx's *Economic and Philosophic Manuscripts of 1844* by more than a decade, Martineau presents the essence of alienated labour, with the Cingalese doubly estranged from their selves, first through their loss of access to taste, and then through having to labour for another's taste and economic gain. Marana, watching her husband's act, hopes that the destruction of the field would drive away the East India Company, or at least "[drive it] from its monopoly, so that every man might plant cinnamon in his garden" (Martineau 1833a: 70). However, Rayo's protest is destined to go unheard: not only is the devastation blamed on a lightning strike during the monsoonal storm that is concurrently taking place, Rayo overhears one of the managers commenting on how much the Company benefitted by the destruction because the crop had been too good. They would have wanted to destroy some of the crop to push up prices anyway, and this destruction meant that they could blame the monsoon, rather than give rise to the ire of the locals, who could not afford to buy it (75). That the prices are pushed up, benefitting the imperialists in the same way that figures like Charles, Antoine and Steele are benefitted in *French Wines*, speaks to the ultimate powerlessness of figures like Rayo and Marana. The monsoon reveals Rayo's lack of agency and control in the way that "the fire he kindled did not catch the green shrubs; but some flakes were carried off by the wind, and fell among the parched grass near the outskirts of the plantation" (72). He has as much control over the fire he sets as he does over the natural world's delay in sending the rains, thus rendering the land in medium-term drought, or the sudden arrival of the storms when he seeks to destroy the crops, as he does over the economic ramifications of his actions for the imperial organisation.

The text's engagement with droughts and monsoons ends suddenly with a policy change that is not explained, but which allows the Cingalese to grow and sell their own cinnamon. It could be assumed that this is the outworking of Marana's hope, if not for the fact that the Company had been aware already of their oversupply. Furthermore, as much as this ending offers some kind of hope of agency, it seems ultimately a false hope, given that Rayo will still die of disease. The convenience of Martineau's ending allows her to conclude with the dangers of a monopolistic economy so that she can assert her belief in free trade; but this ending remains haunted by the image of Marana desperately selling Mr Carr's daughter, Alice, the charmed conch-shell, risking the vengeance of the sea-hag for the dream of "a basket of steaming rice, stewed with cardamoms or peppercorns" (63). Such a simple meal returns to the fact that in times of dearth, some classes of people will suffer more than others. Mr Carr himself explains to his daughter the unequal distribution of wealth and its impact of people being able to receive the necessaries of life:

> There is salt enough for every body here, and for half India besides;
> and large quantities are destroyed every year, to keep up the price,

while many are dying for want of it.... If we could count the number of Hindoos [*sic*] who die in India for want of salt which their own country produces, we should find that a fearful reckoning awaits the Company there, as there does the government here; a fearful balance of human life against a high price of salt.

(45–6)

While Mr Carr is able to attempt compassion across cultural and geo-graphical zones, looking to the Indian context, he fails to recognise his own similar investment in Ceylon's cinnamon trade. As one of Martineau's morally and intellectually aware proponents of political economy, Carr's unwillingness to do anything to disrupt the power of the East India Company is telling: as much as he positions himself as moral and caring, Carr is still driven by self-interest. He will only act in the community in ways that do not disrupt his own economic privilege. Mr Carr is described as being "pleased" by the destruction of the monsoon: "Not that he wishes ill to the natives, or to the eaters of cinnamon in other lands. But he is thinking of the good news he has to send to his employers" (75). Upon hearing that this was the "result of his enterprise", Rayo "rolled himself in the sand", mirroring the ancient act of mourning by covering oneself in dust and ashes.

Conclusion

Throughout Martineau's *Illustrations of Political Economy*, the role of the physical, natural environment operates to overturn any human assump-tion of power, violently usurping hubristic attempts to create order in society and the economy. The natural world will always have precedence. Rather than maintaining the aspect of most political economists, who avoided contending with natural disasters, in Martineau's work, these dis-asters are brought to the fore in order to critique the mathematical simpli-city of economic models, as well as the obsessive willingness of those who professed political economy to maintain the myth of the theory's moral grounding. As much as she may provide details of political economic theory in her tales, Martineau also refuses to deny the human cost that the implementation of such theories would entail. The human cost is most effectively shown through the effects of, and response to, natural disasters – factors that would continue to plague the globe, and are, arguably, even more pertinent in our contemporary world. Although forecasting systems have been developed, and are able to predict storms, floods, and even droughts to an extent, it is not possible to prevent them from happening; it is only possible to mitigate their effect. In this way, the physical environ-ment reflects the global economy; for as much as economics depends on narratives of order, the systems in place are actually volatile, essentially unpredictable and ultimately uncontrollable. Martineau is problematically blind to colonial and cross-cultural sensitivities in a way that could be seen as buying into a similar ethos to the imperialists engaged with the East India Company or other British trade; but this broad stroke is a gambit for her deeper concern regarding the application of economic theories at home as much as abroad. She overturns arrogant assumptions of political economy through her assertion of climatic devastation; yet at the same time, and somewhat idealistically, such disasters have the potential to bring communities together to formulate solutions in their wake. These solutions, however, prove more effective on the local level (although that impact also remains limited), rather than depending on broad national or international structures to assert order into chaos. Ultimately Martineau rejects institutionalised structures of relief in favour of community-based human interdependence.

Notes

1 See a more extended discussion of the critical reception of Martineau's economic tales in this regard in Scholl (2011: 105–10).
2 The Swing Riots took place throughout the south and east of England. Agricultural workers and labourers were protesting against harsh working conditions and the increase of machinery in farm production. The name comes from the fictitious "Captain Swing" in whose name threatening letters were written to landowners and magistrates. The participants were feared by many for their midnight raids and machine-breaking.
3 See Rudé (1964: 108) for a detailed discussion on this impact.
4 The Corn Laws (1815–46) were a tariff on imported grains, designed to keep domestic grain prices higher. The result for many was that bread was unaffordable and much ended up wasted.
5 The way in which droughts resist structural definition affects any kind of institutionalised relief or aid. However, in Martineau's tale, there is an entire absence of institutionalised charity. In general, Martineau distrusted such institutions. Her fictional works emphasise the importance of community-based relief that focused on the individual relationships and interdependence between members of the community across classes.
6 Throughout the first half of the nineteenth century, journalists, politicians and commentators referred to The Terror of the 1789 French Revolution as a point of fear and aversion, particularly in regard to social and political reform. It was a persistent narrative in both official political documents, the periodical press and novels. For further discussion see Scholl (2016: 16–20).
7 In the following chapter, Sanjay Sharma discusses how food insecurity could be exacerbated due to the cultural inappropriateness of food served in north Indian poorhouses during nineteenth-century famines.

7   Poorhouses and gratuitous famine relief in colonial North India

Sanjay Sharma

The second half of the nineteenth century was marked by numerous famines in India that impacted the ways in which the colonial state and its subject population faced issues related to hunger, poverty, and welfare. Indeed, questions of starvation, disease, death, and the responsibilities of the state informed nationalist constructions and critiques as well as colonial claims of progress, improvement, and ameliorative policy interventions. Famines generated debates on the responsibilities and duties of the state, and interventions in the form of relief were accompanied by an acceptance of the idea that famines were not produced by "unmanageable fate, whether natural or supernatural" (Robb, 2007: 50). Driven by these impulses, and a belief in its technological, institutional, and ideological abilities, the colonial state sought to formalise famine relief through commissions and codes in the closing decades of the nineteenth century. The extensive reports and relief policies they generated were arguably "the first written statements of famine policy in the modern era" (Hall-Matthews, 1996: 216). While this may be true of the *formalisation* of relief, there is a rich and elaborate pre-history of the idea of state relief itself and its practice from the late eighteenth century, aspects of which have been explored by a growing number of studies (Damodaran, 1998; Sharma, 2001; Ahuja, 2004). Episodes of scarcities, epidemics, and starvation-deaths since the Bengal famine of 1769–70 generated debates about the relevance of European ideas about the role of the state in managing the markets and the poor subjects of the colony. While famines were blamed on "natural" causes, as well as the inadequacies of the indigenous systems and people, as the nineteenth century progressed, the idea that famines could be mitigated with state intervention grew stronger. Eventually this was enshrined in the famine codes towards the end of the century, and the notion of state responsibility, however limited, was embedded in the idea of relief. Official relief policies were driven by the core idea of offering work to the able-bodied in return for subsistence payment either in cash or kind. However, it was also recognised that many persons in need were not in a position to work and the ameliorative measures that were devised for them came to be officially classified as "gratuitous charity".[1] Gratuitous charity was meant to take care of those in need who were not in a position to work.

Before the 1860–61 famine in northern India, gratuitous relief work was mainly in private hands. The general official view was that the state should refrain from direct involvement in it and if those having links with the colonial establishment wished to indulge in acts of gratuitous relief they should do so in their private capacity. During subsistence crises and other disasters, charitable acts were undertaken by voluntary organisations run by Europeans, missionaries, and administrators along with their families that were often supported by indigenous elite and notables attached to the emergent colonial regime. Simultaneously "native" expressions of kindness and benevolent practices of assistance that were witnessed in normal times, as well as during crises, were perceived to be driven by personal charitable impulses that were intricately embedded in religious and cultural practices of the inhabitants of the colony. Hence, charitable acts that were considered gratis by the early colonial regime were expected to be undertaken as voluntary humanitarian initiatives located in the non-state private realm of the colony. However, a significant shift occurred in the policy towards gratuitous charity during the 1860–61 famine in northern India when the novel institution of the poorhouse made its appearance and it emerged as the most important agency of state-sponsored gratuitous relief (Srivastava, 1968: 343). This chapter tracks this noticeable shift in policy and traces the principles, practices, and institutional trajectory of poorhouses from the second half of the nineteenth century in northern India, most of which was then administratively organised as the North-Western Provinces (NWP) and Awadh.

The region had experienced a severe subsistence crisis accompanied by widespread famine-crime during 1837–38. Official estimates attributed 800,000 deaths to it, a figure that appears to be conservative as its demographic effects lasted well into the 1840s. Hunger, death, and disease were inscribed in popular memory as the famine came to be remembered for a long time as the terrible *chauranvee* ("of the year 94", i.e. the year 1894 in the indigenous *samvat* calendar, corresponding to 1837 CE). Later official accounts of this famine emphasised that the 1837–38 famine was the first one in which a system of famine relief was devised that laid the foundational principles of state-sponsored work-based famine relief programmes in India. Based on the principle of "less eligibility", those considered "able-bodied" were offered subsistence wages in return for work done on what were officially described as "works of public utility". At the core of this was the official view that the famine was caused by a natural calamity (drought) leading to loss of employment, which could be remedied by setting the needy to work in return for wages. It was assumed that this would create demand, and the supply of goods would ensue if the market forces were allowed to operate. Employment of the famished poor was also supposed to prevent crime and vagrancy and, by ensuring sustenance, it would take care of shortage of labour likely to result from death and migration. But above all, benevolent state relief would delegitimise the undesirable charitable practices of indigenous elite and, by establishing the superiority and efficacy of institutional relief, strengthen the ideological claims of the colonial state as the fountainhead of philanthropy and humanitarian governance.

The next major famine occurred in northern India in 1860–61. The region started experiencing "dry and unfavourable" weather conditions from the summer of 1858 leading to successive crop failures. During the summer of 1860, till 13 July 1860, "scarcely a drop of rain had fallen in the Doab" (Girdlestone, 1868: 71). Reports of dwindling stocks of grain and rising prices particularly in parts of Rohilkhand raised an alarm in official circles. On 18 July, Lt. Governor G. Edmonstone issued a Memorandum to all Commissioners as a precaution, but also expressed deep apprehension:

> It is impossible to look forward without deep concern to the serious and general distress which the continued want of rain must inevitably produce, and to the crime which cannot but be anticipated as the natural and certain consequence; and it becomes the duty of the government to devise measures which shall give suitable employment to the poorer classes of the population, and so keep them from starvation and from crime.
>
> (Baird-Smith, 1861: Section I, para 24)

Hence it was made clear that official relief policies were to be structured around the core idea of work, and therefore all those who were needy and wanted state-support were expected to do some work. This policy was thus a continuation of the principles of relief enunciated during the previous famine of 1837–38. Accordingly, during the famine of 1860–61, the departments in charge of irrigation and public works were instructed to employ people on "works of utility". Wages were meant to be as low as possible so as not to adversely impact the wages that a person could get by working elsewhere. In the famine-affected districts, between 40,000 and 50,000 people were employed every day, mainly on the irrigation works being built by the government and by the East Indian Railways that ran through the middle of the central area worst affected in the famine tract. Thus "setting people to work" was the central principle around which relief policies were organised for the "able-bodied".

However, it is in the sphere of gratuitous relief, i.e. for those unable to perform any work (described as "helpless") that the most noteworthy and significant policy decisions were taken for the first time in this region. In the previous famine of 1837–38,

> Commissioners were empowered to disburse unlimited sums on behalf of any and every one who would give labour in return for food; but

gratuitous charity was discountenanced as involving a policy which Government could neither beneficially or generally pursue. The support of the helpless it was argued, was incumbent on private, and not on public, benevolence.

(Girdlestone, 1868: 44)

Departing from this "absolute separation between private and public benevolence and the disowning of all governmental responsibility of the destitute" (Mukherjee, U., 2013: 67), gratuitous relief for the "helpless" during 1860–61 was sought to be given a concrete organisational shape by laying down clear principles to govern it.[2] In December 1860, the government issued orders for the constitution of local relief committees in the headquarters of each district affected by famine. The committees were authorised to invite private contributions, and to coordinate their work a Central Relief Committee was established in the city of Agra that met every week from 9 January 1861 onwards. All district-level relief committees were to report their collections and activities to the Central Relief Committee that allocated funds while making efforts to raise aid in India and in England. The Central Relief Committee devised and advocated a number of steps for gratuitous relief of those considered helpless (e.g. for veiled (*pardanashin*) women) and orphans. However, its most notable and ingenious measure was the establishment of "relief houses" that were also called "poorhouses" (called *mohtājkhāna* in Hindustani; from Arabic *mohtāj*: "poor" or "needy", *khāna*: "place" or "residence"). The first relief/poorhouse was opened in January 1861, and till 30 April 1861, in the famine tract and the districts bordering it, 26 central and 75 district relief houses were established where, on average, a total of 80,000 persons were being relieved daily (Baird-Smith, 1861: Section I, p. 16). The last of the relief houses carried on till September. Of these, the poorhouse of Moradabad, a district in the Rohilkhand region of the NWP, emerged as a prototype that enunciated the core principles around which poorhouse relief came to be structured.

The principles and organisation of poorhouses

The Moradabad poorhouse was created and supervised by its Magistrate and Collector, John Strachey and Syed Ahmad Khan. Khan was the principal Sadar Amin of Moradabad at that time, who subsequently founded the Muhammedan Anglo-Oriental College and emerged as a key social reformer and educationist in the late nineteenth century. Strachey wrote a report on the principles that guided the relief measures undertaken in Moradabad that provides fascinating insights into the theory and practice of poorhouses in the context of famines in the colony (Strachey, 1862). The report conceded that, in principle, a poorhouse was to be a place to provide subsistence to those who were unable to perform any productive labour and were in official terms *not* able-bodied. However, providing free (gratis) support to the "undeserving" was an undesirable idea and indiscriminate public charity was considered to have "evil" consequences. Strachey made this absolutely clear:

> The general principles upon which public charity ought to be afforded are equally applicable to the able-bodied and the infirm. In both cases, it is a great evil that recourse should be had to charity, until no other alternative remains. It is a serious mistake to suppose that every person, apparently unable to work, is a fit object of charity. The evils of indiscriminate private charity are universally admitted. It has been too commonly forgotten that indiscriminate private charity is far worse. The latter has all the evils of the former, in an aggravated shape, and it is doubly injurious, because it is a public recognition of a false and mischievous principle. Under the pressure of extreme famine, it is true that the difficulty of discrimination may become too great to be contended with, and it is possible that in some districts this may have occurred already. But such cases must be extremely rare, and until distress becomes altogether unmanageable, there can be no reason for the disregard of the obvious principles upon which public charity ought to be administered. The problem, as Mr J.S. Mill has said, is, "how to give the greatest amount of needful help, with the smallest encouragement to undue reliance upon it." This is equally true whether relief is given to the infirm in the shape of simple charity, or to the able-bodied in return for labor performed.
>
> (Strachey, 1862: 4–5)

Thus the principle of setting people to work lay at the heart of state relief for those classified either as "able-bodied" or those deemed "helpless". In the rules for the relief of the "helpless" it was made absolutely clear at the outset that those adults and children who were found fit to be able to perform light work, like carrying a basket of earth, were not to receive any gratuitous relief and were to be dispatched to a "labouring gang" (Girdlestone, 1868: Appendix IV, "Rules for the Relief of the Helpless in 1860–61", No. I). The biographer of the 1860–61 famine, Col. Baird-Smith, affirmed that the "principle that all who can work shall work in ways suited to their capacity should be carried out as much as possible" and desired that all relief houses for the "helpless" should be "gradually developed into a true work-house" (Baird-Smith, 1861: Section I, 25 May 1861, para 22). Strachey had also emphasised that "the establishment of a poor-house should at the same time be, strictly speaking, a work-house" (Strachey, 1862: 5). In his view, making relief-seekers do some work would enable the separation of the deserving and undeserving as, otherwise, "professional beggars, fakirs, Brahmins, and imposters" managed to grab a bigger share of relief than those who were "really fit objects of charity".

Clearly the implication was that these groups were disinclined to work and should therefore be discouraged to partake of state charity in poorhouses. By stressing that "charity shall be, as far as possible, only afforded in exchange for labor" (Strachey, 1862: 13), official policy made it apparent that work and labour defined useful living, and unproductive sections of the subject population had weak moral claims on state benevolence. Consequently, poorhouse inmates were engaged in tasks like cotton spinning, manufacture of cloth, *niwar* (coarse broad tapes often used to lace beds) and *durries* (mats), rope-making, grinding corn, road-making and building sheds for the poorhouse (ibid.: 10–11). The products were sold for money, although Strachey observed that these activities were "undertaken without any idea of profit, and even if they had been carried on at a loss, they would not the less had been expedient" (ibid.: 10).

The second crucial feature of poorhouses was the serving of cooked food to its inmates. This had been tried in earlier relief measures and, from the 1830s, arguments in favour of serving cooked food in prisons had found acceptance among officials and doctors of the colonial establishment. Its ideological context was provided by the emergence of the workhouse as the key institution in Britain and its other colonies since the New Poor Law of 1834. Intended to be houses of correction, the workhouses were often described as "prisons", especially in their early years, but where work replaced the whip (Reinarz and Schwarz, 2013: 1–16; Pemberton, 2013). Among other aspects, a distasteful and unappetising diet contributed towards making the workhouse a place of deterrence. These ideas found reflection in the colonial drive to reform prisons in India in the early nineteenth century. For example, the 1838 report of the Committee on Prison Discipline propounded a new structure of prison management in which punishment was intended to ensure what has been described as the "right calculus of terror and deterrence" (Yang, 1987: 30). In this, serving a diet of cooked food was favoured for its disciplinary aspect. The next step in that direction was the introduction of the system of messing that was introduced in Bengal prisons in the 1840s. In this system, convicts were to be divided into groups and cooked food was to be substituted for money or rations. This invited hostility from prisoners for a number of reasons. Cooked food increased the working time of the convict by taking away the time they spent in cooking, reduced the choice of what they ate, how they varied their diet and acquired desirable products like tobacco (Singha, 1998: 281). Above all, cooked food threatened the caste and religious identities of the prisoners and several instances of serious opposition to it were reported from the jails of Bengal Presidency. However, the government was firm in dealing with them and was determined to implement the policy of serving cooked food to its prison inmates. This practice stepped out of colonial prisons and became the defining feature of poorhouses that appeared during the 1860–61 famine in the NWP.

In the model poorhouse at Moradabad, elaborate rules were laid down for doling out cooked food. Cooked food was given only once in 24 hours with little variation in the food that was served. Collector Strachey's report that was much cited in official circles reasoned:

> The general good health of the paupers has shown that there is no necessity for more frequent meals. Hitherto, there has been no variation in the diet, except that different kinds of dáls have, from time to time, been supplied. Persons for whom other food is necessary can obtain it from the hospital.
>
> (Strachey, 1861: 9)

Rations were uniform for all classes of adults and children and the single meal consisted of 10 *chaṭaks* of flour and 2 *chaṭaks* of *dāl* (pulses) for each "working pauper" while "non-workers" received less.[3]

Separate cooking arrangements were made for Muslims and others who had no objections on grounds of caste. For them cooking was done by contract, something that was found to be "least troublesome and most economical". For Hindus with caste-prejudices, *Brahmin* cooks and *kahars* (caste of carriers with low social status) were engaged but the amount served to both the groups was the same. In Strachey's view, the system was so designed to keep out all those who had other means of support and the amount of food was just about sufficient to preserve the health of the poor. He also pointed out that the system of serving cooked meals worked well to ensure checks and reduce fraudulence. The purchase, preparation, and distribution of food were to be supervised by a sub-committee composed of the "respectable members of the Native community, with some trustworthy officer of Government as e.g., A Native Deputy Collector, or Tehseeldar as their President" (Strachey, 1861, No. IV).[4] The government insisted that one or more of its officers should be part of each such local committee to not only "safeguard against waste or abuse of funds" but to ensure that "fundamental rules" were followed and to ensure "uniformity". There are several aspects here that are similar to the administration of the new Poor Law in England. Felix Driver has noted a similar quest for uniformity in his study of the workhouse system in England: standardisation of local procedures, to make local relief practices consistent with and conform to the principles laid down by central authority, and to level out

Table 7.1 Poorhouse food rations

	Flour	*Daal*
Adults of both sexes	8 *chataks*	1½ *chataks*
Children above 10 years	6 *chataks*	1½ *chataks*
Children below 10 years	4 *chataks*	1 *chatak*
Children in arms	2 *chataks*	1 *chatak*

Source: Strachey, 1861: 9.

the variations in pauperism, that was often implied but not explicitly advocated by the architects of the new Poor law as room was left for local variations (Driver, 1993: 47–8).

When Baird-Smith prepared his report on the famine of 1860–61 he stressed that relief should be interpreted liberally and should include relief from hunger and nakedness, and medical treatment and hospital comforts, while the nature of food should be cautiously adapted to the strength of the relief-seekers. However he expressed unreserved support for the practice and principle of cooked food:

> Relief from hunger by the supply of *cooked* food is the main characteristic of the system … in fact it is a corrective of or a preventive to abuses, that the supply of cooked food works so well, and excepting in very special cases, and under very peculiar circumstances. I am satisfied it should be rigidly adhered to; I found an absolute unanimity on this point among Native Committees, and as all personal details connected with the food are left exclusively to them, the plan has not in my experience been the subject of a single complaint.
>
> (Baird-Smith, 1861: Section I, p. 14)

Poorhouses become unpopular

From the mid-1860s a number of famines affected Madras, Bihar, and particularly Orissa, which was struck by a severe famine in 1866. By the time of the next official famine (1868) in the NWP, the principles of famine relief tended to get more standardised. The government of India gave instructions that gratuitous relief was to be provided to those incapable of labour and residence in poorhouses (a term now freely used for relief houses). This was generally enforced (Henvey, 1871: 5). A large number of poorhouses were opened but their function was highly unsatisfactory, as noted by several reports and the Famine Commission (Srivastava, 1968: 75). Mismanagement, lack of funds, and poor living conditions plagued the poorhouses. In most cases, cooked food was served, usually once a day, although rations and money were also distributed occasionally. Cooked food was served as a norm and the amounts were broadly the same as those given by Strachey in Moradabad.[5]

However, serving cooked food in poorhouses became a vexed question and contrary voices appeared soon after its supposedly successful implementation during the famine of 1860–61. Caste Hindus were averse to eating cooked food in poorhouses and regarded it as disgraceful. This was widely reported by lower level officials in charge of administering relief during the Orissa famine of 1866 (Srivastava, 1968: 76).[6] The fear of losing caste and respectability discouraged many people from attending poorhouses during 1877–78 in the affected districts of Rohilkhand. For Moradabad, it was observed that "the Hindu better classes never consent to take bread or anything cooked from any person's hand, other than their own relations" ("Letter from Roy Kishen Kumar of Moradabad", n.d. 1878). This deterred most of the cultivators and others who, it was said, "would rather die of hunger than go and take food in a poor house, as they consider it against their religion and caste" (ibid.).[7] Loss of caste in poorhouses gave rise to fears among poor cultivators that they would be ejected from their lands by *zamindars* on return, and this reportedly did occur ("Petition from Munshi Parmanand, Tehsildar of Aonla, 28 May, 1878").[8]

Significantly, there were several cases of women who were turned out of their houses by their husbands for having gone to the poorhouse:

> Mustt[9] Naseban, wife of Chhidda, caste Sheikh, residents of Bhainsia within the limits of the Moradabad city Police Station, 3 miles distant from the city left her village during the famine and was admitted in the poor house but when the famine was over, she went back to her house, but contrary to her expectations, she was turned out of her house by her husband, for having gone to the poor house and taking bread there. The poor creature thereupon attempted to commit suicide. The case was chalaned [*sic*] to the Court and the woman was sentenced to 3 months simple imprisonment. She died a few days ago of gripes in prison.... The same was the fate of all the women of cultivators who had left their houses during the famine.
> ("Letter from Syed Imdad Ali, Deputy Collector of Moradabad, 2 June 1878")

In a later famine (1897) "disquieting rumours" were circulating in Jhansi suggesting that women, who would accept aid will be required to leave their house, go and render some work either in a relief centre or a poorhouse and that the government would confiscate their property after their death.[10] The upper castes were quite averse to the idea of being housed and confined to the poorhouse space with low caste *chamārs* (leather workers), *bāghbans* (gardeners), and *julahas* (weavers). In Badaun, a poorhouse was opened on 17 September 1877 on the principles laid down by the government, in 1874, where separate cooks were employed for Hindus (*Brahmins* and *Kahars)* and Muslims; but as the Collector noted, the inmates were unwilling to stay on for a number of reasons:

> I can account for the dislike in accepting relief at the Poor House only to the general objection to giving up home and freedom and undergoing the confinement necessary if such relief is accepted and also to the fear of being turned out of caste, a very strong feeling amongst the rural population in this District, but which doubtless been overcome by degrees had the distress continued much longer and had a larger number of paupers thus been able to see for themselves what the

arrangements for cooking the food were. Some recruiters came to the District at the commencement of the cold season and enlisted 205 emigrants for Demerara. I have since heard that this gave rise to a rumour that if the people come to the Poor House they would be sent across the seas.

(Collector Badaun, 21 May 1878)

Despite the efforts of the administration to make appropriate cooking arrangements so that caste equations were not disturbed, poorhouses continued to arouse suspicion and invite hostility. It was reported that "the very name of the poor house is hated by the Brahmins, Chowhans, Jats and other better classes" because of fears of caste interference as there was "a large number of the Chamars, Baghbans, Julahas & the other low born people in the poor house" ("Letter from Raja Jagat Singh of Jajpur, 28 May 1878"). When the Famine Commission initiated its inquiries in the late 1870s, C. A. Elliott, the Secretary of the Commission, asked Syed Ahmed Khan to give his observations on the unpopularity of poorhouses in the NWP, in the light of his experiences of managing the poorhouse at Moradabad during 1860–61. Khan was asked to comment on the reports received from various officials of the NWP and Awadh that recorded the enormous dislike poorhouses generated among virtually all sections of the society except those who were starving wanderers. In 1878 poorhouses had experienced heavy mortality: those who entered them were usually beggars who were already sick before coming to the poorhouses, and many died after leaving them. Poorhouses hardly attracted other classes as they were highly averse to eating food in government establishments and were unwilling to leave their homes ("Reports by Messrs. Benett and Roberts and Captain Pitcher, deputed by Lt Gov. to enquire into the causes of mortality and in North-Western Provinces and Oudh (and) regarding the feeling entertained towards the poor-houses", in *Report of the Indian Famine Commission, Part III, Famine Histories*, 1885).

In his reply, Syed Ahmed Khan recalled his experiences of running the poorhouse in Moradabad in 1861 and enumerated the principles on which it was run. He admitted that as "no arrangement could conveniently be made with regard to caste system at such relief works, therefore only those persons who did not mind caste restrictions, and who were somewhat strong and healthy, were ordered to such works" ("Note by the Honourable Syed Ahmed Khan Bahadur, C.S.I., on the causes of the Unpopularity of the Poor-houses in the North-Western Provinces and Oudh during the famine of 1878", in ibid.: 252). Khan clarified that persons admitted into the poorhouse were separated according to their castes and sub-castes and, in fact, those Hindus who "no longer observed the caste system" as they had accepted alms and food from anyone earlier were clubbed with Muslims. Khan reiterated his opposition to distribution to relief in the form of money and rations as it had "evil" results, like consumption of unwholesome food and embezzlement. He added that one of the best principles of running a poorhouse was to make it a place that only admitted those who could not support themselves in any other way. He also rejected the view that poorhouses should be located near the residences of the needy as this was not practical, and it also negated the basic principle that made poorhouses places of deterrence. He concluded that deviation from or violation of these principles had led to mismanagement of most poorhouses, rendering them unpopular.

However, Syed Ahmed Khan's "Note" to the Famine Commission offered no solution to the problem of caste Hindus in poorhouses. The "model" poorhouse at Moradabad that he managed admitted only those who did not mind caste restrictions, having lost their caste purity prior to entering the poorhouse. Poorhouses established since 1861 therefore found it very difficult to handle the issue of caste because most caste Hindus feared loss of status on entering and leaving poorhouses. Poorhouses mainly attracted those who had run out of other modes of survival: beggars, wanderers, the sick and the infirm, or abandoned old people and children. Mortality was often high, and sometimes also because inappropriate food was served. Thus, for example, bread made of *kachcha* (raw) gram instead of wheat was served to inmates of the poorhouse in Moradabad in 1878. The gram was not parched (it was noted that even horses required parched gram) and as a result "the poor people could not digest such bread and consequently lots of men, women and children died of indigestion, notwithstanding the poor house having been inspected by the station surgeon everyday" ("Letter from Syed Imdad Ali, Deputy Collector of Moradabad, 2 June 1878").[11] Hence a number of factors made poorhouses unattractive: confinement away from home, acceptance of cooked food leading to ostracising from caste, ejection from land, sickness and mortality, and "as a receiving place for enforced emigrants to countries beyond sea and as a means for obtaining converts to Christianity".[12]

Poorhouses beyond famine years

Despite the popular dislike of poorhouses, the colonial administration persisted with them and they became an important part of state-sponsored gratuitous relief. The government was aware of popular feeling, but there was also a belief among some in officialdom that more than considerations of prestige and caste, "natives" were accustomed to free support from their rulers without rendering work. For example, in the Ajmer Division, a large number of Marwaris flocked to the poorhouses between March and August 1869. They reportedly refused to work saying that they had come "to be fed by the Sircar, not to work" (Henvey, 1871: 92). Henvey's report disagreed with the explanation that social pride and aversion to manual work made the Marwaris refuse work. Instead, he was of the view that it was "not the custom of Native States to demand labour from starving paupers". Such people expected alms not wages from the government, British or Native (Henvey, 1871: 92). Hence, though designed for those unable to work, poorhouses were imagined by colonial administrators in principle as workhouses, i.e. places where inmates were to be encouraged and made to do some work. Official animosity persisted towards the "generous dole of lavish and indiscriminate charity" practised by the "richer and better-educated classes", particularly for religious mendicants, that made it "inexpedient to take any steps for the establishment of workhouses" ("Report on Operations of the Central Committee Relief Fund, North-Western Provinces, 1868–69, 1870", in Arnold, 2008: 126). It seems that the colonial regime was averse to any institutional measure that provided succour without work, suspecting that it would lead to undesirable dependence on the government. Thus, as far as possible, poorhouses were expected to be places of work and quite often their inmates were sent off to labour on relief works as soon as they regained a little strength to do so.[13]

Despite being unpopular and riddled with problems, poorhouses were deemed necessary and were not abandoned, and famine codes made a provision for them as they encapsulated desirable values of labour, diligence, and discipline. Described as "the commonest mode of administering gratuitous relief" detailed information was sought by the government from officials about their structure and organisation with the directive that poorhouses were to admit those unfit or unwilling to work with compulsory residence and provision of cooked food ("Circular Asking for Information on Matters connected with the Relief and Prevention of Famine", from C. A. Elliott, Secy. to the Famine Commission, 22 June 1878). The Famine Commission of 1880 posed a set of questions for officials from all parts of British India seeking comprehensive answers about the issues plaguing poorhouses that were classified under "gratuitous relief":

> The commonest mode of administering gratuitous relief is through the poor-house. What is the proper situation for a poor-house so as to secure accessibility, discipline, space, water and proximity to food-supply? Is an enclosure wall or fence necessary, and of what should it be made? What total area is desirable in proportion to the whole number of inmates? What shape and material are best for the huts, and what sleeping space (in superficial area) should be provided for each inmate? How they may best be arranged with a view to ventilation, &c.? How should latrines be placed and managed? What is the maximum number you would accommodate in one poor-house? How should the inmates be separated and classed together, so as to provide for the requirements of caste, for the keeping of families together, and for the separation of the sexes in case of persons who do not belong to families?
>
> (*Report of the Indian Famine Commission, Part III,*
> *Famine Histories,* 1885: Ch. III, Question 23)

Several other questions were asked seeking responses of officials on "conditions of admission to poor-houses", "compulsory detention" in them, rations, organisation, hospital arrangements, and "disposal of convalescent poor-house inmates" (ibid.: Question 24–9). The extensive replies to these questions often displayed sharp differences in opinions and experiences of those responsible for running poorhouses. For instance, highly contrasting opinions on the question of compulsory detention in poorhouses were received from the North-Western Provinces. One official observed that all persons "wandering about and begging" along with those too weak to work "should be compelled to go to a poor-house" (ibid.: 239, reply to Question 25 by Mr Sandys), while another one went to the extent of criminalising them and advocated forceful detention:

> I would allow no discretion to a starving incapable man of refusing poor-house relief, unless of the middle or upper classes. I treat all such as criminal lunatics, and bring them in by force. Once in, it requires force to eject them. Yes, I would certainly have legislative authority for the purpose. I see no risk or fear. All that is necessary is a discretion to the magistrate of the district to issue orders for the sending of this class of people when in danger of starvation, if they belong to the labouring classes.
>
> (Ibid.: Reply by Mr Colvin)

The opposite view was articulated with no less force and backed by arguments:

> It does not appear to me desirable under any circumstances to make residence in a poor-house compulsory. The paupers resident in a poor-house are practically demoralized, being rejected as outcasts by their neighbours, having cast off all sense of respectability or shame, demoralized by want of food, and the mental imbecility which attends starvation, and learning in the poor-house to disregard all ties of family; it is not desirable that persons should be compelled to enter such a place.... It was for a long time ... believed that all the inmates of a poor-house were to be first made Christians, and then transported beyond the seas. Even after this idea was dispelled, the mass of professional mendicants preferred their own independence with the prospect of starvation.
>
> (Ibid.: Reply by Mr Kennedy)

Thus there were conflicting expectations from the poorhouses. While the colonial authorities in principle were not in favour of giving anything gratis and expected work in return for any assistance even in poorhouses, the popular norms and expectations ran contrary to that. Official advice to "native" elites continued to firmly stress that they should avoid indulging in *muftkhairāt* (literally, "free charity") as it made the recipients slow, lazy, and dull (*sust*) (*Qahat Sāli Ke Zābate* [Rules for Famine Years], 1897: 7).[14] During famines, the needy did come to the poorhouses, but once the conditions improved even the poorest stayed away from them because of insistence on work and cooked food. So, for example, an official from Bengal was of the opinion that

> relief through a poor-house, i.e., in an enclosure, in which at stated times cooked food is served out, although suited for beggars, lepers, worn-out prostitutes, and the very lowest castes, is wholly unsuited to meet the requirements of an extensive famine.
> (*Report of the Indian Famine Commission, Part III, Famine Histories,* 1885: 231, reply to Question 23 by Mr Metcalfe)

Beyond the famine years, poorhouses increasingly became hospices for beggars, lepers, the disabled, and those who were physically or mentally ill. Official belief hardened that the poor preferred begging, and many administrators argued that poorhouses were required as they could regulate street begging. Beggars were also allowed in poorhouses in several instances and by some codes (Srivastava, 1968: 170, 180–1). One report from Bijnor observed that even after raising wages in relief works

> yet men do not go to works in large numbers. They are seen begging in villages & towns and after a few days they are so reduced that Tahsildars have to send them to the Poor House which has so overflowed with them that its expenditure is enormous.
> (*Robkar* dated 28 February 1878, in "Abstract of Orders Issued on the Occurrence of famine in the Bijnor district 1877–78")

This was widely reported:

> I have often heard the people say that Govt. aided the people without any work even during the former temporary famines but they were at a loss to know why hard labour was taken this time while the country was suffering from the horrible famine. It appeared to me, that these people expected aid from Govt. without doing any work. But it was impossible to meet their desires and also inexpedient.
> ("Petition from Munshi Parmanand, Tehsildar of Aonla, 28 May, 1878")

Arguing in favour of establishing poorhouses, one official admitted that, to begin with, "the benefits of the poor house may be confined to the blind, lepers and persons otherwise utterly destitute and physically incapable of supporting themselves," but efforts should be made to find some light work they were capable of. In his view, the poorhouse would "regulate street begging since the really indigent would be provided for, and it would become the duty of others to work and not to beg" (P. Carnegy, Officiating Commissioner, Faizabad, 20 August 1870). Newspapers in districts and *mofussil* towns appealed to local administration that beggars should be sent to poorhouses. Thus, the *Bharat Jiwan* from Benaras reported that "famine-stricken women and children are to be found wandering about in the streets of the town and begging alms. The police should send them to the poor house" (*Bharat Jiwan* (Benaras), 4 January 1897, *Selections from the Vernacular Newspapers Published in the North-Western Provinces & Oudh*, IOR L/R/5/74, British Library, London; hereafter *Selections from the Vernacular Newspapers*). Elsewhere in Allahabad, famine-stricken people "wandering on the streets" were caught by the police and sent to the poorhouse. However, it was further noted that many continued to beg for alms and refused to go to the poorhouse, complaining that "the food supplied at the poor-house does not appease even half the hunger of the natives" (*Prayag Samachar* (Allahabad), 7 January 1897, *Selections from the Vernacular Newspapers*). Complaints about insufficient meals at poorhouses were common even when two meals were being served (*Bharat Sudasha Pravartak* (Farrukhabad), December 1896, *Selections from the Vernacular Newspapers*). Yet, generally, many vernacular newspapers were of the opinion that the police should remove the beggars and send them to poorhouses. Requests and appeals for the opening of poorhouses also appeared in the vernacular press. For example, a poem in Urdu published in *Mehr-i-Nimroz* described the wretched famine conditions that were forcing people to eat water-chestnuts, and appealed to the government to open poorhouses otherwise "men may begin to eat one another" (*Mehr-i-Nimroz* (Bijnor), 28 December 1896, *Selections from the Vernacular Newspapers*).[15]

Poorhouses in India may have originated as part of gratuitous famine-relief policy of the colonial state, but they came to have a life beyond the famine years. Their establishment and management were entrusted to municipalities. Provision for establishing municipal corporations in the major cities of India was made in the mid-1860s that also had a close connection with the sanitary and medical management of cities (Mann, 2015: 336). Most poorhouses had a dispensary attached to them to treat the sick. They were usually run by a Trust and while their establishment was initiated by the government or the municipality or sometimes by wealthy Indians, their running costs were met by regular contributions or subscriptions from various quarters. A poorhouse was established at Nawabgunj in Barabanki in 1872 with subscriptions of *taluqdārs* and government servants. Initially its expenses were met by monthly contributions; when a certain amount of money was accumulated, it was decided to stop the subscriptions and invest the capital in government securities and bank. However, when the interest proved insufficient subscriptions were resumed. Some money was also realised by selling fruits and vegetables grown on poorhouse land. The total number of poor (divided into four categories: blind, lepers, poor, and boys) relieved in the poorhouse during the year 1885–86 was Rs. 11,143, but most of them came and left and did not stay for long spells. The number of poor remaining on 30 September was 30, and most of the budget of the poorhouse was spent on the diet of the inmates. In 1885–86, the total annual income of the poorhouse was Rs. 886 while its expenses were Rs. 1,223. Diet accounted for Rs. 510 in the expenses and it had risen because of "dearness of corn & and the increased number of poor". The annual report observed that the poorhouse admitted "only those poor who cannot work" ("Poor House Annual Report of Nawabgunj, Bara Banki for 1885–86"). Elsewhere, another poorhouse in Bahraich was also managed by a Trust that invested its money in Government Promissory Note at an interest of 4 per cent.[16] Most poorhouses were administered by a committee that had Indian members along with a district official but sometimes they were in the charge of civil surgeons.[17]

By the first decade of the twentieth century, the desirability of having a poorhouse in each district or municipality was being expressed by senior colonial administrators. The commissioner of Allahabad wrote to the officers of the districts under him advising them to open a poorhouse in their respective districts (if it was not there already) as it was "a perfectly legitimate way of expending municipal money and the amount of the cost would not be great" (Letter from Commissioner Allahabad, 4 February 1906, Dept. of Scarcity). He also observed that when the price of grains rose it affected "wanderers badly", and then a poorhouse was the "legitimate direction for the expenditure of Municipal Coin and in it a part may be set aside for lepers" in case there was no separate asylum for lepers (Letter from Commissioner Allahabad, 26 January 1906, Dept. of Scarcity).[18] In his reply, one district collector observed that a poorhouse would be started once private charity contracted "to turn paupers adrift" (Letter from Collector Fatehpur to Commissioner Allahabad, 13 January 1906). It was being noted that the creation of paupers was a pragmatic gain to the administration, threatened by the persistence of local private charity. It also seems that local administration came to view poorhouses as places where those living on the margins of society could be confined. Beggars, lepers, paupers, vagrants, and orphans were often clubbed together and excluded as they were stamped with stigma and criminality in varying degrees. Many officials assumed that there was revulsion and fear among Indians who also wanted to shun and avoid these groups. To what extent this prevailed among local communities of Indians, and whether they believed stigma and marginalisation justified confinement, is difficult to assess here.[19] Despite the colonial attempts to stigmatise these groups, support for them within local communities did not diminish drastically. Driven by religious, ritual, and cultural obligations, charitable practices persisted even towards those considered "undeserving" in official perception. In fact, appeals for private charity were often made by colonial functionaries during famines, especially when distress increased to supplement state relief. Europeans and well-off Indians were exhorted to rise to the occasion and donate in line with their eleemosynary impulses. Famine relief funds were created mainly in urban centres for collections which strengthened the idea of organised impersonal charity for public good.

This aided the emergence of "a more precise notion of welfare" in the early twentieth century when the cycle of killer famines abated, especially after the First World War (Arnold, 2008: 128). In the early decades of the twentieth century, day-to-day charity of common Indians was "moving away from personal and largely religious acts to secularised, collective and organised undertakings that were intended to benefit much bigger, transregional groups or 'communities'" (Watt, 2005: 65).[20] Thus, some desacralisation of charity occurred as modes of giving changed and new ideas of *seva* (service) took root that were informed by older ideas of charity and practices and forms privileged by the colonial regime. This led to the evolution of "associational philanthropy" that enabled non-elitist sections to participate in social service, fundraising often suffused with the ideas of sacrifice and love and for nation-building (Watt, 2005: 66; cf. Sundar, 2000).

Conclusion

Unlike in Britain, poorhouses in India had their origins in famine relief, specifically in the famine of 1860–61 in colonial north India. As a part of the policy of gratuitous relief they were organised around the idea of "less eligibility" and were not meant for those who were deemed "able-bodied". Initially, their primary purpose was to prevent starvation-deaths and to just about restore the health of the famished inmates to enable them to work again and return them to a life of productive labour. As a matter of principle, every inmate was expected to do some useful labour, however light, even if she/he was incapable of doing so. This was grounded in the belief that any form of assistance, including gratuitous relief, should not encourage indiscriminate charity. This belief had its roots in the shifts that had been occurring in Europe, particularly from the sixteenth-century post-Reformation period, as a result of which indiscriminate alms-giving and beggary came to be regarded as inimical to the needs of a capitalist bourgeois society (Frohman, 2008: chapters 1 and 2; Hindle, 2001). This led to attempts at rationalisation of charity and the establishment of houses of correction in most European countries.[21] By the nineteenth century, pauperism, vagrancy, and criminality further stigmatised the marginal sections of society and institutional mechanisms emerged in Britain in the form of workhouses after the New Poor Law of 1834 (Driver, 1993). These workhouses, that were products of a specific utilitarian dream, served as the prototype for poorhouses when they were conceived by the colonial bureaucracy in the later decades of the nineteenth century. Physical, geographical, and spatial confinement, insistence on extraction of work from even the most feeble and debilitated inmates, a monotonous daily regulated routine, a frugal subsistence diet and denial of all indulgence characterised the poorhouses. As a corollary, virtues of discipline, diligence, and obedience were sought to be inculcated in the inmates who, in official perception, were to be weaned away from undesirable indigenous charity that encouraged indolence, dependence, and parasitism. Indian charitable practices came to be located in non-Christian religious superstitions, and were described as desultory and arbitrary, in need of reform. Poorhouses were thus presented as alternative models of rational and institutional philanthropy. They served as illustrative examples of the ways in which utilitarian ideas were practised in the colonial context, which in addition to being paternalistic had little regard for the perspectives of the subject population. As Gagnier's influential study of Victorian economics and aesthetics points out, utilitarian reformers treated the poor and the needy as means to an end and for "their own social planning rather than ends in themselves" (Gagnier, 2000b: 224–6).

The successful functioning of poorhouses was marred by a number of factors. The insistence on serving cooked food, and work and confinement away from homes, prevented many needy caste Hindus and women from coming to the poorhouses. Despite official efforts to take care of these objections, over a period of time, poorhouses became unpopular and even hated institutions that were shunned even by those rendered destitute either due to famine or impoverishment. Yet they were not shut down as they came to house the extremely sick, indigent, beggars, maimed, orphans, and often lepers. The colonial administration therefore persisted with the poorhouses beyond famine situations and entrusted their management to municipalities. Exclusion and confinement of these extremely marginalised sections of society found support among, certainly, elite Indians, many of whom also gave donations for the establishment and running of poorhouses. However, poorhouses remained under-funded and too few in number, and assisted only a very small percentage of the population. Though metropolitan in their origins in terms of their core ideas and principles, they eventually failed to address the problem of poverty and hunger in the colony. As institutions, their impact was therefore limited and they hardly served as "tools of empire", but the excavation and recovery of the principles and practices embedded in them sheds light on a lost chapter in the history of hunger and institutional care in India.

Acknowledgements

I would like to thank Pragati Mohapatra, Tanuja Kothiyal, and Ayesha Mukherjee for their comments and suggestions. I am grateful for the input that I received on my paper presented at the conference held in Oxford in 2015, which has resulted in this publication. Thanks are also due to my colleagues at Ambedkar University Delhi for providing the intellectual and institutional milieu in which many of my ideas took shape.

Notes

1 The famine reports of the late nineteenth century classified governmental remedial measures under the category of "gratuitous charity" meant for those considered incapable of work, for example, the old, sick, infirm, maimed, "idiots and lunatics" etc. See among others, *Report of the Indian Famine Commission, Part III, Famine Histories*, 1885 and *Report of the Indian Famine Commission*, 1898. This was distinguished from private charitable acts undertaken by individuals in their personal capacity.

2 The ambivalence about whether and how to separate private and public benevolence had a long history in the provision of English poor relief, going back to the early modern period. Similar debates about the "deserving" and "undeserving poor" led to a separation of private and public charity measures in the context of the 1590s famines in England. For details, see Hindle, 2004: 15–95 and Mukherjee, A., 2015: 10–13, 20–1. For some aspects of hospitality and alms-giving in late Elizabethan England and their complex relationship with the statutory welfare provision, see Hindle, 2001.

3 *Chaṭak*, literally one-sixteenth. One *ser* contains sixteen *chaṭaks*, and is equivalent to approximately 930 grams or 2 lbs, i.e. a little less than a kilogram.

4 For a useful description of gratuitous relief in the NWP and the working of the poorhouses during the famine of 1860–61, see Srivastava, 1968: 38–45.

5 Those who were served cooked food in the poorhouses were divided into three categories: adults (16 oz flour, 4 oz vegetables); children above 10 (12 oz and 2 oz); children below 10 (8 oz and 2 oz) (Henvey, 1871: 6).

6 Apparently the Brahmins of Puri, Cuttack, and Calcutta were consulted on the issue of accepting cooked food during the 1866 Orissa famine. Among the pundits "opinion was unanimous that no act committed to save life occasions loss of caste". However some pundits did insist on purificatory rituals with some payment (Blair, 1874: 200).

7 There is a substantial literature on the cultural and ritual significance of cooked and uncooked food in South Asia. See, for example, Khare, 1993, and Bhushi, 2018.

8 This was, however, denied by others. See, for example, "Letter from Syed Imdad Ali, Deputy Collector of Moradabad, 2 June 1878".

9 Mustt: abbreviation of *Musammat*, an Arabic word meaning "woman" or "wife", usually written before a woman's name, often in official documents.

10 Reported by the Jhansi correspondent of the *Nasim-i-Agra* of 7 January 1897 in *Selections from the Vernacular Newspapers*.

11 In another instance cited in this letter, a *chamar* woman was served the food of seven or eight persons for "immoral purpose" by two brothers known to commit adultery. Ibid.

12 These factors created the "dread of entering the poor house" in Shahajanpur. See "Note on the Scarcity in Rohilkhand Division, 1877–78".

13 An official reported that in the newly opened poorhouse at Orai "over 30 starving waifs and strays having been picked up on the roads, fed and drafted to the relief works when they have become fit for labour" (Collector Jalaun to Commissioner Allahabad, 3 March 1896).

14 I am grateful to my historian colleague Tanuja Kothiyal for sharing this document with me.

15 The original poem is not cited in *Selections*.

16 The Trust also received private contributions from local notables like the raja of Payagpur. ("Poor House Trust in the District of Bahraich during the year 1893–4").

17 When poorhouses were opened in Kalpi and Orai they were under the charge of the civil surgeon who maintained them through his subordinate staff. However, attempts were being made to administer the poorhouses according to famine code rules and not leave them under the civil surgeon. See Collector Jalaun to Commissioner Allahabad. Div., 13 February 1896.

18 Some collectors were in favour of keeping lepers out of poorhouses as money was given to leper asylums separately.

19 For colonial and indigenous attitudes towards leprosy and confinement, see Buckingham, 2002.

20 In early nineteenth century Europe, after the Napoleonic secularisation of many religious institutions in Germany, Switzerland, and Austria, benevolent societies and charities increasingly played an important role "paving the way for an institutionalised public welfare in the coming decades that eventually superseded Christian *caritas*" (Collet and Krämer, 2017: 111).

21 In this context, a re-reading of Foucault's classic account "The Great Confinement" is rewarding (1965: chapter II).

Part IV

Contemporary voices and memories

8 Farming tales

Narratives of farming and food security in mid-twentieth-century Britain

Michael Winter

The history of British agriculture in the twentieth century is now established as a strong and vibrant genre within modern British history. Much scholarly attention in the last thirty years has been given to the political economy of agriculture, with some strong accounts of the policies and economic factors that have shaped the technologies and patterns of production that have characterised the industry, and to the politics of agriculture (examples include: Brassley *et al.* 2012; Grigg 1989; Holderness 1985; Martin 2000; Smith 1990; Wilt 2001). As a result, a reasonably strong consensus, a dominant discourse, has emerged on the general aggregate characteristics of the agricultural industry and the key policy and economic drivers of change. The sources of data for these accounts are perhaps rather predictable – the economic and physical data available from censuses and surveys, and a wide range of policy papers. On occasions, these official sources are supplemented with material drawn from "less official" contemporary accounts or interpretations as gleaned, for example, from the pages of farming magazines or from books published by contemporaries. But such sources are almost invariably used for general illustrative purposes. They are not the subject of close and sustained analysis in the manner accorded to time-series runs of numeric data, for example. As a result, there is a tendency to draw on certain better known narratives without any attempt being made to justify their favoured status, still less adequately to contextualise their contributions.

This reliance on "official" and "aggregated" data means that the voices and experiences of farmers are often neglected or at best taken for granted. Moreover, alternative or subversive views and interpretations are neglected. Murdoch and Ward (1997) have suggested that this amounts to the construction of a "national farm", and as result the heterogeneity of both farming and farmers alongside competing political views of agriculture have been neglected. Some serious attempts are now being made to remedy these deficiencies. Voice is being given to farmers through oral history (Riley and Harvey 2007). Alternative views of agriculture are being explored through the lively interest in the origins and politics of organic farming (Conford 2001) and the land question (Griffiths 2010). As a means of tackling the deficiencies identified, oral history and the history of the organic or land reform movements provide excellent correctives to some of the dominant trends in agrarian history. But there are additional ways to take forward new ways of looking at twentieth-century agriculture and giving voice to others.

This chapter represents one such attempt through an examination of some of the written works of those who set out to relate their own personal experiences of farming, and there were many of these in the 1940s and 1950s, most, if not all, hitherto entirely neglected by agrarian and social historians as shown in the second section of the chapter. In particular, I focus on "working farmers", a category developed further in the third section of this chapter. In the remaining section of the paper I provide case studies of three writers whose divergent and particularistic voices offer an insight into the drive for food security in war-time and post-war Britain.

Questions about the role of markets, policies, and ownership structures, that seemed "settled" as Britain dealt with the food security challenge of the 1950s and 1960s, appear as far from settled in these works. Given that food security requires productive and successful farmers, the category of writers examined here are those who explicitly or implicitly set out with a pedagogic purpose to introduce or prepare would-be farmers to the world of farming. The chosen three for case studies are George Henderson, Clifton Reynolds, and Frances Donaldson. I have not included a host of other examples from the same genre including James Gunston (1941, 1943, 1945, 1947, 1948, 1950), Robert Homewood (1947), and Frederick Smith and Barbara Wilcox (1940, 1942, 1942, 1947, 1948), all of whom would repay further study in the future.

My choice of three writers has been influenced by a number of factors. On the one hand, I needed to have some contextual information, and this appears to be sadly lacking for Gunston, Homewood, and Smith and Wilcox. By contrast, Donaldson and Reynolds both wrote autobiographies, and Henderson – the best known in farming circles of the three – excited various written reviews and comment. On the other hand, I wished to avoid relatively well known literary figures such as Adrian Bell, Thomas Firbank, A. G. Street, and Henry Williamson, whose primary motivation was not to "instruct" farmers, and whose sphere of influence extended far beyond the farming world. Bell is openly literary, indeed he insists his works are fictional, although as his son Martin Bell (of BBC reporting and independent MP fame) indicates in the preface to the 2000 edition of *Corduroy*, the trilogy is largely autobiographical. Firbank (1940) is somewhat populist, with plenty of "human interest" elements, and more than a hint of hyperbole in places. Henry Williamson wrote one book about farming (1941), amidst a wide canon of literary output such as the famous *Tarka the Otter*. A. G. Street wrote many books, from novels to commentaries on farming life (for details, see Street 1969); if they have a pedagogic purpose it is to educate urban dwellers on the realities of farming, not would-be farmers.

The neglect of farmers' writings in standard agricultural histories

Of the three writers dealt with in detail in this chapter, Donaldson is the only one to warrant a mention by John Martin, in his important post-war agrarian history of Britain, and this in a discussion of economies of scale: "overhead expenses of more specialized machines could only be justified on a minimum of 121 ha of cereals" (17). This remarkably, indeed improbably, precise figure is drawn from page 71 of *Four Years Harvest* (Donaldson 1945) and seems a meagre harvest from such a rich book. Martin (2000) cites A. G. Street twice, in passing, and in both instances from Street's most famous book *Farmer's Glory* (1932). Again it seems a modest use of such a prolific and topical writer on agriculture throughout the period from the publication of his first book in 1932 to his last in 1964, just two years before his death. Moreover, Street's radio broadcasting, including appearances on the topical current affairs programme "Any Questions", alongside leading politicians of the day, gave him a national reputation, and this perhaps accounts in part for the occasional references to him in agrarian history. Nor does Street fare any better with Philip Conford (2001), whose seminal history of the organic farming movement contains one citation for Street. Street was not an advocate of organic farming, though in this instance he is cited by Conford as a supporter of the closer integration of agriculture and health policies as advocated by many advocates of organic farming (Street 1954). Neither Grigg (1989) nor Holderness (1985) draw at all on Street or any of the three writers.

The main point of mentioning Street is merely to illustrate how minimal has been the use made of contemporary writers of agriculture in the developing historiography of twentieth-century agriculture. Street was prolific. He wrote thirty-six books, including autobiographical farming accounts, novels, and collections of his journalism and broadcasts. He was a regular columnist for *Farmers Weekly* over many years. A controversialist by nature, he wrote *inter alia* a novel championing the rights of farmers in the face of war-time bureaucracy, particularly evictions (Street 1952), as well as providing pithy comment on agricultural policy, technology, and economics. Arguably, he was the last "born and bred" and "lifelong" farmer to be a genuine public figure known to millions. He has yet to be the subject of a full-length paper, even if he gets the occasional reference. Most of his contemporaries, as indicated, have fared even worse.

One group of agrarian writers has, however, attracted considerable attention – those who pioneered the advocacy of organic farming. Conford's history of the origins of the organic farming movement is very much an account of key personalities and their written works. The book contains an appendix listing the leading figures and providing brief biographical details. In his final chapter he issues a call to other scholars to investigate further the various individuals and organisations introduced in his book. There has been a response, with some fine papers on seminal figures in the organic movement. H. J. Massingham (Moore-Colyer 2002), Rolf Gardiner (Jefferies and Tyldesley 2011; Moore-Colyer 2001a), Jorian Jenks (Moore-Colyer 2004), and others were fascinating figures, as were the organisations they spawned, such as Kinship in Husbandry (Moore-Colyer 2001a; Moore-Colyer and Conford 2004) but, as those who have devoted so much recent effort to exploring their ideas, concede, their impact on mainstream agriculture was minimal.

So we have two contrasting approaches to writers and their ideas about farming represented in contemporary agrarian historiography. On the one hand, explorations of the origins of the organic movement have emphasised key people and their ideas; on the other hand, mainstream economic historians of agriculture barely give them a mention.

What is so lamentably lacking is any investigation of writers and thinkers who might conceivably have had an influence on the lives and mores of conventional farmers, farmers who were surely not solely influenced by the diktats of economic policy instruments or the salesmanship of agricultural suppliers, farmers too whose gradual professionalisation (Brassley 2005) exposed them to competing commentators on their complex industry. In other words, what about the voices, if not of ordinary farmers, certainly of those who engaged in mainstream agriculture and wrote about it? In fact, the war and immediate post-war years saw a flowering of rich writing about farming, chronicles of agricultural life that helped to shape the aspirations and opinions of farmers and would-be farmers, as well as the perceptions of a much wider public. Their neglect in the pages of agricultural history deserves rectifying, and the purpose of this chapter is to begin that process. The popularity and marketability of the literary representations of farming, which flourished in the immediate pre- and post-Second World War periods, probably rests on a combination of a nostalgic ruralism, the importance of agriculture to the war effort, and the attractions of farming to returning service personnel. There is also no hiding the ideological roots of some of the writings. Of his own compulsion in the 1930s to farm, Henry Williamson wrote in the *Daily Express* of dreaming "of English fields feeding English people. It seemed so natural, so true. I hoped that I might help awaken the English to this natural truth. I wanted a revolution, in thought and action" (*Daily Express*, 14 December 1938). A quote from Oswald Mosley on the title page of Williamson's *The Story of a Norfolk Farm* confirms the direction of Williamson's thinking at this time, but this should not detract from the power of his book nor, surprisingly given this was 1941, did it prevent a generous review in the *Times Literary Supplement* (*TLS Review*, 1941: 82; on Williamson's fascism, see Farson 1986; Higginbottom 1992).

The agricultural context and the emergence of family and working farmers

Britain's food security has for more than a century and a half been largely dependent on its ability to import food from around the world, acting as both a colonial and a trading nation. From the 1870s until 1939 (with the exception of the years of the 1914–18 war) domestic agriculture suffered as result of this free trade ideology (Perry 1973; Turner 1992; Whetham 1978). And at the same time, changes in taxation, particularly death duties, and agricultural tenancy law resulted in a decline in the proportion of land let by landlords to tenants and a corresponding rise in owner-occupied farming (Cannadine 1990; Sturmey 1955). Thus the 1939–45 war commenced with Britain producing barely a third of its own food supplies as a consequence of twenty years of agricultural depression (Short *et al.* 2007) and a rapid process of restructuring of ownership and occupation. The agricultural industry was in a fragile state and farmers remembered only too well the so-called "great betrayal" in 1920, when the Government suddenly removed the protectionist price policy that had helped stimulate food production in the war (Whetham 1972). It was clear that any new drive to increase food production, vital to the war effort, would demand a high level of intervention, both regulatory and in terms of price policy, combined with a firm assurance that the government would not walk away from the industry at the end of the war (Winter 1996). However, the precise nature of the state–agriculture relationship that would emerge in the post-war period was not clear, and it was deeply contested with some advocating land nationalisation, others a new social contract between the state and farmers, and many a market solution, albeit with price guarantees to avoid a return to depression (Smith 1989; Tichelar 2003).

I have argued that out of this political turbulence and national emergency a rejuvenated agriculture was born and, key to this, was the idea of *family* or *working* farming which emerged as result of a particular conjuncture of cultural, political, and socio-economic forces (Winter 1996). Culturally, the notion of family farming was promulgated in the period roughly from the 1930s to the 1950s in literary representations in a manner quite unparalleled before or since. In the same period, a politics of agricultural support was forged which saw family farming as a means of circumventing the traditional tri-partite class-based politics of landed capitalist agriculture. Economically, family farming emerged as a result of the relative fixity of the land-holding structure along with the declining size of the hired labour force due to mechanisation. In short, family farming emerged almost simultaneously as a cultural ideal, a political project, and a socio-economic reality.

Between 1851 and 1951 the proportion of the full-time agricultural labour force in England and Wales comprising hired farm workers fell from 80 to 63.7 per cent (Grigg 1989: 144). The number of famers remained roughly constant. Notwithstanding, the decline in the use of hired farm labour as a result of mechanisation, the process still had a long way to go in the 1940s and 1950s. All three of our writers employed labour but all three were actively involved in farm work and management too. Were they family farmers then? Understanding the notion of family farming has been a strong theme in rural sociology, rural geography, and agricultural economics for some time, with the literature continuing to be added to in an incremental manner (Brookfield and Parsons 2007; Djurfeldt 1996; Moran *et al.* 1993). But academics of all disciplines are prone to capture certain terms and to create (and contest) meanings in such a way that attention is diverted away from everyday usage. Indeed, sometimes the disparity between everyday use and academic definition and conceptualisation becomes almost unbridgeable. Things may not have gone quite that far for "family farming", but social scientists have lamented the imprecision with which the term is used and, in the search for definitional rigour, have selected certain characteristics for particular scrutiny. For example, conceptually, the deployment of family labour has been seen as crucial. Consequently, the use of hired labour on "family" farms has presented particular intellectual challenges to social scientists – does not the presence of hired labour shift a farm from one category to another (simple commodity production to capitalist)? If not, why not? Sociologists and political economists have agonised over these questions, tying themselves in definitional knots, with views ranging from those who see farms with any employment of labour as outside the pure family farming category, to those who see hired labour as a prerequisite for the continuity of family farming, allowing families to cope with the peaks and troughs of family labour availability across the family life cycle (Friedmann 1978).

But outside of academia, the issue seems to present no such difficulties. On the contrary, there is a quite different definitional focus within the farming community itself to do with the importance of physical work as a defining characteristic of a *working* farmer. To a working farmer, the presence or not of hired workers (unless the numbers are large) is irrelevant to their self-understanding. The opposing category is certainly not that of a capitalist famer extracting surplus value (these may or may not be referred to by "family farmers" as agri-businesses). The contrast to a working farmer is usually seen as either a "gentleman farmer" or a "hobby farmer" (Winter 1986; see also Williams 1963).

The changing social and economic conditions of agriculture in the 1930s and 1940s provide an important context to the flowering of farming tales. Although still a (growing) minority of farmers in the 1940s, the majority of the writers of farming tales were owner-occupiers, and a common feature of their accounts is the trials and tribulations of finding a farm to purchase. This is true for George Henderson and Frances Donaldson, two of the writers featured in this chapter, and also for

Thomas Firbank and Adrian Bell. An interesting and little known exception is Robert Homewood, whose book illustrates well some of the challenges of tenant farming, including a mobility in farming now a rarity, in
the inter-war and war period. But in the main, owner-occupation is a
powerful feature of the working farming narratives. As noted earlier, cultural notions of family or working farming appeared frequently in literary
representations from the 1930s to the 1950s, at a time when the class-based
politics of landed capitalist agriculture was being challenged by a politics
of agricultural support focussed on family farming.

In exploring contrasting representations of "working farming" in the
farming literature of the period, my focus is on those who wrote about
their "real-life" experiences of farming often with an element of instruc-
tive intent – lessons about "how to farm" in the context of a need for
improving food security in a pre-war, war, and post-war context. Their
accounts of farming were drawn from first-hand experience, not just of
owning or managing land but of working the land too. It is the experience
of physical work that pervades the books and gives them their quality and
their appeal, particularly to those who want to farm to produce food and a
commercial profit, rather than those who aspire to farming and landholding in terms of social position (the country squire) or recreational opportunity (country sports). My own interest in this literature dates back to
aspiring to be a farmer in boyhood. Henderson in particular appealed to
me and my father had copies from his days as an agricultural student in
the immediate post-war period.

Henderson: the "self-made" working farmer

George Henderson was born in 1904 into a seemingly lower middle-class,
and definitely urban, family. His love of farming and of scrupulous business practices emerged early when as a boy in the 1914–18 war he and his
brother, Frank, took on the job of tending some poultry for an enlisted
neighbour:

> This we were quite happy to do, without also realizing that we would
> continue day by day for nearly five years before our trust would be
> completed. Every day we fed and watered the birds, collected the eggs,
> entering the number in a book, selling them each week..... We set two
> broody hens, reared the chickens, sold the surplus birds, and banked
> the profits.
> … until 1919, when a somewhat battle-scarred warrior returned to
> civil life, and we expected to return the stock and hand over the
> profits..... Somewhat huskily, he made over the birds and profits for
> our trouble.... The stock had grown from six birds to twenty-seven a
> good strain of real old-fashioned Light Sussex.
>
> (*The Farming Ladder*, 40–1)

Henderson had no doubt that farming was what he wanted to do and, as he recounts in *The Farming Ladder*, following this early success with urban poultry, he set out both to learn about different types of farming and in due course to find his own farm. He spent a year on a lowland mixed farm, then a few months on a dairy and poultry farm. Then on an upland sheep farm he learned more from the shepherd than he did from the failing, and periodically drunken, farmer who eventually offered the young man a partnership, which Henderson rejected because of his commitment to a partnership and purchase of a farm with his brother. His quest during these two years of learning, and in the farming career that followed with his brother, was marked by a single-minded work ethic that might now-adays be seen as verging on the obsessive:

> Working from five in the morning to nine o'clock at night, I had few opportunities for spending money. .... I was very happy in my work, finding no toil or drudgery in it.
>
> (*The Farming Ladder*, 18)

> We intended to work about eighty hours a week, or twice the output of the ordinary labourer, allowing for the fact that twenty per cent of their time is wasted for want of careful planning and real interest in the job.... On the other hand, we proposed to live on half a labourer's wages, which is quite easy if a good part of one's food is produced on the farm.... One acquires the serenity of outlook usually found in a monastery. One is not troubled with second-hand opinions absorbed from the daily newspaper. In fact for first five years we did not buy one..... In the hours when other young men of our class were shooting, playing cards and tennis, or taking a girl to the pictures or on the river, we were working.
>
> (*The Farming Ladder*, 39)

Certainly his hard work gave him the requisite knowledge and, with the help of capital from his mother, he and his brother bought their Cotswold farm in 1924 at the height of the inter-war agricultural depression. In the years that followed he demonstrated how a small farm could be made to pay, an experience which he set out in meticulous detail in his books.

Henderson is the quintessential "working farmer" writer. He wrote solely about practical farming and confined his writing to his three published books; no journalism, no novels, and certainly no romanticised accounts of country living. His was a philosophy of self-reliance and the spiritual and material values of hard work. He saw farming as both a way of life – that was character-building and fulfilling – and a demanding business. His is the classic story of the self-made man, and his ability to forge business success at a time when many agricultural businesses were failing – with consequent calls for government support for agriculture – led to an ambivalent or even hostile attitude to the war-time and post-war consensus that developed around a state supported agriculture to secure food security:

> To say that only the State has the means to rebuild and equip our farms is ridiculous; any farm which is fully productive can earn the capital necessary to restore it, and build on for future requirements, as my brother and I have proved on our own holding.
>
> (*The Farming Ladder*, Postscript to 1955 edition, 241)

Between 1939 and 1945 the urgent need to feed the nation resulted in unprecedented levels of state intervention in agriculture, with a raft of measures designed to encourage and cajole farmers to raise levels of production and to focus on calorie-rich crops such as potatoes and cereals (Collingham 2011). Crucial to these efforts were the County War Agricultural Executive Committees (CWAEC) with tough powers to impose supervision orders and even to evict farmers unwilling or unable to comply with the CWAECs' requirements (Short 2014). Such an approach was anathema to a free market proponent such as Henderson:

> No chapter on wartime agriculture would be complete without some reference to the War Agricultural Committees. We deplore that they should have been considered necessary; it is a very great reflection on British agriculture as a whole that each individual farmer was not prepared to make the best possible use of his land in the national interests, which are, of course, identical with his own..... Freedom of speech was one of the Four Freedoms in which President Roosevelt crystallized the needs of the world – freedom of Speech, of Religion, from Want, and from Fear. I wish with all my heart he had included freedom from Bureaucracy, for in the committees this is found at its worst..... What is most annoying is to have an order served upon you compelling you to carry out something, with all the force of the law behind it, when this something is what you are only too willing and anxious to do.
>
> (*The Farming Ladder*, 157–9)

However, it is hard to discern from Henderson's writings quite what means he would have preferred to have been deployed to increase food production in wartime, given that many farmers lacked his drive, confidence, intelligence, and skill. He does commend the Committees for their commitment to advance good practice through demonstration and advice, and shows obvious delight that his farm is cited in the CWAEC's monthly "Farm Notes" as an example of good practice:

> Some striking comparisons were made with the Agricultural Returns for Oxfordshire; showing that, although the percentage of arable to

grass has always been higher than that for the whole county, the farm can carry three times the cattle, four times the breeding ewes, ten times the pigs, and twenty-five times the poultry for the acreage compared with the pre-war figures compiled by the Ministry of Agriculture for the county.

(*The Farming Ladder*, 161)

But, on the whole, he appears perplexed and outraged, in war-time and in peace, as to why others cannot or will not emulate his example:

I am inclined to think that any measure of success I achieved, a town-bred boy, with no special ability, capital, friends or influence in the industry, is simply due to the fact that I had to try so much harder; the effort became habitual and so I have gone steadily on, while others with every advantage showered upon them have just drifted along expecting someone else to do the hard work, and the National Farmers' Union to do their thinking for them.

(*The Farming Ladder*, Postscript to 1955 edition, 218)

Good character, good habits, and industry, are impregnable to all the ill luck this world ever dreamed of, proof against every misfortune, including, I believe, legalized robbery by a state that caters for the lazy, the selfish and the idle and penalizes the efficient, thrifty and industrious.

(*The Farming Ladder*, Postscript to 1955 edition, p. 219)

Thus, his outlook is primarily built around a strong political morality of self-reliance. He is clearly on the liberal right politically, in terms of his antipathy to the state and of interventionist policy, but his disdain for privilege means he is no natural Conservative either. He introduced a profit-sharing scheme for the succession of farm pupils or apprentices that worked on the farm. Again principles of self-reliance and moral merit are of great significance:

Individual merit is the only consideration. With sufficient money anyone can boast that he was educated at Eton and Baliol; only a boy of character and ability can say he learned his farming at Oathill.

(*The Farming Ladder*, 113)

His disdain for the dominant consensus about a state-supported agriculture is nowhere more powerfully put than in this section where he both lambasts the National Farmers' Union and applauds the opportunities offered by depression:

Is it to be wondered at that we have never joined a union that contends that "world conditions are such that farming in this country cannot be self-supporting, and the policy of protection and subsidies has not been in operation long enough to bring about improvement in methods of weaker farmers"? ... Much has been written about depression in agriculture and that it must be avoided at all costs in the future, but few realize that it is the depressions that give the weaker farmers, such as ourselves, the opportunity to get a start. Slumps eliminate the lazy, inefficient, and sport-loving farmer, together with the man who wants to devote his time to politics and local government, giving a heaven-sent opportunity to the man from the poorer and harder districts of the north and west to take the better land in the south and east of these islands. Also it is the opportunity of those of us who were reared in the towns, but regard the land as our birthright, and which we are prepared to earn in spite of every difficulty which may be placed in our way..... Ability to farm the land should be the main qualification for holding it, and a man who can take a farm with limited capital in a depression and make a success of it should not be kept out, at the expense of the taxpayer, by a man whose sole qualification is that his grandfather farmed it before him, and who is unable to adapt his methods to the times.

(*The Farming Ladder*, 163–4)

The Farming Ladder remained in print for over thirty years into the late 1970s, and *Farmer's Progress* was nearly as popular. Copies were to be found in the libraries of farm institutes, agricultural colleges, and universities, and the books were read by numerous aspiring farmers, farm advisors, and the like. It cannot have failed to have influenced the thinking of many, and yet so many of its fundamental premises were at odds with the corporatist agricultural settlement, championed by the NFU, that had emerged as the seemingly undisputed answer to the UK's food security (Cox *et al.* 1986, 1991).

Reynolds: the "sceptical" working farmer

I now turn to Clifton Reynolds. Reynolds wrote a volume a year for four years during the war, as he embarked, by his own account a complete novice, upon a farming adventure (Reynolds 1943, 1943, 1944, 1945; and his biography of 1947). He provides vivid accounts of the trials and tribulations of taking to farming for the first time during the Second World War. He develops an account that is highly critical of many of the practitioners of farming – farmers, workers, and indeed commentators such as A. G. Street and Henderson – and candid about his own failings and difficulties. An engineer by profession, he laments the lack of scientific knowledge and the application of its principles in the agricultural industry. Farming a small tenanted farm of 100 acres, he deplores what he considers the lack of scale economy and efficiency inherent in small farming.

He occupied what now seems a highly contradictory position. A successful entrepreneur – when he embarked on farming he seemed as determined to make money from his pen as from the land – he also believed in land nationalisation and a centrally planned socialist economy, having visited Soviet Russia in the 1930s:

> Many people have expressed surprise that I, an apparently successful business man, should write the kind of stuff I do about our social and economic system. I have tried to explain that I do so because I have a higher regard for the truth than for self-interest: that I refuse to be a victim of a system I despise.
>
> (*Autobiography*, 117)

> Although I have played as successfully as most of my critics at the game of Individual Enterprise, I hate it, ... I am prepared to devote the rest of my life to preaching against it.
>
> (Reynolds, 1945: 37)

> I inflict all this upon you because I foresee that by the time this book gets published you will almost be deafened by bleatings about the virtues of individual enterprise. An excellent exponent of it amongst farmers is Mr. George Henderson..... It might be taken as a Liberal Party tract....
>
> (Reynolds, 1945: 93)

But Reynolds had one thing in common with Henderson, his disdain for the NFU:

> no one, including myself, seemed to regard the N.F.U. as a body capable or desirous of facing the great questions affecting the future of farming with determination or fire. It may be that I am prejudiced in favour of the view that any action of real worth must and will come from the workers. The officers of the N.F.U. were, on the whole, the more prosperous farmers; men who could spare the time.
>
> (Reynolds, 1944: 114)

Although critical of small farming, Reynolds takes credit where he seems to have made progress and had success in his undertakings, but often falls back to his underlying critique of the system when things don't go well. At times, Reynolds seems to be on a perverse mission to demonstrate the folly of private farming through his own experiences of the operation of the market, hardly a free one, it should be added, given the level of state involvement in war-time agriculture. This is certainly picked up by A. G. Street, who describes the third year book in the *Farmer's Weekly* as:

a complete manual of how not to do everything connected with British farming, and such an exposure of the ineptitude of the townsman when confronted with the real problems of the countryside. No farmer ... could have been so cruel as to depict even a *fictional* townsman beginner as such a hopeless incompetent at farming .... the book is a long tale of truly pathetic foolishness.

(Quoted in Reynolds, 1945: 94–5)

These are harsh words indeed, and Reynolds responds robustly. It is hard to avoid the conclusion that Street, a conservative and traditionalist voice, was responding as much to Reynolds' subversive politics as to his actual farming experiences. Street was mounting a spirited defence of conventional agriculture and conventional agricultural politics.

Donaldson: the "intellectual" working farmer

Frances Donaldson (née Lonsdale, born 1907) could not be further removed from Henderson in terms of background and subsequent career, although they had one thing in common in that both came to farming from a non-farming background. Donaldson was an intellectual who cut her writing teeth in books about her war-time farming, but is now far better known for biographies of P. G. Wodehouse, Evelyn Waugh (both of whom she knew personally), and Edward VIII (Donaldson 1967, 1974, 1982). She was from a cultured literary background, which did not suggest in any way the likelihood of farming as a profession. Her father, (Lionel) Frederick Lonsdale (1881–1954), was a playwright. Her second husband, a left-wing intellectual and social worker when they married in 1935, later became a Labour cabinet minister, and subsequently received a peerage. He was also, in the words of Michael De-la-Noy (2004), a "dilettante Gloucestershire farmer", with the farm prospering "when the Second World War intervened and Jack Donaldson was called up, his wife so taking to agricultural life that in 1941 she achieved her real ambition to be a writer by producing her first book, *Approach to Farming*". However, the impression given here by De-la-Noy – that Jack was farming before his marriage to Frances and that his absence in the war gave Frances her chance to flourish in this occupation – is not borne out in any way by her own account either in her autobiography (Donaldson 1992) or in *Approach to Farming* (Donaldson 1941). Nor is there any evidence in his own obituary (Dalyell 1998) that Jack was the original farmer. In any case, Gipsy Hill Farm was in Warwickshire, near Stratford-upon-Avon, and the Donaldsons' Gloucestershire farm was their second farm and not purchased until 1947.

Approach to Farming went into six editions in as many years, and was followed by three more farming books, *Four Years Harvest* (1945), *Milk Without Tears* (1955), dismissively characterised by De-la-Noy as "hardly titles to tempt the literati", and the jointly authored *Farming in Britain*

Today (Donaldson *et al.* 1969). As practical accounts of starting out in agriculture they contain much in common with Henderson and Reynolds – dealing with tackling practical farm work, the labour "problem", the flows of the seasons, the trials of the weather. Also like Henderson and Reynolds, Donaldson takes the opportunity to spell out her thinking about agriculture in political terms, in her case in the context of thinking about the future as the war came to an end. She looks for an agricultural industry to deliver social justice – a better life for farmers and farm workers and better food for consumers, and she sees the state as having a key role to play:

> If the people of England are to be properly fed, not merely on a sufficiency of food but on high quality food cheaply produced, the farmers of England must have time not only to administer but also occasionally to take a holiday. And what does this all mean? It means electric light and water laid on, it means a decent standard of housing for both the farmer and his men, it means roads, it means schools, it means skill. It means equipment worthy of a great undertaking, it means a reasonable remuneration for every job properly done, it means an utterly different conception of an efficient standard of living. In one word it means capital. And from where is all this capital to come? I can only conceive of one answer – the state. And if the state is to supply it, then, it follows … that we must nationalize the land.
>
> (*Four Years Harvest*, 113)

But unlike Reynolds, Donaldson's arguments are not to do with collectivisation and state-run enterprise. Rather the state would become the landowner and all farmers would be tenants of the state. Adequate investment would be made by the landlord to encourage profitable private farm enterprises to ensure adequate food supplies for an urban nation. This is, in broad principles, the social welfarism that came to prominence in the post-war period, but with the necessary investment coming not from the state as landowner but as provider of grants and subsidies.

Conclusions

The three farming writers explored in this chapter demonstrate that the voices of agriculture were by no means united in their views. In 1996, I wrote of a "firm and coherent policy community, capable of defending and promoting the interests of farmers" (Winter 1996: 102). I identified the factors that brought about this coherence based on a mutuality of interests in post-war Britain. The farming industry was

> seen to be of key importance by civil servants because of food shortages and the industry's importance for overall economic performance;

to politicians because electoral prospects were so dependent on economic and food security factors; and to the key interest groups because of their livelihoods.

(Ibid.: 102)

As I have explored divergent farming voices in subsequent years, I have come to realise that the emergence of key interest groups representing farmers does not mean that all farming voices are as one. The post-war agricultural settlement was indeed based on some powerful dominant cultural and political forces which consequently shaped subsequent historical accounts. But it is not the whole picture. Of the three writers explored here, Henderson and Reynolds espoused visions of agriculture that were radically at odds with the dominant view and with each other. Donaldson is closer to the mainstream which, given her close connections with parts of the British political establishment, is perhaps not surprising. But even Donaldson can ring surprises such as in her support for land nationalisation.

Politically the election in 1945 of a Labour government committed to policy intervention and state planning across economy and society as a whole ensured there would be no repeat of the "great betrayal". Neither the radical free market voice of Henderson nor the land nationalisation advocacy of Reynolds and Donaldson found much support once corporatism had closed down options and electoral politics had set in motion a legislative programme that ultimately transitioned to membership of the European Union and the Common Agricultural Policy. It is doubtful that Henderson or Reynolds would have had much confidence in either, Donaldson possibly more so. Few can doubt that the post-war decades proved to be highly successful in protecting the food security of the British people. There are of course numerous questions that could be raised about the sustainability of the agriculture that emerged and the nutritional quality of mass produced food, but in terms of the crude provision of calories it was a success story based on price support policies and the application of science and technology. But could the alternative visions provided by Henderson, Donaldson, or Reynolds have led to similar or "better" outcomes? Counterfactuals present notorious challenges to historians. One thing is clear, though; powerful political forces mean that Henderson and Reynolds were side-lined as political voices even though their books were widely read. The last edition of *The Farming Ladder* was published as late as 1978 after thirty years of highly interventionist policies that inflated land values and made farming ever more of a closed shop, the precise opposite of what Henderson would have wished. Despite the seeming consensus on agriculture during this period, might it be that Henderson's free market vision did have an impact in the collective psyche of the farming community, and might this have influenced many farmers to vote for a likely radical reform to agricultural support policy by voting Brexit in 2016? An impossible question to answer, but the identification of competing food security policy narratives in this chapter at least suggests it is a possibility. As farmers will often remind non-farmers, farming is a long-term business and long shadows are cast by land management practices, farm business decisions, and cultural mores over many, many years.

9 The economy of hunger

Representing the Bengal famine of 1943

Amlan Das Gupta

The Famine of 1943 is imprinted in the Bengali memory in a way that no other natural catastrophe is. Those who actually witnessed the event are today a dwindling lot, but in many cases their childhood memory of disaster is still clear. Many of their anecdotes form part of family lore: at least for the following generation they are familiar and often repeated, as also are, for instance, accounts of the trauma of the Partition of Bengal (1947) and the Great Bengal Killings of 1946. More to the point, however, is the fact that the famine was written permanently into popular consciousness by the powerful cultural productions of the time. These range from fiction and drama to woodcuts, drawings, and photographs. Even a list of the most important writers and artists who responded to the famine would run into scores, and their works into many hundreds. It needs to be emphasized that these works are still very much in circulation; some of the literary works, in which we are here primarily interested, form part of everyday reading habits, such as they still exist.[1]

The 1940s in Bengal was a time of vigorous literary production, with both established writers at the height of their powers and a new generation of artists making their mark. Saratchandra Chattopadhyay died in 1938 and Rabindranath Tagore in 1941, between them having taken Bengali fiction to new heights of distinction. But some of their younger contemporaries remained active through the troubled period of the 1940s – a decade which maps, at a national level, the Quit India Movement of 1942 and Indian Independence in 1947, and in Bengal particularly, a number of traumatic events culminating in the large-scale confusion of Partition and mass migration.[2] For at least two more decades, Bengali fiction shows remarkable resilience and power in representing historical events that engender extremes of despair and hope. Fuelled alike by socialist ideas and nationalist dreams – often in curious conjunction – this body of fiction reinforced individual memories of loss and horror. Nevertheless, literary representation, even in the idioms of realist fiction, remains indirect and aspirational, and therefore not to be thought of as a surrogate for the recounting of historical fact. What it does do, and very powerfully so, is to shape our ethical responses, even after two generations.

For individuals of my generation, the understanding of the Bengal famine itself is shaped by its powerful artistic representations. One thinks of the photographs of Sunil Janah, who as a student accompanied the Communist leader P. C. Joshi in his travels through the ravaged villages of Bengal, or the ink drawings of Chittaprosad which miraculously survived the British censor, or the woodcuts of Zainul Abedin.[3] Searing in their anger and compassion, these images complement the fictional accounts of famine and disaster. I would like in this chapter to briefly consider the problems of representing famine, devoting attention to a short story by Manik Bandyopadhyay (1908–56) and a novel by Bibhutibhushan Bandyopadhyay (1894–1950), *Ashani Sanket* (1944). The selected texts are among the finest literary productions of the time, but clearly they form a small sample for judging a large body of evidence. Yet, the cultural productions speak in a relatively unified manner, in the way they understand the causes of the calamity, attribute responsibility, and document its human impact. There are few mentions of crop-failure or blight, and the overwhelming sense is that the famine was "man-made". The disappearance of rice, and then all other items of daily consumption, was due to government policy and hoarding: we repeatedly come across descriptions of the vast stocks hidden away in warehouses and granaries. Popular anger was further fuelled by the disastrous colonial policies of rice removal and boat denial.[4] There was thus a breakdown in traditional systems of entitlement, particularly in villages. In the summer of 1943, the Bengali journal *Prabasi* angrily noted:

> The intervention of the government has caused confusion and corruption in every aspect of business and trade in the country; the people have not been benefited at all, profits have been made only by grasping traders and a section of government employees.
>
> ("*Ek shata koti tākār khādyashasya kroy*" in "*Bibidha Prasanga*", *Prabāsi*,
> Calcutta, *Jyaistha* 1350/May–June 1943: 153)

The famine of 1942–43 (known as "*Ponchasher Monnontor*"[5]), and succeeding famine-related diseases, resulted in some 3 million deaths.[6] The famine was principally a rural phenomenon, spread over the length and breadth of undivided Bengal. Nearly every district suffered (Sen, 1981b: 441, citing the Census of 1951), and those who survived suffered enormous economic hardship and loss of social status, having had to sell land, livestock, utensils, tools, and agricultural implements and ornaments. The rise particularly in urban destitution, with large armies of rural poor moving into cities like Kolkata and Dhaka, was very marked. M. M. Islam writes:

> Contemporary non-official observers were almost unanimously of the view that the famine was "man-made", no natural factors such as drought or flood caused such a shortage of rice as to make large-scale

starvation and death inevitable. As the Calcutta daily, *The Statesman*, put it, "This sickening catastrophe is man-made. We say with deliberation that the present Bengal famine constitutes the worst and most reprehensible administrative breakdown in India since the political disorders of 1930–31."

(Islam, 2007: 422, citing *The Statesman*, 23 September 1943)

One fact that needs to be noted is that famine conditions seem to have been limited to Bengal and its environs, not the whole of India. Yet the surplus stocks from major producing regions like the Punjab did not reach Bengal, reportedly because of the complicity of traders, politicians, and government officials.[7]

In an article in *The Hindu* (13 February 2013), written on the eve of the passing of the National Food Security Act by the Indian Parliament, the eminent agricultural scientist M. S. Swaminathan looked back at his decision to abandon medical studies and become a soil scientist. The most powerful forces behind his decision, he pointed out, were the Quit India call by Gandhiji and the photographs of dying multitudes in Bengal:

> I am narrating this event in a crucial stage in my life only to point out the life-changing impact the Bengal Famine and Gandhiji's vision of a hunger free India had on young minds. Looking back, I am glad I made this change and also that I am living today when a historic transition from the Bengal Famine to Right to Food with home grown food is taking place.

Swaminathan recounted the reasons behind the calamity succinctly and with scientific dispassion:

> A constellation of factors led to this megatragedy, such as the Japanese occupation of Burma, the damage to the *aman* (kharif) rice crop both due to tidal waves and a disease epidemic caused by the fungus *Helminthosporium oryzae*, panic purchase and hoarding by the rich, failure of governance, particularly in relation to the equitable distribution of the available food grains, disruption of communication due to World War II, and the indifference of the then U.K. government to the plight of the starving people of undivided Bengal.

Swaminathan avoided taking sides in the most prominent of academic debates that have been conducted on the Bengal famine, associated with the work of Amartya Sen. Sen's argument was that "The traditional approach to famines looks for a decline in food availability.... However, starvation is a matter of some people not *having* enough food to eat, and not a matter of there *being* not enough food to eat" (1981b: 434). The argument that the Bengal famine was caused by the breakdown of traditional systems of entitlement rather that of food supply per se has received a great deal of critical attention and dissenting voices are many and varied. There is little to be achieved by rehearsing those arguments here.[8] What strikes me particularly is a comment cited in a recent article by Islam: "What Professor Sen has said about famine, was known to my grandmother."[9] Indeed, that may be the reason why Sen's description of the causes of famine has been similar to the analyses of cultural commentators in Bengal, and largely fits with the literary evidence available. That is neither to say that the literary evidence can claim any measure of scientific "accuracy", nor that Sen's arguments are in any way advanced or nullified by literary opinions. Dearth is a familiar and recurrent trope in representations of agrarian economies: famine too is hardly new, for as Swaminathan (2013) points out: "Famines were frequent in colonial India and some estimates indicate that 30 to 40 million died out of starvation in Tamil Nadu, Bihar and Bengal during the latter half of the 19th century." But it was not just the extent of the 1943 famine that made it stand out. Images of skeletons in lush paddy fields, tales of hoarders secreting away vast reserves of grain, of an inhuman colonial administration burning standing crops, capsizing fishing boats, and seizing the regular stocks of rice in agrarian households, and above all the sharp disparity between the fates of city and country produced a discourse of an *exceptional* breakdown.

Literary representations of the famine in Bengal render this breakdown in profoundly moral terms, seeking to come to grips with its inmost workings in human motivation and action. Much of it is factually accurate, and based upon reported events. More relevantly, the fictional tales of suffering and destitution written in the years immediately following the famine must be seen as a response to perceived reality. In a moving scene of Bijon Bhattacharya's play *Nabanna* (1944), human beings and street dogs fight for the refuse of the rich from rubbish bins; a familiar theme in the literary representations of the famine is the arrival of starving multitudes in Kolkata and Dhaka in the hope of casual charity. Oral accounts of urban middle-class witnesses inevitably recount the harrowing cries of the poor for a spoonful of rice-water; where they were able to get relief from food camps, the fare seems to have been both inadequate and inedible. Health stations, even when operated by dedicated doctors and nurses, struggled with shortages of the most basic medicines. In a later scene in the same play, set in a health camp, patients die like flies. The doctor, watching over a dying patient, says in despair: "I know ... he will die. He, and the whole lot of them. The *future* [my emphasis] is being murdered, deliberately, murdered by thieves and bunglers" (Bhattacharya, 2000: 105).[10] At the same time, the utter helplessness of the starving multitudes is underlined in the scene in which the tout Haru Datta and the trader Kalidhan Dhara traffic in destitute women by getting them to put their thumb impressions on forged papers (85–9). The plan is ultimately foiled by the intervention of the police, and Bhattacharya's play ends with the return of the hungry villagers to their original homes with the hope that they will celebrate a new harvest there. The play is something of an exception in the literature of the time, offering hope for a more equitable future, but only after we have seen extremes of human suffering, as well as a variety of responses to it that range from utter indifference to active malice and brutality. Hoarding, profiteering, and trafficking in women are common themes in the literature of the times, vices found both in the city and in the villages. Yet for all the play's socialist fervour, Bhattacharya's villagers are a law-abiding lot. The villains in the play are the black-marketeers and dishonest businessmen, rather than the colonial government as such.

The reader may be minded here of a point powerfully made by Paul Greenough through a contrast with the experience of European food shortages and food riots. He writes:

> In Europe the quasi-legal notions of subsistence "rights" and the "just price" gave legitimacy to food riots, a legitimacy sometimes conceded by officials, who refused to punish enraged looters and leaders of hungry crowds. ... In Bengal such legal notions were absent; the demands by starving dependents upon their destined providers were purely moral and customary, and abandoned victims did little more than to beg and dramatize their helplessness in the hope of stimulating a flow of benevolence. Hence mendicancy, imploring gestures, cries and wails; hence the passive confrontation of starving victims with the well-fed in front of "bulging" grain shops.
>
> (1983: 847)[11]

The reference to "bulging grain shops" invokes the testimony of a British medical officer who testified in front of the famine inquiry commission of 1944 that Bengalis died in front of "bulging food shops" because they could not buy and because "it was due to the passive, fatalistic attitude of those people that there were no riots and they were dying" (ibid.: 847).

Greenough's analysis of the rupture of the "moral economy" of rural Bengal has received much praise, and its main contentions have been accepted by many scholars (for instance, reviews by Appadurai and Chaudhuri, both 1984). Greenough takes issue with James Scott's study of the "moral economy" of the Asian peasant on several counts, but the question of passivity is an important one. Scott argues that starving peasants, when not restrained by force or law, will rise violently against their social superiors. This was clearly not the case in Bengal:

> If state-supplied relief subsequently fails, there is then a collapse of the social bonds uniting landlords with tenants, parents with children, and husbands with wives. Thus, in an advanced state of unrelieved famine, landlords and heads of households coolly abandon their clients and dependents, imposing suffering and starvation on the very persons

who are ordinarily their wards. Yet these resource-controlling and decision-making males do so without fear of resistance or retribution; in fact they appear to obtain their victims' acquiescence even as they pursue their own self-interest. Far from eliciting rage and violence, famine abandonment in Bengal is accompanied by widespread "passivity" and "fatalism", a fact that has always dismayed non-Bengali witnesses.

(Greenough, 1983: 832–3, citing James Scott,
The Moral Economy of the Asian Peasant, 1976)

In Bengal, states Greenough, peasants are unfamiliar with the simple ideas of scarcity and subsistence, preferring to refer to the notion of *Laksmi*, standing for prosperity or well-being, which is realized when there is abundance, and consequently the networks of mutual obligation that tie together members of families – and families with the larger community – are intact. Prosperity, he goes on to say, is expressed by the presence of three related qualities "indulgence" (*prasraya*), "abundance" (*raj-laksmi*), and "good health" (*sri*). The Bengal famine, that paradigmatic moment of *absence* of well-being sees not violent peasant upsurges, but rather a widespread breakdown in the ethic of care that normatively should be present:

Caught in these pincers of high prices and unemployment, a larger and larger proportion of the rural population was driven to sell its possessions, to foraging, and to beggary and theft. In a second, even more terrible phase of abandonment, individual households began to collapse, the male heads either driving off their dependents or leaving them behind. Sales of children and the abuse of women and children also occurred.

(Greenough, 1980: 234)

Given the widespread acceptance for Greenough's arguments – by Indian (including Bengali) and western scholars – a private sense of unease may be wholly irrelevant. Neither would an attempt to provide counter-instances drawing upon scattered anecdotal knowledge be of much use in countering the labours of a professional historian. In his recent counter-argument to the narrative of "passivity", Janam Mukherjee recounts hungers marches, and the looting of grocery and ration shops, and vehicles transporting grain (2015: 12–13, 40–1). However, this evidence appears to be drawn from an earlier stage of the crisis in 1942, before the physical extremes of famine were fully felt. The evidence of "resistance" to official attempts at providing relief and rounding up victims for shelters and poorhouses, on the other hand, comes from reports dating from October and November 1943, a later phase at the height of the crisis. These reports suggest that victims were "resisting" capture by relief officials and "kept running away" (ibid.: 203). Such "disciplinary challenges", as Mukherjee terms them, are described by one official as follows: "when we used to come with police lorries, they used to get frightened, the mother would run in one direction and the child in another". The resistance, once famine conditions had fully set in, thus appears to take the form of fear and confusion about official intentions – which is rather different from organized (or spontaneous) food riots. What one might say, however, is that the assumption of a coherent set of values – and Greenough is strong on this point – which characterizes the Bengal peasantry, or even the entire agricultural class, seems counter-intuitive. At the same time, the claim that the Bengal peasantry was unlike their counterparts in other parts of India and that their responses to famine were in some unique way different, is also worth pondering. We might for a moment consider the response of E. P. Thompson, the "original" propounder of the idea of the "moral economy":

> But Greenough hangs his interpretive apparatus upon slender evidence – a few accounts of the "banishment" of wives or desertion of families – and alternative interpretations are not tested. And he affirms his conclusions in increasingly confident form, as if they were incontestible findings. What were "desperate" measures on one page becomes, fifty pages later, the sweeping assertion that "authority figures in peasant households abandoned numerous dependents deemed inessential for the reconstitution of family and society in the post-crisis period". What is found in extremity is now offered as if it were the norm: "husbands and heads of families appropriated domestic assets and abandoned their spouses, and parents sold children for cash". We must leave these questions to specialists in Bengali culture.... But they strongly influence Greenough's comparative findings as to riot.
>
> (1993: 345)[12]

The point about *desperation* is important: neither droughts nor floods nor rapacious landlords and traders are unusual in Bengal, and scarcity is very much a condition of being for the greater number of its inhabitants. The exceptionality of the 1943 famine is what the literature of the period documents, and the question of moral agency is unlikely to have a simple answer.

Let me then briefly consider two representations of the moral consequences of famine in Bengali literature, not for their exemplary value, but to propose that literature habitually suggests alternate ways of response. The temporal closeness of the events to artists and audiences alike might argue for a kind of mimetic force, even if fables – like *Nabanna* – have ends that seem forced and propagandist. One should also point out that representations of the human conduct in extreme crisis are extremely varied, given the sheer bulk of literary famine narratives. The first text that

I wish to briefly examine is Manik Bandyopadhyay's short story "*Chiniye khayni keno*" (Why didn't they snatch and eat?), first published in the 1947 volume of short stories, *Khatiyan*.[13] In her detailed documentation of the representations of the famine in Bengali literature, Binata Roychowdhury observes that of all contemporary writers, Manik Bandyopadhyay composed the greatest number of stories on the famine (1993: 55). The present tale recounts a conversation between an unnamed narrator, and Jogi, who has the fearsome reputation of having been a brigand in the idealized traditional mode: he robbed the rich and fed the poor. Even during the famine, he looted food to distribute to the hungry, and into the bargain, saved several women from being sold into prostitution. He is certainly not the docile Bengali peasant, mutely suffering extreme deprivation. He has only recently been released after serving a prison sentence for robbing a government supply boat.

Supriya Chaudhuri examines this story in the context of her study of the moral economy of wellbeing, and finds in it a peculiar mimetic anxiety:

> The harsh, sometimes polemical realism of these stories can be seen to evidence a kind of representational anxiety, a response, I would suggest, to the pressure of a real event that exceeds fictional understanding or adequacy. "Chhiniye khayni keno?" pushes this struggle for representational common sense, as we might describe it, to the edge of a question that is put to history: why do people starve if there is food before them? The 1943 famine is above all the event that has raised this question, asked at the time by western observers as well as somewhat distanced Indians, and repeated subsequently by sociologists, economists and historians trying to come to terms with the cruelty of the contradiction that history has so faithfully recorded: food in the warehouses, deaths on the streets.
>
> (2014: 113)[14]

Chaudhuri concludes:

> Beyond that liminal point where the body crosses into the exhaustion and physical depletion of hunger, the body is its own food, hunger consumes it like an other, and in so doing it estranges and alienates the self, so that it appears to have no worldly recourse.
>
> (Ibid.)

I have chosen to revisit this tale because of the way it formulates and answers the issue of passivity: "Not one, not ten, but hundreds and thousands and millions of them went under … yet they didn't move an arm to snatch and eat their food, to grab it" (204). Jogi's tone is ironic, and at times openly derisive of the middle-class intellectualism of his interlocutor.

The city *bābus* (urban Bengali gentlemen and intellectuals) shouted themselves hoarse about the "food" crisis. For the poor, it was not a question of food in the abstract, its many refined varieties, but of rice; for if there had been the coarsest, maggot-ridden grain, even then people would have lived, hung on to life somehow. There are wild roots, plants, and leaves in the forest: all they needed was a little rice. Jogi is a privileged speaker, for two different reasons. First, he is a witness in the double sense that Giorgio Agamben uses the term of the survivors of the Holocaust, both *testis* and *superstes*, witness and survivor (1999: 17); second, as a brigand and organizer of revolt, he claims a distinct kind of agency, one that sets him apart from his suffering fellows. There is thus a fierce pride in his claim that he, and only he, can truly say why there was no violence, no forcible seizure of food: "Now I – I know why they didn't snatch – I alone do. No one else has a clue" (206).

Jogi provides in fact a mocking commentary on urban middle-class responses to this question, "all nonsense, just so much hot air" (206). Jogi reports to his companion both the opinions of the "*bābus*" and his own angry rejoinders. One lot say, these are poor and inoffensive farmers, they can't even dream of looting and robbing. Jogi's response is appropriately mordant. Who thinks of the law, he says, in the face of death? They would sell their wives and daughters, they would strangle a dying sharer, just to have that much more for themselves. To be arrested is to be saved, for at least there is food in the prisons. Another *bābu* tells him that ordinary people believe in fate, and accept it unquestioningly. But Jogi asks: Don't people seek recourse against snake-bite? Don't they take precautions against floods and try to save themselves from fire? So why wouldn't they at least try to save themselves by seizing the food in front of them? The narrator feels a little uncomfortable at this vein of mockery: "I know what such people say, Jogi. What about you?" (206) But Jogi is relentless. The third opinion, voiced by a *bābu* whose heart bleeds for the poor, attributes the docility of the peasants to their age-old habit of living with dearth. They were used to not eating when there was no rice to be had. Jogi's response is appropriately savage: "So I told him, sir, they may have been used to starving, were they also used to dying?" (107).

Jogi comes to the relief camp in the city as an outsider, having failed earlier in his attempt to get together a gang to loot food rather than money and ornaments. He dresses in rags, even though he clearly looks better fed than the others. Some try to chase him away, others flatter him for possible advantage. Jogi witnesses the condition of the relief-seekers, and true to his recalcitrant nature tries to instill in them a rebellious spirit. "I go around telling everybody, why don't you snatch and eat? … We are dying anyway, so let us die fighting" (210). Most of the supplies sent for the relief kitchen disappear into the hands of the hoarders. But his incitement appears to have little effect. The starving lot, feeding on miniscule helpings of a watery concoction of rice and lentils, pays little heed to what he says, not because they do not want to but because they simply can't. They nod off, and in between ask him to repeat what he was saying. Only some, after consuming the degrading fare doled out, are stirred into a show of temper, but by evening it has all died again and all they are able to do is to feebly jostle for a place in the queue.

Jogi arranges by contacting his earlier criminal associates to have a full shipment of food sent to the camp. This seems to work wonders. The food improves dramatically, the gruel is nice and thick, there is a potato per head in the bargain:

আর এটাই আসল কথা মন দিয়ে শোনেন বাবু। ছিনিয়ে খেয়ে বাঁচবার কথা যারা কেউ কানে তোলে নি, দুটো দিন দু-বেলা এক মগ ডাল আর একটু করে আলুসেদ্ধ খেয়ে সকলে কান পেতে শুনতে লাগল আমার কথা, সায় দিয়ে বলতে লাগল যে এই ঠিক, এ ছাড়া বাঁচবার উপায় নেই।

(176)

[*ār eṭai āsal kathā man diye śonen bābu. chiniye kheye bāñcbār kathā jārā keu kāne tole ni, duto din du-belā ek mog dāl ār ektu kore āluseddha kheye sakale kān pete śunte lāgla āmār kathā, sāy diye bolte lāgla je ei ṭhik, e chaṛa bāñcbār upay nei.*]

And then, sir, comes the most important part of my story, so listen carefully. The same people who had paid no heed when I told them to come and loot now grew attentive to my words, now that they were getting two square meals ... for the last couple of days. They started agreeing that what I said was true, that there was no other way but this.

(211)

They were ready to loot and plunder; they would take over the camp themselves and cook their own rations; even the children were oozing bravado. Jogi takes upon himself the task of training this rag-tag lot the art of professional brigandage with the same care that had taught his bandit crew. He settles on Baikuntha Saha's warehouse as the target of his attack, and spends a couple of days surveying the spot. When he gets back, he finds to his shock that food has run out, the old ration of thin gruel resumed. The very people who had sworn violent deeds are back in their state of inaction: "Hooked on to the thought of their watery pish-pash once again they were. Lost the power of thinking of anything else" (211).

This then is the core of Jogi's answer to the question that he formulates himself: "Why didn't they snatch and eat?" The question apparently exercised nationalist leaders as well. Malini Bhattacharya observes that Jawaharlal Nehru is supposed to have asked the same question (headnote, 203). The answer that Jogi finds is based on the nature of hunger itself: in a state of radical privation, hunger inhibits its own redress.

সেদিন বুঝলাম বাবু কেন এত লোক না- খেয়ে মরছে, এত খাবার হাতের কাছে থাকতে ছিনিয়ে খায়নি কেন। এক দিন খেতে না পেলে শরীরটা শুধু শুকায় না, লড়াই করে ছিনিয়ে খেয়ে বেঁচে থকার তাগিদ-ও ঝিমিয়ে যায়। দু-চার দিন একটু কিছু খেতে পেলে সেটা ফের মাথাচাড়া দিয়ে ওঠে। দুদিন খেতে না পেলে ফের ঝিমিয়ে ওঠে। তা এতে আশ্চর্য কি। এত সহজ সোজা কথা।

(177)

[*sedin bujhlām bābu keno eto lok nā-kheẏe morche, eto khābār hāter kāche thākte chiniẏe khāẏni keno. ek din khete nā pele śorirṭa śudhu śukāẏ nā, laṛāi kore chiniẏe kheẏe bēce thākār tāgid-o jhimiẏe jāẏ. du-cār din ektu kichu khete pele setā pher māthācāṛā diẏe othe. dudin khete nā pele pher jhimiẏe jāẏ. ta ete aścorjo ki. eto sahaj sojā kathā.*]

So then I knew, sir, why people starve to death, why they never snatch and eat even with food within their reach. When one goes without a meal, it is not just the body that gets dried up, the urge to fight for life and grab food goes down too. Then you get something to eat once more, and the urge is back. Then you starve for a couple of days, it goes down again. No wonder. It's all quite simple really.

(212)

Jogi's answer is based on that most unavoidable of constraints: the body itself. One must also realize that this is not a passage from prosperity to misery either: just that tipping of the scales between life and death. As Manik Bandyopadhyay's writings so eloquently testify, the condition of the marginal peasant in Bengal, Hindu or Muslim, is habitually attended by conditions of dearth. The 1943 famine then is understood in terms of its exceptionality; a people inured to the vagaries of flood and drought, of rapacious landlords and grasping money-lenders, of a callous and brutal colonial government, now experience a situation that renders the "implicit rules of crisis conduct" irrelevant. In its inhabitation of the condition of mere life the body become unresponsive to moral calculation.

That may also be the point of the ending of the story. Jogi's wife is visibly pregnant, and the narrator remembers that he has been released from prison only three or four months ago. Jogi answers the unspoken question that hangs in the air, by retelling a tale from the *Mahabharata*: of the sage Jaratkaru who, realizing his duty to bear a child for the perpetuation of his family, touches the womb of his wife, before departing for the forest, saying only *asti*, "it is there". In Jogi's cryptic retelling the sage has been worn out with asceticism and the union has no fruit: when he chides his wife about her childlessness, she berates him about his penances and tells him it takes strength to father a child. The sage, suitably penitent, feasts for a year on butter and cream, and only then is able to fulfil his conjugal duties. Walking back with Jogi to the railway station, the narrator wonders whether his companion knows that is biologically impossible for him to be the father. But then he realizes:

আজে-বাজে খেয়ালে - যেসব খেয়াল তাদেরই মানায়, তাদেরই ফ্যাশান, যারা ছিনিয়ে খেয়ে বাঁচার প্রবৃত্তিটা পর্যন্ত কেঁচে দিয়ে মারতে পারে লাখে-লাখে মা-বাপ ছেলে-মেয়ে - অনর্থক অখুশি হতে রাজি নয় মানুষ।

(178)

[*āje-bāje kheẏāle – jesob kheẏāl tāderi mānāẏ, tāderi fyaśān, jārā chiniẏe kheẏe bāñcār prabrittiṭa parjanta kĕce diẏe mārte pāre lākhe-lākhe mā-bāp chele-meye – anārthak akhuśi hote rāji noẏ mānush.*]

Who would bother to grumble about silly fancies, fancies that suit only those who can kill off billions of mothers, fathers and children simply by crushing their instinct to snatch food and live?

(214)

The backdrop of famine narratives, recorded and fictional, is frequently constituted by the multitude, the mass of "living skeletons" that Jogi describes, unnamed and unnameable. Human action in their case is reduced to a feeble scratching for a crust of bread, or finding a place in the queues outside the relief kitchens. Literary representations of the famine are marked on the one hand by the extinction of ethical calculation, a recognition of the most fearsome force of necessity, founded neither on cosmology or character, but on the human body itself. On the other hand, literary representations do foreground the question of agency: whether the outcomes are understood in terms of courage or of cowardice, of self-sacrifice or of self-preservation, they habitually challenge our moral responses, rather than ascribe praise and blame. It may be worth noting that the Bengal famine appears to place upon its witnesses and survivors the *duty* of representation, and thereby intervention in the debates it generated, clearly different from the responses to the Holocaust, to which it has been sometimes compared.[15] The character of Jogi is dramatized by Bandopadhyay as both narrator and agent who actively intervenes in the events of the famine as well as their interpretation.

I will conclude by briefly considering Bibhutibhushan Bandyopadhyay's novel *Ashani Sanket* (1944). I have chosen it not only because it is, through Satyajit Ray's celebrated film version,[16] relatively familiar outside Bengali speaking audiences. It marks something of a departure from the author's representational style, for he appears to have been unresponsive to political issues in the previous decade, claiming that the artist's role was to examine the "deeper realms" of aesthetic truth. Like most of his fellows, the famine of 1943 appears to impose on him the duty of response. Celebrated for his lyrical representations of rural Bengal, Bibhutibhushan chooses to chart the change from relative well-being to utter disaster instead of immediately plunging us into the world of starving multitudes. The novel ends with one death, and one death only; but in its prophecy of disaster, it remains one of the most powerful works of its time.[17]

The plot of *Ashani Sanket* has to do with the changing fortunes of a Brahmin family in rural Bengal. The central character is Gangacharan Chakravarty who has recently set up home in the prosperous and fertile *Natun Gan* ("new village") with his wife Ananga and his two young sons. Theirs is the only Brahmin family in a community inhabited by agricultural labourers; Gangacharan is held in high esteem and the first section of the novel describes his growing success as teacher, physician, and priest. Gangacharan is shown to be a man of a somewhat unsettled disposition, who has come away from his ancestral home because of family disputes and has been unable to prosper in other villages where he has tried his luck. The humble village suits him well as his authority here is unquestioned; it is easier for him to impress the village folk with the evidence of his wisdom and power. He is not averse to using both common sense and mild trickery to bolster his reputation. His willingness to take up the task of administering religious rites to the lowly Kapali villagers is, as his wife anxiously thinks, fraught with danger, for consorting with Shudras might invite high-caste censure. Gangacharan looks at it from a pragmatic viewpoint: "Who'll be the wiser? Who do you think is going to find out?" The villagers in return bring him gifts of the choicest vegetables, fish, and oil, and Ananga's pride in her husband's authority knows no bounds.

By chance more than design, Gangacharan's religious and medical ministrations seem to succeed, and his reputation grows daily. But the first intimation of disaster comes without warning and has little impact. Gangacharan goes to the neighbouring village of Kamdebpur to perform purificatory rituals after an attack of cholera, and there he hears that the rice is selling at higher rates than usual. Nobody believes that rice can sell at two rupees a *maund*, and the conversation turns to other things. But on the way back, Gangacharan meets a Brahmin acquaintance who tells him that he is starving: "I'm dying of hunger. There isn't a grain of rice at home. Prices are rising like anything – it was four and half rupees just then and now it's six" (83). Gangacharan is mildly worried and comes to understand that all this is happening because of the War. News comes of the fall of Singapore, a place that he has never heard of. The anxious villagers debate whether it is near Jessore or Khulna or Puri, a conversation in which Gangacharan remains superior and non-committal.

Like most narratives of the time, the question of sustenance in *Ashani Sanket* is founded on the trope of *rice*, its presence and absence. A multitude of wrong decisions leads up to the crisis. At one level it shows greed and short-sightedness. Farmers sell their produce, trying to cash in on the increasing prices, the warehouse owner Khan Saheb sells his stock to government contractors for profit. Biswas, the trader, tries to smuggle his rice out of the village, and finally abandons the village altogether. Gangacharan's prestige and social standing ensure that he is still able to buy rice when others cannot, but within weeks he finds that there is simply nothing to be had. Few accounts of the famine year match *Ashani Sanket* in conveying the immediacy and relentlessness of the spread of panic in the rural areas of Bengal. Equally shocking is the speed of the breakdown. The progress of the novel is measured in days and weeks, each stage marking new depths in suffering. This is comparable to the pattern of narration, in traditional Mughal chronicles, of famine horrors (see Chapter 4). However, the modern Bengali novel form allows its author to emphasize and reconstruct what the past imperial chronicles could elide – a precise teleology or progress of human suffering and degradation of values during particular famines.

The price of rice continues to rise unabated: from six to ten and then to twenty, thirty, forty and finally up to sixty or sixty-five rupees a *maund*. Looting breaks out in the rural markets, traders hide their stocks, hordes of starving people roam the countryside. Other foodstuffs also disappear; the villagers eat boiled gram and pulses, then yams and wild vegetables from the forest, and at the end are reduced to eating leaves and roots. Hordes of people forage in the ponds for snails and clams, while the children cry on the banks. "So many died eating these." Gangacharan discovers that there is simply no rice to be had, even for ready money. The inevitable pressure on social values is mapped tellingly in the relationship that develops between the young Kapali housewife and the grasping contractor Jadu Pora. She tells Ananga: "I can't bear it any more – if I die of hunger, what's the use of anything? I don't care – let me go, it's better for me to sin and rot in hell." Ananga, used to a life of ease and privilege, is reduced to labouring in the Kapali households, and while Gangacharan is racked with helpless shame, he does not refuse a meal at the house of a parishioner even while his own children starve.

The final turn of the story is the death of Moti, a woman from the lowest of castes, that of leather workers (*muci*). She is an old associate and companion of Ananga, and her appearances in the story map the gradual worsening of the situation. When we first see her she is happy and vivacious: in her subsequent visits to Ananga's house, her condition progressively deteriorates, her changing perceptions of her wasting body serving in the novel as the site of the famine's depredation. Her death causes a shift in perception among the villagers, who now understand that the accustomed habits of dearth and lack have been changed utterly.

গ্রামে থাকা খুব মুশকিল হয়ে পড়ল মতি মুচিনীর মৃত্যু হওয়ার পর। অনাহারে মৃত্যু এই প্রথম, এর আগে কেউ জানত না বা বিশ্বাস করে নি যে অনাহারে আবার মানুষ মরতে পারে। এত ফল থাকতে গাছে গাছে, নদীর জলে এত মাছ থাকতে, বিশেষ করে এত লোক যেখানে বাস করে গ্রামে ও পাশের গ্রামে, তখন মানুষ কখনো না খেয়ে মরে? ... কিন্তু

মতি মুচিনীর ব্যাপারে সকলেই বুঝল, না খেয়ে মানুষে তাহলে তো মরতে পারে। এতদিন যা গল্পে-কাহিনি তে শোনা যেত আজ তা সম্ভবের গন্ডির মধ্যে এসে পৌঁছে গেল। কই এই যে একটা লোক মারা গেল না খেয়ে, কেউ তো তাকে খেতে দিল না? সকলের মনে বিষম একটা আশঙ্কার সৃষ্টি হল। সবাই ত তাহলে না খেয়ে মরতে পারে !

(Repr. 2014: 149)

[*grāme thākā khub muśkil hoẏe porlo Moti Mucinīr mrityu hoẏār par. anāhāre mrityu ei pratham, er āge keu jānta nā bā biśwās kare ni je anāhāre ābār mānush morte pāre. Eto phal thākte gāche gāche, nadir jale eto māch thākte, biśesh kore eto lok jekhāne bāsh kore grāme o pāsher grāme, takhon mānush kakhono nā kheẏe mare? … kintu Moti Mucinīr byapāre sakolei bujhlo, nā kheẏe mānushe tāhole to morte pāre. etodin jā golpe-kāhinite shonā jeto, āj tā sambhaber gandir modhye ese poūche gelo. koi ei je ektā lok mārā gelo nā kheẏe, keu to tāke khete dile nā? sakoler mone bisham ektā āśangkār srishti holo. sabāi to tāhole nā kheẏe morte pāre!*]

It became difficult to live in the village after Moti Muchini's death. This was the first death from starvation, before this nobody knew or believed that people could die of hunger. So many fruits in the trees, so much fish in the river, above all so many people in this village and the next – how could anyone die of starvation? … But after Moti Muchini's death everybody understood that people could die of hunger. What was the stuff of fiction now became part of plausible reality. A person dies from lack of food – nobody came to help her! Nobody could feed and save her from death! People were gripped with fear. Everybody could die of starvation.

The novel ends with two events. Moti's body lies under the mango-tree, people come to see and shudder, but ultimately it is Gangacharan and Durga Bhattacharya, another Brahmin, who along with Ananga and the Kapali woman, arrange for the last rites. Finally, Jadu Pora offers to take the Kapali woman to the city and safety, but she refuses to go. One might speculate about the possibility here of a "weak" ethical position, carefully distinguished from numb passivity and heroic choice. Gianni Vattimo, the propounder of the idea of "weak thought" writes of Benjamin's angel in the ninth thesis from the "The Concept of History":

The angel in Klee's painting that Benjamin speaks of in Thesis 9 feels enormous compassion [*pietà*] for the ruins that history has accumulated at its feet. … This follows not from the fact that these relics seem precious in view of some ideal construction, but from the fact that they are traces of something that has lived.

(2018: 42; cf. Benjamin, 2006: 389–400)

Ashani Sanket is the most unheroic of tales, unrelenting in its examination of the debilitating moral effects of hunger. This recuperation of value, however slight it might be, is as much part of the received wisdom of the 1943 famine.

The Great Famine is still part of our lives and memories in Bengal. Perhaps relatively few remain to share with us their lived experiences, but the cultural production that the Famine prompted is still strongly embedded in our collective consciousnesses. I have tried to argue that the Great Famine marks a moment of exceptionality, its greatest representations can memorialize and mourn the event, but never exhaust its significance. What then might be truly shocking is the facility with which many of us are able to think of the persistence of these powerful images of deprivation and loss in the aspirational fiction that is the South Asian metropolis: the lines of the poet Premendra Mitra documenting the cry of multitudes on Kolkata streets crying for rice-water (*phyan*), from householders, evoke ghosts that still inhabit our worlds.

নগরের পথে পথে দেখেছ অদ্ভুত এক জীব
ঠিক মানুষের মতো
কিংবা ঠিক নয়
যেন তার ব্যঙ্গচিত্র বিদ্রূপ বিকৃত
তবু তারা নড়ে চড়ে, কথা বলে, আর
জঞ্জালের মতো জমে রাস্তায় রাস্তায়
উচ্ছিষ্টের আস্তাকুঁড়ে বসে বসে ধোঁকে
          - আর ফ্যান চায়।

(1989: 98)

[*nagarer pathe pathe dekhecho adbhut ek jīb*
ṭhik mānusher mato
kingbā ṭhik noẏ
jeno tār byangacitra bidrup bikrita
tabu tārā naṛe caṛe, kathā bale, ār
janjāler mato jame rāstāẏ rāstāẏ,
ucchishṭer āstākūṛe bose bose dhõke
- ār phyan cāẏ.]

You have seen on the city streets
Strange beings,
Human, yet not quite –
Cruel caricatures, twisted in scorn!
Yet they move, and speak
And pile up like garbage on the roads.
They sit, weary, on mounds of refuse
And cry for rice-water.

Notes

1 The Bengal famine is powerfully represented in the cultural production of Bengali intellectuals from the 1940s onwards. A full list is unfeasible here, but even the most cursory survey would include the work of the novelists Tarashankar Bandyopadhyay, Bibhutibhushan Bandhopadhyay, Satinath Bhaduri, Manik Bandhopadhyay, and Sulekha Sanyal; poets like Kazi Nazrul Islam, Subhash Mukhopadhyay, Jibanananda Das, Premendra Mitra, Sukanta Bhattacharya, and Birendra Chattopadhyay; the playwright Bijan Bhattacharya; the work of artists such as Zainul Abedin, Chittaprosad, and Somnath Hore; the photographs of Sunil Janah and the films of Ritwik Ghatak.

2 The wider context of the famine has been extensively dealt with; see for instance: Sugata Bose (1986) on the politics of Agrarian Bengal, and (1990) on the Bengal famine; Joya Chatterji (1995), Partha Chatterjee (1984), and Suranjan Das (1991, 1995) on land ownership, communalism, nationalism, and riots in the period.

3 Janah's photographs of the Bengal famine are discussed in V. K. Ramachandran (1998) and published in Janah (2013); Chittaprosad Bhattacharya's sketches were published in *Hungry Bengal: A Tour Through Midnapur District, by Chittaprosad*, in November, 1943; on Zainul Abedin, see Ela Sen, *Darkening Days* (1944) and Sanjukta Sunderason (2017).

4 The British, fearing a Japanese invasion, adopted a scorched-earth policy, destroying crops or buying them up forcibly in areas that were thought to be sensitive; they also seized boats for the same reason, seriously affecting river transportation and fishing. See A. Sen, "Ingredients of Famine Analysis: Availability and Entitlements" (1981), who describes

> the unquantified, but reported to be large, decline in the amounts of fish caught and river transportation because of the government's "boat denial" policy ... carried out in 1942. That policy, like the "rice denial" policy, was also aimed at the elusive Japanese, and took the form of destroying or removing boats capable of carrying ten passengers or more in a vast area of river-based Bengal; it did not touch the Japanese, but played havoc with river-transport ... and fishing.
>
> (445)

5 This refers to the year 1350 in the Bengali calendar; often used specifically to distinguish it from the other great scar in the history of colonial Bengal, the famine of 1770, "*Chhiattarer Monnontor*".

6 This famine was thus similar in scale and impact to the other calamity discussed earlier in Chapters 3 and 4, the Gujarat famine of 1630–32, which also had reportedly 3 million deaths.

7 See for instance, Yong, 2005: 292–3. The Famine Inquiry Commission (1945a: 53) claimed that 294,000 tonnes of rice moved into Bengal from other parts of the country in 1943.

8 Some key positions, post-Sen, are: Greenough (1982); Bose (1986); and more recently, Mukerjee (2010) and Mukherjee, J. (2015).

9 Qadrat-i-Ilāhi, "Amartya Sen's Famine Philosophy", *The Daily Star*, May 12 2005, cited in Islam, 2007: 422, n.6.

10 All translations from the Bengali are mine, unless otherwise specified.

11 The inset reference is to E. P. Thompson's "The Moral Economy of the English Crowd in the Eighteenth Century" (1971). Ideas stated here and in other essays are presented fully in Greenough's *Prosperity and Misery in Modern Bengal, the Famine of 1943–44* (1982).

12 See also Thompson's comment: "Greenough derives his account from Hindu cosmology and is silent as to any differences between Hindu and Moslem villagers" (345, n. 3).

13 I have used the English translation in *Manik Bandyopadhyay: Selected Stories*, ed. Malini Bhattacharya, Kolkata: Thema, 2003. Page numbers in brackets after the citations in the text.

14 See also Supriya Chaudhuri, 2011. For a recently articulated contrary view that passivity was not the overriding response during this famine, see J. Mukherjee (2015). My arguments regarding his position have been outlined above.

15 On the question of "unsayability" and the Holocaust, see, for instance, Agamben, 1999: 31.

16 Satyajit Ray, *Ashani Sanket* ("Distant Thunder"), released 1973.

17 The Bengali edition used is Bibhutibhushan Bandyopadhyay, *Ashani Sanket*, Kolkata: Mitra and Ghosh, 7th reprint, 2014. Page numbers are in brackets after the citations in the text.

10 Are we performing dearth or is dearth performing us, in modern productions of William Shakespeare's *Coriolanus?*

Julie Hudson

Human beings securely provisioned with food and water may feel in control of their environment, thus unaware that they are "performed by ecologies", to borrow a phrase from Baz Kershaw (2015). In his article Kershaw argues, with reference to the work of Jane Bennett (2010) and Gregory Bateson (1972 and 2000), that the environment is "internal to human beings", and thus shapes everything human beings do (Kershaw, 2015: 125). The pun in my chapter title suggests that when human beings are in the grip of famine and hunger, controlled by and no longer controlling their resources, those affected become painfully aware of being performed by dearth thus also by earthly ecosystems (d'Earth). What may be forgotten in benign conditions is that this applies at all times, for the Earth contains, encompasses, and subsumes everything we do and, as James Lovelock suggests in his writings on Gaia (2006), ultimately, is far more powerful than any individual species on the planet. Thus, the only sense in which we should see ourselves as "performing the Earth" is responsively, sensitively, collaboratively, and in tune with natural forces thus recognising the bit part we play in the whole.[1]

When satisfying our daily need for food, we could not be more intimately embedded in earthly ecosystems, even when we are consuming modern-day processed food products that seem to be far removed from the earth. It is an unavoidable fact that the consumption of food involves human physiology at many levels – mechanical, chemical, and cellular, to name three. As this implies, the ecosystem is (embedded in) the human body and the human body is (embedded in) the ecosystem. In live theatrical performance, the human body is centre stage, both on stage and in phenomenological spectatorial responses in the audience. Thus, Raymond Williams, discussing naturalism on stage, and describing the "lives of the characters" as having "soaked into their environment" and the environment as having "soaked into" their lives (Williams and Axton, 1997: 127), could be talking about any live theatrical performance or, indeed, about life in a more general sense.

As a term, the "environment" is anthropocentric and throws into focus the fundamental problem underpinning this chapter. This is the impossibility of being integral to a system and at the same time having the perspective to understand it. Perhaps because of this, the term environment is many-layered. It can be used to denote the natural environment (separate from or combined with humans); social structures formed by living beings (including humans) within and as part of the natural environment; the hard and soft infrastructure of human society or the complex system of conditions surrounding and infused through the human mind and body. Such subtleties notwithstanding, the environment, however defined, needs to be understood as "fundamentally performed by Earth's ecologies" (Kershaw, 2015: 113). Sometimes, the way the term "environment" is used in the context of activities performed by human beings mistakenly implies that we are in control, performing earthly ecologies rather than being performed by them. Dearth has the power to destroy this illusion as demonstrated by many examples of eye-catching real-life events theatrically delivered through the media. To give just two of many possible examples, Michael Buerk's striking eyewitness account of the 1984 Ethiopian famine (YouTube) and, much later, the 2005 media pictures of the after-effects of Hurricane Katrina showing New Orleans residents stranded on rooftops (Snyder, 2005), were memorable reminders of the fragility of human beings disconnected from their ecologically reshaped support systems. Twenty-first century commodity price volatility (also performed by d'Earth, as discussed below) has resulted in outright dearth in some countries, a recent example being the Mexican Tortilla Riots (BBC News, 2007). Moreover, climate modelling predictions suggest that dearth will be an inevitable consequence of uncontrolled global warming in some regions (IPCC, 2013). Considering such examples, it would be surprising to find an absence of dearth in performance even in a seemingly unlikely place such as modern theatre performed in conventional theatre spaces.

In this chapter, I identify a small number of plays that came to the stage many years ago at times of famine or harvest failure, and could, because they thematise dearth, be described as dearth plays (cf. Mukherjee, A., 2015, "literatures of dearth"). This chapter considers what happens to them in modern-day productions. If no food-insecurity resonance can be identified in the production or reception of modern productions of early-modern dearth plays, even perhaps to the extent that they are no longer dearth plays in production, I want to argue that this may say something potentially significant about the twenty-first century environmental and social cultural context. My reading of the absence of such resonance where it would reasonably be expected is that it signals a society (or at least a group of people within that society) in denial. Absence or under-emphasis would suggest a disturbing lack of awareness of the approaching collision between growing populations and increasingly resource-hungry economies, on the one hand, and constrained resources potentially under threat from over-exploitation, on the other.

The methodology applied in this chapter borrows an idea from statistics, where the impossibility of proving a negative proposition (such as the absence of a theme in a play) requires the framing of research questions in an affirmative form. Hence the need to identify older dearth play texts in which dearth can be clearly identified in the text (as well as the context) that are still in production. In theory, plays that came to the stage any time from 1500 onwards are potentially relevant to this exercise; in practical terms, I found the early-modern period to be the best source of earlier plays still regularly performed. Works that came to the stage at this time hold promise in this work for two reasons. First, it is a matter of record that harvest failures and commodity price volatility were frequent in England in the late 1500s and early 1600s. (For example, Mukherjee, A. (2015: 309) cites Appleby (1978) as identifying 1587–88, 1597–98, and 1623 as "severe crises in the northwest".) Second, several of them are still in production. Where they still appear in production repertoires on a regular basis, they present the possibility of informative empirical research in the area of food insecurity in performance in modern times, thus indirectly they may also reveal the extent to which we understand that we are "performed by" the Earth we live on.

Grain prices performed by earthly ecologies

Grain prices are generally regarded as "performed by" economics. In reality, economics and grain prices are shaped by natural forces – human beings set up market systems and earthly ecologies play through them. The early-modern chronology of harvest failures and social duress can thus be understood from arable crop price data running from 1450 to 1649, compiled by Peter Bowden (see Thirsk, 1967: Table I, 815–28; cf. Hoskins, 1964: 28–46).[2] These data are suggestive of the price-squeeze suffered by labourers on relatively fixed wages in the context of commodity price volatility. The segment of data relevant to this chapter shows grain prices between 1534 and 1630 (Thirsk, 1967: 818–21). The same volume also compiles Southern English wage rates for agricultural labourers and building craftsmen for the same years (Table XVI, 865). It should be noted that Bowden tabulates grain prices annually, and wages only for each decade, so it is quite possible that the data are overstating the parlous situation people could find themselves in when grain prices rose and their wages failed to follow; however, it seems safe to assume that wages would be relatively static. Some years – for instance 1600–03 – would provide relief (grain prices fell while wages stood still) but hunger pains would never be far away for those working in these sectors, and, at times (e.g. 1595–96, 1600, and 1612) grain-based staples would have been downright unaffordable.

Early modern plays potentially influenced by dearth

I will briefly discuss two well-documented Shakespearian examples of dearth-relevance – *The Merry Wives of Windsor* (1597–99) and *King Lear*

(1606) – as well as modern examples of dearth in performance, then move on to consider a specific scene in William Shakespeare's play *Coriolanus* (1605–08) in greater detail.[3]

Merry Wives may have been written somewhere between 1597 and 1599 (Melchiori, 2000), thereby immediately following a severe deterioration in food affordability (see Hoskins, 1964: 32). Kinney explores differences between the folio and quarto editions of the play that seem to be largely explained by the impossibility of staging the play as first written and where first intended (Windsor) because of the political sensitivity of laughing at a fat, profligate wastrel at a time when food was no laughing matter (Kinney, 1993).[4] An awareness of the interconnectedness of failed politics and failed agriculture is shown to run through *King Lear*, and other plays, by Archer *et al.* who comment:

> Following *1 Henry VI* (1592) and *Henry V* (1598–9), *King Lear* is the third and final of Shakespeare's plays to include an allusion to darnel. The first two plays […] use darnel and related imagery to […] interrogate contemporary issues of food supply and national security.
>
> (Archer *et al.*, 2012: 530)

A relatively well-known illustration of the topicality of dearth in the Shakespearian cultural context shaping the plays lies in the connection between events in William Shakespeare's own life, and the riots depicted in the opening scenes of the *Coriolanus*. This play is thought to have been written in the first decade of the seventeenth century, some five to ten years after the events contextualised by E. K. Chambers, and cited below:

> The dearth appears to have been particularly felt in South-West Warwickshire […]. Sturley reports to Quiney on 24 Jan.1958, that the people were growing "malcontent", and were approaching neighbouring justices with complaints against "our maltsters". There was wild hope of seeing them in a halter, and "if Lord God send my Lord of Essex down shortly, to see them hanged on gibbets at their own doors".
>
> (Chambers, 1930: 100–1)

It is not known whether Shakespeare saw this exchange, but unlikely that he was unaware of public sentiment in respect of the grain traders of his day. Indeed, subject to the play's having come to the stage early on in 1608, the 1607 anti-enclosure riots may have brought the issue of unequal access to food and food-related resources back into focus again. One can imagine the feelings of William Shakespeare, the well-to-do 1598 trader in "ten quarters of malt" (cited by Chambers (99) with reference to documentation of "Returns made to the authorities" on 4 February 1598), contemplating the anger of hungry people performed by dearth: "Let us revenge this with our pikes, before we become rakes" (I.i.20–1). There are strong arguments, as Steve Hindle demonstrates (2008), for associating *Coriolanus* with the Midlands Rising, and Shakespeare is also thought to have engaged with the immediate context of food riots in London in his earlier play *Romeo and Juliet* (1599; cf. Fitter, 2000).

In our times, technology has provided new approaches to food production and preparation, but there is plenty of evidence to suggest that this has not banished food insecurity as a social concern. The profits made by food commodity traders are as sensitive now as they were in early modern England: so much so that some global banks have closed down their agricultural commodity funds, in a good example of markets in the grip of ecologies (Archer *et al.*, 2012). Food security and nutrition are front of mind for politicians as I write this for a number of reasons, including: the prominent discussions in the media of the food-related effects of the economic downturn (hunger in Greece, food banks in the UK, and political change under way in both countries); long-standing discussions of climate change (to which the food habits of some nations contribute) and its likely impacts on unequal societies; science reports such as the Assessment Reports of the Intergovernmental Panel on Climate Change suggesting that severe water shortages are likely in major food-producing parts of the world; and debates about the nutritional quality of sugar, and processed food.[5] Having enough food, but not of a quality sufficient to meet nutritional standards sufficient for good health, may be a problem the early moderns would have regarded as nice to have when the challenge was to find the next meal, yet it can also be framed as a modern-day form of dearth. In the twenty-first century micronutritional inequality is highlighted by the fact that people continue to suffer the effects of malnutrition in developing countries alongside a worldwide obesity epidemic (also a form of malnutrition) in the west. Scientific evidence suggests that the causes of the obesity problem are unlikely to be Falstaffian – that is to say, caused by greed. Considering that NHS (National Health Service) statistics find that the majority of British people have an unhealthy Body Mass Index, and in 2011/12 a tenth of 4–5 years olds were obese as they started school, it is more likely that something systemic is at work. One of the causes named on the NHS (2013) website is as follows: "There is easy access to cheap, high-energy food that is often aggressively marketed to people." Superficially speaking, economics (thus, a social failure) seems to have something to do with this problem. A 2015 report of the UK Overseas Development Agency by Wiggins and Keats analysing food prices between 1990 and 2012 reported that junk food had become significantly cheaper while the price of fruit and vegetables had risen significantly. The effects of this on nutrition are inevitably unequal because of the variation of shares in family income with wage levels, thereby reminding us of the rise in prices at the end of the sixteenth century.

In general terms, then, even if definitions of food insecurity vary with specific geographical and cultural contexts, dearth still appears to be a sufficiently sensitive issue to be present in theatrical performances in developed countries. Moreover, there are enough modern-day catalysts in the broader context to magnify potential sensitivities, such as the significant global economic downturns that occurred in 1973–75, 1980–81, 1990–91, and 2008–10 (with continuing effects right up to the time of writing), and the commodity price shocks of 1971–73 and 2005–08. Ingram *et al.* cite the Food and Agriculture Organization of the United Nations (FAO): a "rapid rise in food prices in 2007–8 [...] increased the number of hungry people to 923 million" (2010: 554). Globally speaking, the 2008 credit crunch exacerbated the problem by constraining incomes available for food, taking the number of hungry people to over 1 billion world-wide.

Food insecurity in performance

The year 1973, the first of the economic downturn triggered by the oil crisis, was an appropriate moment in which to retell the story of Shakespeare the landowner's stance with respect to enclosures in 1614/15, as in the modern example that follows. Edward Bond's play *Bingo* was first performed in Northcott, Exeter on 14 November 1973 and in the Royal Court, London in 1974 (Bond, 1987), and revived at the Young Vic in February 2012. Enclosures (in which the rich and powerful assumed ownership of and consolidated small landholdings in the name of productivity) had a number of unfortunate effects. As described by Greenblatt they "tended to make grain prices rise, overturn customary rights, reduce employment, take away alms for the poor, and create social unrest" (2004: 368–9). The period 1614/15 marked the enclosures battle in which Shakespeare had come to a financial arrangement with potential enclosers of Stratford land that would leave him no worse off, as an owner of certain tithes, whatever happened. Thus protected, he did not join forces with the Stratford Corporation to protect others more vulnerable to its effects (Greenblatt, 2004: 377).

A directly ecocritical reference to the ecological themes underpinning food security and identifiable in *King Lear* appeared in the 1994 Western Literature Association Conference entitled "Defining Ecocritical Theory and Practice" (ASLE, 1994). One of sixteen ecocriticism position papers happened to talk about a performance of *King Lear*: "Olivier's Lear", recently seen "again" (Black, 1994). For its author, the ecopolitical problem he noticed in the recording of the 1983 television performance was, I believe, a catalyst for his 1994 paper. The recording seems to have resonated deeply. He describes it as a "transgression" that "the commodified landscape is sliced up and parceled out to the highest rhetorical bidder". He thus connects the play to a modern-day ecocritical discourse of (natural and human) exploitation and oppression, within which food insecurity is embedded. The conference of the Western Literature Association at which this and fifteen other position papers were presented came not long after the early 1990s economic downturn (thus a reminder of frugality) and the all-important 1992 Rio Earth Summit, which succeeded in putting climate change on the map.[6] The year 1994 was also when Caryl Churchill's climate change play *The Skriker*, which strikingly connects environmental degradation to cannibalism, first came to the stage.[7]

Another production putting food and power centre stage arrived in 2012: a modern post-script to *King Lear* in the form of a new play by David Watson. This play explored what "sustaining that 'gored state' might mean" in an epilogue to the play. In this play, the traitor Edmund is confined to an "isolated prison". An envoy from the crown – named Abina – arrives to oversee the trial and is refused entry until his credentials can be checked (Drew, 2012). As this requires a messenger to ride back to the city, the suspicion is that his mission is being subverted by the prison guards. Most significantly, in this context, the Warden also asks whether, because they are starving, they can eat Abina's horse, the agreement being that it will be replaced by a new one from the city. In this reading – which can be seen as a response to the ecological thread of meaning observed by Black – the "gor'd state" seems to imply social collapse and dearth.

Overall, the above evidence suggests that dearth-awareness has not become less relevant on stage notwithstanding major cultural shifts such as modern approaches to food procurement and preparation. Food continues to be a politically sensitive issue, identifiable in conventional theatre spaces.

Coriolanus

William Shakespeare's play *Coriolanus* stands out in the canon as clearly connecting politics to food, thus it can be seen as a potentially interesting litmus test of twenty-first century dearth awareness, described above. The key scene I identified in this play as an informative focal point for modern attitudes to food security is Act One, Scene One. The riot in the opening scene is peopled by "mutinous" citizens armed with "staves, clubs and other weapons". These "plebians" are protesting against hunger, and its inequitable distribution between the well-fed patricians and the rest.

> If they would yield us but the superfluity while it were wholesome, we might guess they relieved us humanely; but they think we are too dear: the leanness that afflicts us, the object of our misery, is as an inventory to particularise their abundance; our sufferance is a gain to them.
>
> (1976: I.i.16–21)

In the context of social inequality leading to food-related power imbalances, the arguments metaphorically presented to the Citizens by Coriolanus' friend Menenius Agrippa readily connect to the idea that human beings are performed by "d'Earth", to use the terminology of this chapter.

He assigns a physiological dimension to food power-politics, through the famous fable of the dominant stomach and the inferior extremities. This extended metaphor is important in being closely connected to three key themes running through the play: power imbalances in the context of food; bodily distemper and disease; and imbalances in the body politic.[8] Menenius' playful description of the patrician view of an appropriate balance in the domain of food power – in which the senators of Rome are benign distributors of food according to need – comes up repeatedly in the context of Coriolanus' tirades, as an idea he strenuously disagrees with. Corn handed out for free "nourished disobedience" (III.i.117); it was not deserved by those who had not fought for the city when needed (III.i.125). The scorn in which Coriolanus holds the lower orders is reinforced by such comments. However, they also reflect tensions in the body politic, which is thrown out of balance by Coriolanus' world view and uncontrolled behaviour. Thus, for the tribunes he is (in yet another ecological metaphor) a "disease that must be cut away" (III.i.292). Elsewhere, it is made clear that he comes of a choleric stock – his mother describes anger as her "meat", and like the cannibal, devouring herself "[she] starve[s] with feeding". Cannibalism – yet another overturning of the natural order of things – appears repeatedly in the play's imagery. The shocking moment when Volumnia kneels to her "corrected son" is yet another. Coriolanus' own description of this moment connects it to the hunger driving the opening scene:

> Then let the pebbles on the hungry beach
> Fillip the stars. Then let the mutinous winds
> Strike the proud cedars 'gainst the fiery sun.
>
> (V.iii.67–9)

The fact that the opening scene in *Coriolanus* is so core to the play raises key questions about its modern performance and reception. What modern productions do with this scene (whether it is emphasised or excised for instance) is likely to say something about the cultural positioning of those involved, in respect of dearth awareness, because productions that de-emphasise it are removing a deeply embedded part of the overall structure. After all, a key point about *Coriolanus* as a dearth play is that food security – defined as the opposite of dearth – is presented as depending upon the social order. The achievement of balance between the extremes of dearth and plenty also depends on an ordered relationship with nature. This also depends, in turn, upon a balance in the body politic – the opposite of which is depicted in *Coriolanus*. In this play, bad governance or stewardship, which leads to the opposite of stability, is at the root of the dearth suffered by the plebeians. The play thus thematises broken-down social and natural relationships and their consequences. In modern parlance, dearth in performance is ultimately about system (and ecosystem) collapse.

In the following section, I assess this by focusing on the relatively well documented production history of *Coriolanus*, studied through evidence discovered in performance archives and critical reviews.

The 1745 production of *Coriolanus* by Thompson dispensed with the first three acts in the name of "neoclassical unity of action" (Ormsby, 2014: 16), thus dismissing food politics to the margin.[9] In contrast, in Brecht's 1959 post-war adaptation of the play, the opening scene dwells more on food than on the lead protagonist Caius Martius, with the addition of a dialogue with The Man with the Child ready to flee the city for "water, fresh air and a grave", as well as lines that reinforce the importance of food prices and food power-politics. This weaves in contemporary socialist politics at the same time (Shakespeare and Brecht, 2014):

> First Citizen: Are you prepared to stand fast until the senate agrees it's us citizens who decide the price of bread?
> Citizens: Yes, yes.
> First Citizen: And the price of olives?
> Citizens: Yes.

Brecht's 1953 analysis of the first scene of the play makes it clear that, for him, this scene is absolutely indispensable to the play, and that the first scene is in no way a superficial excuse for the battles that follow:

> I don't think you realise how hard it is for the oppressed to become united. [...] Later on this unity of the plebeians will be broken up, so it is best not to take it for granted at the start but to show it as having come about.
>
> (Willett, 1957, 1963, 1964: 252)

The context in which Brecht's adaptation of *Coriolanus* developed – post-war East Germany where people spent long hours queuing for food – seems to be topical to Brecht's ideas on the dynamic driving riot.

Direct evidence is unlikely to be available in respect of whether the *Coriolanus* in production at the National Theatre (NT) in 1984–85 was explicitly connected by anyone involved to the modern-day famine (documented by Michael Buerk, as discussed above) that happened to be evolving at the same time. Timing however suggests that these events had the potential to connect. The Buerk interview was broadcast on 23 October 1984. *Coriolanus* rehearsals had begun three weeks beforehand (Bedford, 1992: 193), and opening night was 15 December 1984. For Robert Ormsby (2014: 140–56), the important politics lay in the volatile mix of the 1984–85 miners' strike and Arts Council funding cuts, suggesting that local, rather than global, issues may have had a dominating influence on the reception of this production. On the other hand, Kristina Bedford's description of the "haphazard" system of "costuming the mob" suggests that even if hunger-awareness was not consistently present in the minds of the production team, it does seem to have been on her mind, considering the reaction she describes to this piece of the production design. Her rehearsal notes on Menenius' "fable of the belly" speech show how important it was to the Company to "crack" this speech and this scene. Thus its importance to the whole was recognised. Involving members of the audience, putting them on stage as citizens, was likely to connect them to the hunger problems of the Citizens in the text. However, for Bedford, this seemed to backfire in the London performances:

> "Hunger" [...] issues solely from the mouths, not the souls and bodies of the rebellious plebeians. The attire of several citizens plants them firmly in the ranks of the middle class; [...] and dissipates the tension of acting "in hunger for bread, not in/Thirst for revenge".
>
> (Bedford, 1992: 31)

Greg Hicks (who played Tullus Aufidius) was interviewed by Bedford and, in a similar vein, thought that "[...] the director [hadn't] made an opinion about what kind of citizens they are" (ibid.: 149–50). This production could thus be described as out of tune with the play's many ecosystems, both natural and metaphorical.

As the discussion of Black's response to *King Lear*, above, suggests, the Royal Shakespeare Company's (RSC) 1994 *Coriolanus* was well-positioned in terms of its timing to reflect difficult economic conditions in the years immediately preceding it. By all accounts, this *Coriolanus* was a memorable production that put the issue of food security front and centre. So striking was the opening – in which corn "[poured] like gold from the flies when the play [opened] and [was] carried off in wooden bowls after the protagonist's banishment" (Nightingale, 1994) – that an employee of the Stratford-upon-Avon Shakespeare Bookshop responded (in February 2015), to my question about whether the latest edition of the play was in stock, by spontaneously describing this as a memorable moment in the most outstanding production he had seen (starring Toby Stephens) no less than two decades ago. Thacker's second innovation – to stage the play in France in the years leading up to the French Revolution, in which food insecurity brought out by crop failures in the summer of 1788 was one of the catalysts for social unrest (Neumann and Detwiller, 1990), could hardly be more in tune with the idea that human society is (and has historically also been) "performed by" the ecosystems driving food systems. Nevertheless, this cross-connection between starvation and politics was not appreciated by several newspaper critics (Coveney, Spencer, Hagerty, and Peter, 1994) who variously described this transposition as "fatuous", "irritating", "incongruous", and "quite the wrong setting". All did not agree; for Irving Wardle (1994) the point was:

Famine, warfare, plenty: these are the mainsprings of human action, and they dominate the stage from the opening sight of doors slamming shut on the grain store, to the city gates closing on the blood-soaked hero.

As the above suggests, dearth-awareness (or the lack thereof) seems to show itself in different ways in the production history of this play. Sometimes, even the direct constraints of economic downturns in western countries fail to remind of other, worse privations, such as starvation. Michael Dobson describes the mob scenes in David Farr's 2002/03 RSC production (about three years on from the global stock market crash of 1999/2000) as follows:

> [In] today's economic climate, when two is a retinue, and three's a crowd, this play's inclusion of an angry mob as a main character can make it extremely difficult to stage with the sort of naturalistic violence for which its street scenes call.
>
> (Dobson, 2004: 285)

Questions left hanging in the air by this comment are whether this representation of the mob weakened the position of the plebeians, thus reinforcing the imbalance of power generally encountered by the poor in the context of food insecurity; and whether this (human) resource cut happened to be harsher on the plebeians than the patricians within the production.

A few years on, there were two productions of *Coriolanus* in 2007. Both took place early in the year, a few months before 15 September 2007, which was the day savers queued round the block to try and get their money out of Northern Rock, thus dramatically marking the start of the credit crunch (Rayner, 2008). These productions both took place at a time when irrational exuberance was still in full swing, increasing the likelihood of reduced dearth (thus d'Earth) awareness. Gregory Doran's March 2007 production came just before the three-and-a-half year, £113 million refurbishment of the Royal Shakespeare Theatre (Levy, 2010), and as suggested above, also happened to coincide with peak of the financial bubble at work in markets. It "cluttered the stage with a big old-fashioned set" and, recalling the 1984 production of *Coriolanus*, featured "woefully clean and polite plebeians [...] dwarfed by the set and unable to make up in energy of menace what they lack in numbers". Michael Dobson's brief description ironically suggests an emasculated mob in the presence of plentiful production resources. In contrast, the Ninagawa Company (Barbican, 25–29 April) made good use of what must (also) have been a good production budget for design and set and actors, but in a different spirit. The magnification of the mob was achieved by a clever visual trick without physically adding to the numbers involved:

> As the house lights faded this immense, precipitous structure [resem-
> bling an oriental ziggurat] was suddenly populated by an entire
> brown-clad plebeian riot, twenty strong and doubled and redoubled
> again by the side mirrors, converging down the centre of the stairs,
> and all shouting at [enormous] volume.
>
> (Dobson, 2007: 345)

Even in the context of an impressive set, a hint of frugality that is absolutely consistent with the play runs through Dobson's description.

Moving on past the bubble to its aftermath, the 2012 World Shakespeare Festival was well-timed to contain food security-related reactions to
the 2007–10 credit-crunch and the commodity price-shock that immediately preceded it. Food indeed was centre-stage in the Chiten Theatre
Company's World Shakespeare Festival production in Japanese at Shakespeare's Globe. In this production, a cast of five, taking up different roles,
performed *Coriolanus* as a chorus. With such a small cast this comes across
as a frugal (post-crunch) production, and the same can be said of the
props budget. As described by Adele Lee (2013: 49), reviewing it in *A Year
of Shakespeare*:

> The use of baguettes as props was [a] notable feature of this produc-
> tion. All cast members brandished the baguettes as weapons while
> their constant consumption of the bread reflected not just greed, but
> the destruction and emasculation of Coriolanus (the baguette, after
> all, can be a phallic symbol).

Watching a film of this production on Globe TV, I found that the
baguettes had interesting effects. Someone speaking powerfully and brandishing bread as a sword could look strong and vulnerable at the same
time (a good description of Coriolanus); conversely a hungry person
armed with a baguette (and brandishing it rather than eating it) reminds
that hungry people can bring down governments. Although significant
parts of the play were excised as a consequence of Chiten's choric
approach, food insecurity was prominent, and consistently embedded, in
this production.

Later in the year the National Theatre Wales and the RSC's World
Shakespeare Festival Production in the Vale of Glamorgan "welded" the
work of two hunger-sensitised playwrights with *Coriolan/us*. This production also did a tremendous job of magnifying the mob by (in effect) recyc-
ling the audience:

> As the massive hangar sliding-door slid open and the 300-strong sell-
> out crowd who'd been huddling outside, buffeted by a Welsh wind
> driving straight down the open valley, surged forward, we met our-
> selves coming towards us. We were being filmed. We were being

projected, onto the big screen on the far wall and two smaller screens closer to us.

(Chillington Rutter, 2013: 390)

Fusing the deprived mob and the audience seems all too appropriate in a place disproportionately hit by the credit crunch because of the structure of the job market and lower median levels of pay than elsewhere in the UK (Fitzpatrick *et al.*, 2013: 19).

In the physical Meadow Meanders created by Baz Kershaw, participants who enter the maze are cryptically informed that the maze contains a puzzle in the form of an earthly system, invisible from the ground, but potentially visible to the mind's eye of those who walk through it (2015: 127). In a similar vein, the production history of Act One, Scene One of *Coriolanus* is often about a collision of aesthetics and economics, but, meandering through (and reading between the lines of) production archives, I found a clear pattern. Some productions performed dearth responsively, sensitively, and collaboratively. In such productions, dearth-awareness can be described as "ecologically systemic". When the reverse seems to be the case, this can be seen as a deeply ironical flouting of the natural order of things, in the context of *Coriolanus* in particular. There is a small note of hope in this chapter. This lies in the fragments of dearth-awareness discerned in some of the productions discussed above: perhaps human beings sometimes have sufficient insight to stage dearth (or d'Earth) as if human life depends on it.

Notes

1 This chapter draws on an early draft of material in chapter 4 of my Warwick University PhD (2017), "An Ecotheatrical Perspective on Dearth in Performance".
2 The collection and interpretation of price data during dearth and famine in early modern England has a long and complex historiography, which is summarised in Walter and Schofield (1989) and Mukherjee, A. (2015).
3 This chapter does not provide an exhaustive list of dearth plays, and there is significant scope for further research in this area.
4 Falstaff has most frequently been interpreted in relation to the "grotesque" and the "festive", without engaging fully with the context of dearth in which he appears. Exceptions are: Whitney (1994); Mukherjee, A. (2015: 45–9, 189–91). Critical debates on Falstaff in relation to festivity and order in *Henry IV* are usefully summarised in Ruiter (2003: 1–39).
5 See, for example: Smith, 2013; Hartocollis, 2015; Trussell Trust, 2017; Miller, 2017; United Nations, Water and Climate Change. On nutritional debates, see, for example: Lustig, 2012; Hudson and Donovan, 2014: ch. 9.
6 Rio Earth Summit, UN Conference on Environment and Development (1992). "Resulting document" included the "United Nations Framework Convention on Climate Change" (UNFCCC). See www.un.org/geninfo/bp/enviro.html.
7 On the environment in general, see, for example, Churchill, 1994: 48: "It was always possible to think whatever your problem there's always nature. [...] But it's not available any more." In the banquet scene (35), a "hag" looks desperately for her dismembered body – "head", "heart", "arm", "leg", "finger" – on the banquet table.

8 Of the many literary and historical discussions of this infamous trope, the following are especially pertinent to the politics of food: George, 2000; Wilson, 1993; Patterson, 1991; Sharp, 2007, Hindle, 2008. My analysis focuses on *Coriolanus* as a "dearth play", replayed in contemporary contexts of food insecurity, when performances appropriated, in differing degrees, the rhetorical and political nuances of Menenius' fable of the belly.

9 The date of this production coincided with the time (mid-eighteenth century onwards) when famine and dearth started to become less frequent occurrences in the history of England, although food shortage remains a significant problem in British colonies, such as India (Hoskins, 1964; Walter, 1989, and Chapter 1 of this book; Mukherjee, A., 2015).

Bibliography

Primary sources

Manuscript

Bodleian Library, Oxford

Mundy, Peter. *Itinerarium Mundii.* MS. Rawlinson A.315.

National Archives, Kew

State Papers Domestic, Elizabeth I. SP 12/188/47.
State Papers Domestic, James I. SP 14/138/35.

Oriental and India Office Collections, British Library, London

Bengal Proceedings, General Ledgers and Journals, P/175/83 to P/176/29.
Bengal Revenue Consultations, P/49/47 (30 August 1774); P/49/48 (30 November 1774); P/49/52 (7 April 1775); P/51/15 (28 January 1787); P/51/17 (4 March 1788); P/51/19 (17, 21 April 1788); P/51/40 (15 July 1789); P/52/27 (23 November 1791); P/52/50 (19 October 1792).
Home Miscellaneous. IOR/H/465.
Letters Received, E/4/24, letter of 29 December 1759.
MSS.Eur.E.12, F.95, G.11, D.74.

Persian MSS, British Library, London

Khān, Sādiq. *Tawārīkh-i-Shāhjahāni.* MSS. Or.174, Or.1671 (ff. 2–96).
Lāhawrī, ʿAbd Al-Ḥamīd. *Pādshāh nāma.* MS. Add.6556.
Qazwīnī, Md. Amīn. *Pādshāh nāma.* MSS. Add.20734, Or.173.

Uttar Pradesh Regional Archives, Allahabad

"Abstract of Orders Issued on the Occurrence of Famine in the Bijnor District 1877–78". COR (Rohilkhand). Dept. XII. File Nos. 82–2/90, Serial Nos. 1 to 8, Box No. 87.

Carnegy, P. Officiating Commissioner, Faizabad, 20 August 1870. COF (Faizabad). File on "Poor Houses", Serial. No. 3, Bundle No. 68.

"Circular Asking for Information on Matters Connected with the Relief and Prevention of Famine". From C. A. Elliott, Secretary to the Famine Commission. 22 June 1878, Simla. COF (Faizabad). Serial No. 17, Box No. 24.

Collector Badaun. "Note on the Distress Prevailing in the Badaun District from 1st November 1877 to 31st March 1878, Its Effect and the Measures Taken to Relieve the Sufferers". 21 May 1878. COR (Rohilkhand). Department XII. File Nos. 82–2/90, Serial Nos. 1–8, Box No 87.

Collector Jalaun to Commissioner Allahabad. Div. 13 February 1896. "Famine Relief Works & Poor Houses 1896–97". COA (Allahabad). File No. 4, Serial. No. 1, Bundle No. 262, Box No. 359.

Letter from Collector Fatehpur to Commissioner Allahabad. 13 January 1906. COA (Allahabad). "Dept. of Scarcity". File No. 97, Serial. No. 15, Bundle No. 164, Box No. 228.

Letters from Commissioner Allahabad. 26 January 1906, and 4 February 1906. COA (Allahabad). "Dept. of Scarcity". File No. 97, Serial. No. 15, Bundle No. 164, Box No. 228.

"Note on the Scarcity in Rohilkhand Division, 1877–78". COR (Rohilkhand). File No. 90, Serial No. 7, Box No. 87.

"Poor House Trust in the District of Bahraich during the Year 1893–4". COF (Faizabad). Serial. No. 26, Box No. 55.

"Translation of a Letter from Raja Jagat Singh of Jajpur, 28th May 1878". COR (Rohilkhand). Department XII. File Nos. 82–2/90, Serial Nos. 1–8, Box No. 87.

"Translation of a Letter from Roy Kishen Kumar of Moradabad" (n.d. 1878). COR (Rohilkhand). Department XII. File Nos. 82–2/90, Serial Nos. 1–8, Box No. 87.

"Translation of the Letter from Syed Imdad Ali, Deputy Collector of Moradabad, 2nd June 1878". COR (Rohilkhand). Department XII. File Nos. 82–2/90, Serial Nos. 1–8, Box No. 87.

"Translation of a Petition from Munshi Parmanand, Tehsildar of Aonla, 28 May, 1878". COR (Rohilkhand). Department XII. File Nos. 82–2/90, Serial Nos. 1–8, Box No. 87.

"Translation of the Poor House Annual Report of Nawabgunj, Bara Banki for 1885–86" by Syed Tajmmul Hossain Khan, Assistant Commissioner in charge of the Poorhouse, 20 November 1886. COF (Faizabad). Sl. No. 12, Box No. 37.

West Bengal State Archives, Calcutta

Proceedings of the Board of Customs (6 August–29 December 1783; 7 November 1783).

Proceedings of the Board of Revenue (Grain), vol. 1 (1794).

Proceedings of the Board of Revenue (Miscellaneous), vols 20–9 (1787); 30–57(1788).

Proceedings of the Controlling Committee of Commerce, vol. 1 (1771).

Proceedings of the Controlling Committee of Revenue (Murshidabad), vols 5–6 (1771).

Proceedings of the Provincial Council of Revenue (Murshidabad), vol. 1 (1774).

Print

Asiatick Researches; or, Transactions of the Society Instituted in Bengal for Enquiring into the History and Antiquities, the Arts, Sciences, and Literature of Asia (1816). Vol. XII. Calcutta: Calcutta Gazette Office.

Bābur (1995). *Bābur-nāma.* Ed. E. Mano, Kyoto: Shokado.

Bābur (1996). *Bāburnāma: Memoirs of Babur, Prince and Emperor.* Ed. and trans. W. M. Thackston, Oxford: Oxford University Press.

Baird-Smith, R. (1861). *Report on the Famine of 1860–1.* 2 Parts. Calcutta: Home Department.

Bandyopadhyay, Bibhutibhushan (2014). *Ashani Sanket.* 7th reprint. Kolkata: Mitra and Ghosh.

Bandyopadhyay, Manik (2003). *Manik Bandyopadhyay: Selected Stories.* Ed. Malini Bhattacharya. Kolkata: Thema.

Bedi, Freda (1944). *Bengal Lamenting.* Lahore: Lion Press.

Bell, A. (1930). *Corduroy.* London: Cobden-Sanderson.

Bernier, François (1934, 1972). *Travels in the Mogul Empire, A.D. 1656–1668.* Ed. Archibald Constable. New Delhi.

Bhattacharya, Bijon (2000). *Nabanna.* 8th edition. Kolkata: Proma.

Bhattacharya, Chittoprasad (1943). *Hungry Bengal: A Tour through Midnapur District, by Chittaprosad.* Bombay: New Age.

Blair, Charles (1874). *Indian Famines: Their Historical, Financial and Other Aspects.* Edinburgh and London: William Blackwood and Sons.

Bond, E. (1987). *Bond Plays 3: Bingo; The Fool; The Woman; Stone.* London: Methuen.

Bourne, G. H. (1943). *Starvation in Europe.* London: Allen and Unwin.

Calcutta Gazette (1943). Supplements: 13 (1 April), 14 (8 April), 15 (15 April), 16 (22 April), 17 (29 April), 27 (8 July), 34 (26 August), 36 (16 September).

Campbell, George (1868). *Extracts from the Records in the India Office Relating to Famines in India, 1769–1788.* Calcutta: East Bengal Secretariat Press. British Library, India Office Records V/27/830/14.

Carew, Richard (1602). *Survey of Cornwall.* London: John Jaggard.

Chaterjee, Santosh Kumar (1944). *The Starving Millions.* Calcutta: Asoka Library.

Chattopadhyay, Bankim Chandra (1872). *Anukaran* [Imitation]. In *Bankim Rachanavali.* Ed. Jogesh Chandra Bagal. Calcutta: Sahitya Samsad, 1969. Vol. 2: 198–207.

Churchill, Caryl (1994). *The Skriker.* London: Nick Hern Books.

Clive, Robert (1764). *An Address to the Proprietors of the East India Stock.* London. British Library. OIOC, *Tracts*, vol. 113.

Colebrook, Henry Thomas (1794, rev. 1804). *Remarks on the Husbandry and Internal Commerce of Bengal.* Calcutta.

Corbett, Richard (1807). *The Poems of Richard Corbett.* Ed. Octavius Gilchrist. London.

Danvers, F. C. (1877). *A Century of Famine.* British Library, India Office Records, L/E/5/69.

Donaldson, F. (1941). *Approach to Farming.* London: Faber and Faber.

Donaldson, F. (1945). *Four Years Harvest.* London: Faber and Faber.

Donaldson, F. (1955). *Milk without Tears.* London: Faber and Faber.

Donaldson, F. (1967). *Evelyn Waugh: Portrait of a Country Neighbour.* London: Weidenfeld & Nicolson.

Donaldson, F. (1974). *Edward VIII.* London: Weidenfeld and Nicolson.

Donaldson, F. (1982). *P. G. Wodehouse: A Biography.* London: Weidenfeld & Nicolson.

Donaldson, F. (1992). *A Twentieth Century Life.* London: Weidenfeld & Nicolson.

Donaldson, J. G. S., F. Donaldson, and D. Barber (1969). *Farming in Britain Today.* London: Allen Lane.

Drummond, Jack (1946). *Problems of Malnutrition and Starvation during the War.* Nottingham: Clough and Son.

Drummond, Jack (1948). *Malnutrition and Starvation in Western Netherlands, September 1944–July 1945.* The Hague: General State Printing Office.

East India Gazetteer (1828). London; Reprint, Delhi: D. K. Publishers, 1993.

Eastward Ho! The First English Adventurers to the Orient. Richard Chancellor – Anthony Jenkinson – James Lancaster – William Adams – Sir Thomas Roe, etc. (1931). Ed. Foster Rhea Dulles. London: John Lane.

Elliot, Henry Miers (1875). *Shah Jahan.* Lahore: Hafiz Press.

Elliot, Henry Miers and John Dowson (1877). *The History of India as Told by Its Own Historians.* London: Trübner and Co.

Englands Parnassus (1600). Compiled by Robert Allott. London: N. L[ing]., C. B[urby]., and T. H[ayes].

Famine Inquiry Commission, India (1945a). *Report on Bengal.* New Delhi: Government of India.

Famine Inquiry Commission, India (1945b). *Final Report.* Madras: Government of India.

Famine Relief Committee (1942). *Hunger in Europe: A Statement of the Case for Controlled Food Relief in German-Occupied Countries.* London: Famine Relief Committee.

Famine Relief Committee (1943). *A Year's Work: An Account of Efforts to Obtain Permission for Controlled and Limited Food Relief In German-Occupied Countries.* London: Famine Relief Committee.

Fazl, Abul (1907–39). *The Akbar Nāmā of Abu-l-Fazl.* Trans. H. Beveridge. Vols 1–3. Calcutta: Bibliotheca Indica.

Fazl, Abul (2015–19). *Akbarnāma. The History of Akbar.* Vols 1–5. Murty Classical Library of India. Cambridge, MA: Harvard University Press.

Fiennes, Celia (1984). *The Illustrated Journeys of Celia Fiennes, c.1682–c.1712.* Ed. Christopher Morris. London: MacDonald.

Firbank, T. (1940). *I Bought a Mountain.* London: Harrap.

Foster, W. (1906–27). *The English Factories in India, 1618–1669.* Oxford: Clarendon Press.

Gangulee, Nagendranath (1940). *Bibliography of Nutrition in India.* Oxford: Oxford University Press.

Geddes, J. C. (1874). *Extracts from Official Papers Containing Instructions for Dealing with Famine. Compiled under Orders of the Government of Bengal.* Calcutta: East Bengal Secretariat Press.

Ghosh, Tushar Kanti (1944). *The Bengal Tragedy.* Lahore: Hero Publications.

Girdlestone, C. E. R. (1868). *Report on Past Famines in the North-Western Provinces.* Allahabad: Government Press, North-Western Provinces.

Gunston, J. (1941). *To be a Farmer.* London: Methuen.

Gunston, J. (1943). *Farming Month by Month.* London: Methuen.

Gunston, J. (1945). *Farm Friends and Foes.* London: Methuen.

Gunston, J. (1947). *Farming Today and Tomorrow.* London: Methuen.

Gunston, J. (1948). *How to Run a Small Farm.* London: Methuen.

Gunston, J. (1950). *Profitable Smallholdings.* London: John Lehmann.

Hamilton, Walter (1828). *The East India Gazetteer.* Vol. I. London: Allen.

Hansard. *Commons.* Vols 393 (1943) and 444 (1947).

Harrison, William (1587, 1968). *The Description of England.* Ed. George Edelen. Ithaca: Folger and Cornell University Press.

Henderson, G. (1944). *The Farming Ladder.* London: Faber and Faber.

Henderson, G. (1950). *Farmer's Progress: A Guide to Faming.* London: Faber and Faber.

Henderson, G. (1960). *The Farming Manual: A Guide to Farm Work.* London: Faber and Faber.

Henvey, Frederick (1871). *A Narrative of the Drought and Famine which Prevailed in the North-West Provinces during the Years 1868, 1869 and Beginning of 1870.* Allahabad: Government Press, North-Western Provinces.

Hindustan Times, 7 November 1943 edition.

Holwell, J. Z. (1764). *India Tracts.* London: Printed for T. Beckett and P. A. de Hondt, near Surry-street, in the Strand.

Homewood, R. (1947). *Three Farms.* London: Latimer House.

Hume, D. (1757). "Of the Standard of Taste". *Four Dissertations.* London: Millar.

Hunter, W. W. (1869). *Famine Aspects of Bengal Districts.* Calcutta: Ballantyne and Company.

Jahāngīr (1909–14). *Tuzūk-i Jahāngīri.* Trans. Alexander Rogers. Ed. Henry Beveridge. 2 vols. London: Royal Asiatic Society.

Jahāngīr (2006). *Tuzūk-i Jahāngīri.* Ed. Syed Ahmad Khan. Aligarh: Aligarh Muslim University.

James VI and I (1994). *King James VI and I: Political Writings.* Ed. J. P. Somerville. Cambridge: Cambridge University Press.

James, Richard (1845). *Iter Lancastrense; A Poem, Written* AD *1636.* Ed. Thomas Corser. Cheltenham: Cheltenham Society.

Janah, Sunil (2013). *Photographing India.* Oxford: Oxford University Press.

Jugāntar (6 November 1943). Vol. 7; Issue 47. British Library, EAP262/1/2/1614, https://eap.bl.uk/archive-file/EAP262-1-2-1614.

Jugāntar (7 November 1943). Vol. 7; Issue 48. British Library, EAP262/1/2/1615, https://eap.bl.uk/archive-file/EAP262-1-2-1615.

Jugāntar (8 November 1943). Vol. 7; Issue 49. British Library, EAP262/1/2/1616, https://eap.bl.uk/archive-file/EAP262-1-2-1616.

Jugāntar (11 November 1943). Vol. 7; Issue 52. British Library, EAP262/1/2/1619, https://eap.bl.uk/archive-file/EAP262-1-2-1619.

Jugāntar (4 December 1943). Vol. 7; Issue 75. British Library, EAP262/1/2/1622, https://eap.bl.uk/archive-file/EAP262-1-2-1622.

Lāhawrī, ʿAbd Al-Ḥamīd (1867–68). *Bādshāh Nāmah.* Ed. ʿAbd Al-Raḥīm, Kabīr Al-Dīn Aḥmad, and W. Nassau Lees. Calcutta: Asiatic Society of Bengal, Bibliotheca Indica.

Lewes, G. H. (1859). *The Physiology of Common Life.* Edinburgh: Blackwood.

Long, Rev. J. C. (1868). *Selections from Unpublished Records of Government for the Years 1748 to 1767 Inclusive, Relating Mainly to the Social Condition of Bengal.* Calcutta: Calcutta, Office of the Superintendent of Government Printing.

Malthus, T. R. (1836). *Principles of Political Economy Considered with a View to Their Practical Application.* Second edn. London: Pickering.

Malthus, T. R. (2007). *An Essay on the Principle of Population.* Dover: Mineola.

Martineau, H. (1833a). *Cinnamon and Pearls,* London: Fox.

Martineau, H. (1833b). *French Wines and Politics.*London: Fox.

Martineau, H. (2004). *Sowers Not Reapers.* In *Illustrations of Political Economy.* Ed. D. A. Logan. Toronto: Broadview, pp. 295–381.

Martineau, H. (2007). *Autobiography.* Ed. L. H. Peterson. Toronto: Broadview.

Methwold, W. (1926). *A Relation of Golconda.* In Samuel Purchas, *Purchas, His Pilgrimage.* London: n.p.

Mitra, Premendra (1989). "Phyan". In *Kabitā Samagra.* Kolkata: Granthalay.

Monserrate, Antonio (1922). *The Commentary of Father Monserrate, S. J., on His Journey to the Court of Akbar.* London: Milford.

Mundy, Peter (1907–36). *The Travels of Peter Mundy, in Europe and Asia, 1608–1667.* Vols 1–5. Ed. Richard Carnac Temple and Lavinia Mary Anstey. London: Hakluyt Society.

Nautical Magazine (1832). Issue 1. London.

Platt, Hugh (1596). *Sundry New and Artificiall Remedies against Famine. Written by H. P. Esq. upon the Occasion of This Present Dearth.* London: Peter Short.

Platt, Hugh (1607). *Certaine Philosophical Preparations of Foode and Beverage for Seamen, in Their Long Voyages: With Some Necessary, Approoued, and Hermeticall Medicines and Antidotes, Fit to Be Had in Readinesse at Sea, for Preuention or Cure of Diuers Diseases.* London: H. Lownes.

Prabāsi (1350/1943). *Jyaistha*/May–June: 153.

Price, J. C. (1876). *Notes on the History of Midnapur: As Contained in the Records of the Collectors Office.* Calcutta.

Qadrat-i-Ilāhi (2005). "Amartya Sen's Famine Philosophy". *The Daily Star.* 12 May.

Qahat Sāli ke Zābate (1897). *Rules for Famine Years.* Bombay: The Caledonian Steam Printing Company.

Ray, Satyajit, dir. (1973). *Ashani Sanket* [Distant Thunder]. Film.

Rennell, James (1793). *Memoir of a Map of Hindoostan.* London: George Nicol and W. Richardson.

Report of the Committee on Prison Discipline (8 January 1838). Calcutta: Baptist Mission Press.

Report of the Indian Famine Commission, Part I, Famine Relief (1880). London: Eyre and Spottiswoode.

Report of the Indian Famine Commission, Part III, Famine Histories (1885). London: Eyre and Spottiswoode.

Report of the Indian Famine Commission (1898). Simla: Government Central Printing Office.

Reynolds, C. (1943a). *Glory Hill Farm: One Hundred Acres Farmed by an Amateur, the First Year 1940–1.* London: John Lane.

Reynolds, C. (1943b). *Glory Hill Farm: One Hundred Acres Farmed by an Amateur, the Second Year 1941–2.* London: John Lane.

Reynolds, C. (1944). *Glory Hill Farm, Third Year.* London: John Lane.

Reynolds, C. (1945). *Glory Hill Farm, Epilogue: One Hundred Acres Farmed by an Amateur, Fourth Year, 1943–4.* London: John Lane.

Reynolds, C. (1947). *Autobiography.* London: Bodley Head.

Roe, Thomas (1732). *Sir Thomas Roe's Journal of His Voyage to the East Indies and Observations There during His Residence at the Mogul's Court as Embassador from King James the First of England.* London.

Roxburgh, William (1832). *Flora Indica, or Descriptions of Indian Plants.* London.

Santhanam, K (1944). *The Cry of Distress.* New Delhi: The Hindustan Times.

Selections from the Records of Government, North Western Provinces, Part 36 (1862). Allahabad: Government Press, North-Western Provinces.

Selections from the Vernacular Newspapers Published in the North-Western Provinces & Oudh. British Library, IOR, L/R/5/74.

Sen, Ela (1944). *Darkening Days: Being a Narrative of Famine-Stricken Bengal, with Drawings from Life by Zainul Abedin.* Calcutta: Susil Gupta.

Shakespeare, William (1976). *Coriolanus.* Ed. Philip Brockbank. London: Bloomsbury, Arden.

Shakespeare, William (1983, 1984). *King Lear.* Granada Television Production (1983). DVD, Kultur Video (1984).

Shakespeare, W. and B. Brecht (2014). "Coriolanus". In *Berliner Ensemble Adaptions.* Ed. D. Barnett and J. Willett. Trans. R. Manheim. London: Bloomsbury.

Smith, F. and B. Wilcox (1940). *Living in the Country.* London: Adam and Charles Black.

Smith, F. and B. Wilcox (1942a). *Back to the Country: How to Make a Living on the Land.* London: Adam and Charles Black.

Smith, F. and B. Wilcox (1942b). *Family Farm.* London: Adam and Charles Black.

Smith, F. and B. Wilcox (1947). *The Family Farmer.* London: Adam and Charles Black.

Smith, F. and B. Wilcox (1948). *Farming Is Still a Gamble.* London: Adam and Charles Black.

Spaccini, Giovanni Battista (1911–19). *Cronaca Modenese, 1588–1636.* Ed. G. Bertoni, T. Wandonnini, and P. E. Vicini. Modena.

Strachey, J. (1862). "Note on the Measures Adopted for the Relief of the Poor in the District of Moradabad". 30 June 1861. *Selections from the Records of Government, North Western Provinces, Part 36.* Allahabad: Government Press, North-Western Provinces.

Street, A. G. (1932). *Farmer's Glory.* London: Faber and Faber.

Street, A. G. (1952). *Shameful Harvest.* London: Faber and Faber.

Street, A. G. (1954). *Feather-Bedding.* London: Faber and Faber.

Taylor, James (1840). *A Sketch of the Topography and Statistics of Dacca.* Calcutta: G. H. Huttmann, Military Orphan Press.

Taylor, John (1618). *The Pennyles Pilgrimage, or The Money-Lesse Perambulation.* London: Edward Allde.

Taylor, John (1621). *The Praise, Antiquity, and Commodity, of Beggery, Beggers, and Begging.* London: Edward Allde.

Taylor, John (1630). *All the Workes of John Taylor the Water Poet.* London: James Boler.

Taylor, John (1637). *The Carriers Cosmographie.* London: Anne Griffin.

Terry, Edward (1665). *A Relation of Sir Thomas Roe's Voyage into the East Indies.* London.

Times of India (23 November 1943). "Stricken Bengal III: How Famine Cases Are Relieved", p. 4.

Twining, Thomas (1893). *Travels in India.* London: J. R. Osgood, McIlvaine and Company.

van Twist, Johan (1937). "Johan van Twist's Description of India". Trans. W. H. Moreland. *Journal of Indian History* 16.1: 63–77.

Walker, Roy (1941). *Famine over Europe: The Problem of Controlled Food Relief.* London: Andrew Dakers.

Walpole, Horace (1910). *The Last Journals of Horace Walpole during the Reign of George III 1771–1783.* Ed. A. Francis Stewart. 2 vols. London: John Lane.

Weever, John (1599, 1911). *Epigrams in the Oldest Cut and Newest Fashion.* Ed. R. B. McKerrow. London: Sidgwick & Jackson.

Williamson, H. (1941). *The Story of a Norfolk Farm.* London: Faber and Faber.

Yazdī, Sharaf al-Dīn 'Alī (1957). *Zafarnāma.* Ed. Mohammad Abbasi. Tehran.

Yazdī, Sharaf al-Dīn 'Alī (1989). *Zafarnāma.* Ed. and trans. W. M. Thackston. *A Century of Princes: Sources on Timurid History and Art.* Cambridge, MA: Aga Khan Program for Islamic Architecture.

Online

Climatological Database for the World's Oceans, 1750–1850. http://webs.ucm.es/info/cliwoc/intro.htm.

Famine and Dearth in India and Britain, 1550–1800: Connected Cultural Histories of Food Security (2016). http://famineanddearth.exeter.ac.uk/index.html.

FAO (Food and Agriculture Organization) (1996). *World Food Summits.* www.fao.org/docrep/003/w3613e/w3613e00.htm.

FAO (Food and Agriculture Organization) (2002). *World Food Summits.* www.fao.org/worldfoodsummit/english/index.html.

FAO (Food and Agriculture Organization) (2009). *Declaration of the World Summit on Food Security.* www.fao.org/fileadmin/templates/wsfs/Summit/Docs/Final_Declaration/WSFS09_Declaration.pdf.

FAO (Food and Agriculture Organization) (2012). *The State of Food Insecurity in the World.* www.fao.org/docrep/016/i3027e/i3027e.pdf.

International Comprehensive Ocean Atmosphere Data Set. http://icoads.noaa.gov.

International Atmospheric Circulation Reconstructions over the Earth. ACRE Initiative. www.met-acre.org.

IPCC (Intergovernmental Panel on Climate Change) (2013). *Assessment Report 5.* www.ipcc.ch/report/wg1/mindex.shtml.

Old Weather. www.oldweather.org.

Rio Earth Summit. UN Conference on Environment and Development (1992). www.un.org/geninfo/bp/enviro.html.

Trussell Trust (25 April 2017). "UK Foodbank Use Continues to Rise". www.trusselltrust.org.

Twentieth Century Reanalysis. Earth System Research Laboratory. NOAA. www.esrl.noaa.gov/psd/data/20thC_Rean/#_blank.

United Nations. "Water and Climate Change". www.unwater.org/water-facts/climate-change.

Universal Declaration on the Eradication of Hunger and Malnutrition (1974). www.ohchr.org/en/professionalinterest/pages/eradicationofhungerandmalnutrition.aspx.

Weather Detective. www.weatherdetective.net.au/about.

Secondary sources

Agamben, Giorgio (1999). *Remnants of Auschwitz: The Witness and the Archive.* Trans. D. Heller-Roazen. New York: Zone Books.

Agarwal, C. M. (1983, 2006). *Natural Calamities and the Great Mughals*. New Delhi: Kanchan Publishers.

Ahuja, Ravi (2004). "State Formation and 'Famine POLICY' in Early Colonial South India". In *Land, Politics and Trade in South India*. Ed. Sanjay Subrahmanyam. New Delhi: Oxford University Press, pp. 147–84.

Alam, M., and Sanjay Subrahmanyam, eds (1998). *The Mughal State, 1526–1750*. New Delhi: Oxford University Press.

Alamgir, Moiuddin (1980). *Famine in South Asia. Political Economy and Mass Starvation*. Cambridge: Cambridge University Press.

Alfani, Guido, and Cormac Ó Gráda, eds (2017). *Famine in European History*. Cambridge: Cambridge University Press.

Allan, R. J., C. J. C. Reason, J. A. Lindesay, and T. J. Ansell (2003). "Protracted ENSO Episodes and Their Impacts in the Indian Ocean Region". *Deep Sea Research. Part II* 2: 2331–47.

Atwell, William (1990). "A Seventeenth Century General Crisis in East Asia". *Modern Asian Studies* 24.4: 661–82.

Atwell, William (2001). "Volcanism and Short-Term Climatic Change in East Asian and World History, c.1200–1699". *Journal of World History* 12: 29–98.

Appadurai, Arjun (1984). "How Moral is South Asia's Economy? A Review Article". *The Journal of Asian Studies* 43.3: 481–97.

Appleby, A. B. (1978) *Famine in Tudor and Stuart England*. Liverpool: Liverpool University Press.

Appleby, A. B. (1979). "Grain Prices and Subsistence Crises in England and France 1590–1740". *Journal of Economic History* 39: 865–87.

Archer J. E., R. M. Turley, and H. Thomas (2012). "The Autumn King: Remembering the Land in *King Lear*". *Shakespeare Quarterly* 63.4: 518–46.

Archer J. E., R. M. Turley, and H. Thomas (2014). *Food and the Literary Imagination*. Basingstoke: Palgrave.

Arnold, David (1988). *Famine: Social Crisis and Historical Change*. Oxford: Blackwell.

Arnold, David (1993). "Social Crisis and Epidemic Disease in the Famines of Nineteenth-century India". *Social History of Medicine* 6.3: 385–404.

Arnold, David (2008). "Vagrant India: Famine, Poverty and Welfare under Colonial Rule". In *Cast Out: Vagrancy and Homelessness in Global and Historical Perspective*. Ed. A. L. Beier and Paul Ocobock. Athens: Ohio University Press, pp. 117–39.

Ascher J., P. Laszlo, and G. Quiviger (2012). "Commodity Trading at a Strategic Crossroad". *McKinsey Working Papers on Risk* 39 (December): 1–14

ASLE (Association for the Study of Literature and Environment) (1994). *Defining Ecocritical Theory and Practice*. www.asle.org/wp-content/uploads/asle_Primer_DefiningEcocrit.pdf.

Balabanlilar, Lisa (2012). *Imperial Identity in the Mughal Empire: Memory and Dynastic Politics in Early Modern South and Central Asia*. New York: I. B. Tauris.

Bateson, G. (1972, 2000). *Steps to an Ecology of Mind*. Chicago: University of Chicago Press.

Baxendale, J. and C. Pawling (1996). *Narrating the Thirties: A Decade in the Making, 1930 to the Present*. Basingstoke: Palgrave.

Bayly, C. (1993). *Rulers, Townsmen and Bazars: North Indian Society in the Age of Expansion*. Cambridge: Cambridge University Press.

BBC News (2007). "Mexicans Stage Tortilla Protest". 1 February. http://news.bbc.co.uk/1/hi/6319093.stm.

Bedford, K. (1992). *Coriolanus at the National: "Th'Interpretation of the Time"*. Selinsgrove: Susquehanna University Press.

Beier, A. L. and Paul Ocobock, eds (2008). *Cast Out: Vagrancy and Homelessness in Global and Historical Perspective*. Athens: Ohio University Press.

Beinart, William and Lotte Hughes (2007). "Irrigation in India and Egypt". In *Environment and Empire*. Oxford History of the British Empire Companion Series. Oxford: Oxford University Press, pp. 130–47.

Beloff, Max (1963). *Public Order and Popular Disturbances 1660–1714*. London: Oxford University Press.

Benjamin, Walter (2006). "The Concept of History". In *Selected Writings*. Ed. Howard Eiland and Michael Jennings. Vol. 4. New York: Harvard University Press, pp. 389–400.

Bennett, J. (2010). *Vibrant Matter: A Political Ecology of Things*. Durham and London: Duke University Press.

Bhattacharya, S. (1982). "Eastern India". In *The Cambridge Economic History of India*. Ed. Dharma Kumar. Vol. 2, c.1757–c.1970. New Delhi: Cambridge University Press, pp. 279–80.

Bhushi, Kiranmayi, ed. (2018). *Farm to Fingers: The Culture and Politics of Food in Contemporary India*. New Delhi: Cambridge University Press.

Black, R. W. (1994). "What We Talk about When We Talk about Ecocriticism". *Defining Ecocritical Theory and Practice*. Electronic Publication: ASLE. www.asle. org/wp-content/uploads/asle_Primer_DefiningEcocrit.pdf.

Boltanski, Luc (1999). *Distant Suffering: Morality, Media and Politics*. Trans. Graham D. Burchell. Cambridge: Cambridge University Press.

Bose, Sugata (1986). *Agrarian Bengal: Economy, Social Structure, and Politics, 1919–1947*. Cambridge: Cambridge University Press.

Bose, Sugata (1990). "Starvation amidst Plenty: The Making of Famine in Bengal, Honan and Tonkin, 1942–45". *Modern Asian Studies* 24.4: 699–727.

Boshstedt, John (2010). *The Politics of Provisions: Food Riots, Moral Economy, and Market Transition in England, c.1550–1850*. Farnham: Ashgate.

Brassley, P. (2005). "The Professionalisation of English Agriculture". *Rural History* 16: 235–51.

Brassley, P., Y. Segers, and L. Van Molle, eds (2012). *War, Agriculture and Food: Rural Europe from the 1930s to the 1950s*. London: Routledge.

Brewis, Georgina (2010). "'Fill Full the Mouth of Famine': Voluntary Action in Famine Relief in India 1896–1901". *Modern Asian Studies* 44.4: 887–918.

Brookfield, H. and H. Parsons (2007). *Family Farms: Survival and Prospect*. London: Routledge.

Buckingham, Jane (2002). *Leprosy in Colonial South India: Medicine and Confinement*. Basingstoke: Palgrave.

Buckley, B. M., R. Fletcher, S.-Y. S. Wang, B. Zottoli, and C. Pottier (2014). "Monsoon Extremes and Society over the Past Millenium on Mainland Southeast Asia". *Quaternary Science Review* 95: 1–19.

Buerk, M. (1984). *Report on the Ethiopian Famine*. BBC News, 23 October 1984. YouTube recording.

Camporesi, Piero (1989). *Bread of Dreams: Food and Fantasy in Early Modern Europe*. Chicago: University of Chicago Press.

Camporesi, Piero (1996). *The Land of Hunger*. Trans. Tania Croft-Murray and Claire Foley. Oxford: Polity Press.

Cannadine, D. (1990). *The Decline and Fall of the British Aristocracy.* New York and London: Yale University Press.

Chambers, E. K. (1930) *William Shakespeare. A Study of Facts and Problems.* Vol. II. Oxford: Clarendon Press.

Chatterjee, Partha (1984). *Bengal 1920–1947: The Land Question.* Calcutta: K. P. Bagchi and Company.

Chatterji, Joya (1995). *Bengal Divided: Hindi Communalism and Partition 1932–1947.* New Delhi: Cambridge University Press.

Chaudhuri, Pramit (1984). "Review of *Prosperity and Misery in Modern Bengal: The Famine of 1943–1944* by Paul R. Greenough". *Third World Quarterly* 6.2: 529–30.

Chaudhuri, Supriya (2011). "Hunger: Some Representations of the 1943 Bengal Famine". In *The Writer's Feast: Food and the Cultures of Representation.* Ed. R. B. Chatterjee and S. Chaudhuri. Delhi: Orient Blackswan.

Chaudhuri, Supriya (2014). "Moral Economies of Well-Being". In *Shrapnel Minima: Writings from Humanities Underground.* Ed. Prasanta Chakravarty. Calcutta: Seagull, pp. 107–18.

Chillington Rutter, C. (2013) "Shakespeare Performances in England (and Wales) 2012". *Shakespeare Survey* 66: 354–94.

Clark, Peter (1976). "Popular Protest and Disturbance in Kent, 1558–1640". *Economic History Review* 29: 365–82.

Clingingsmith, David and Jeffery G. Williamson (2005). "Mughal Decline and Climate Change, and Britain's Industrial Ascent: An Integrated Perspective on India's 18th and 19th Century Deindustrialization". Working Paper 11730. www.nber.org/papers/w11730.

Clingingsmith, David and Jeffery G. Williamson (2008). "Deindustrialization in 18th and 19th Century India: Mughal Decline, Climate Shocks and British Industrial Ascent". *Explorations in Economic History* 45.3: 209–34.

Collet, Dominik and Daniel Krämer (2017). "Germany, Switzerland and Austria". In *Famine in European History.* Ed. Guido Alfani and Cormac Ó Gráda. Cambridge: Cambridge University Press, pp. 101–18.

Collingham, L. (2011). *The Taste of War: World War Two and the Battle for Food.* London: Allen Lane.

Conford, P. (2001). *The Origins of the Organic Movement.* Edinburgh: Floris Books.

Cotts Watkins, Susan and Jane Menken (1985). "Famines in Historical Perspective". *Population and Development Review* 11.4: 647–75.

Coveney, M. (1994). "*Coriolanus* Review". *The Observer.* 29 May.

Cox, G., P. Lowe, and M. Winter (1986). "From State Direction to Self Regulation: The Historical Development of Corporatism in British Agriculture". *Policy and Politics* 14.4: 475–90.

Cox, G., P. Lowe, and M. Winter (1991). "The Origins and Early Development of the National Farmers' Union". *Agricultural History Review* 39.1: 30–47.

Crawford, E. Margaret (1989). *Famine: The Irish Experience 900–1900. Subsistence Crises and Famines in Ireland.* Edinburgh: John Donald.

Cullen, Karen J. (2010) *Famine in Scotland: The "Ill Years" of the 1690s.* Edinburgh: Edinburgh University Press.

Dale, Stephen (2010). *The Muslim Empires of the Ottomans, Safavids, and Mughals.* Cambridge: Cambridge University Press.

Dalyell, T. (1998). "Obituary: Lord Donaldson of Kingsbridge". *The Independent.* 10 March.

Damodaran, Vinita (1998). "Famine in a Forest Tract: Ecological Change and the Causes of the 1897 Famine in Chota Nagpur, Northern India". In *Nature and the Orient: The Environmental History of South and Southeast Asia.* Ed. Richard H. Grove, Vinita Damodaran, and Satpal Sangwan. New Delhi: Oxford University Press, pp. 853–90.

Damodaran, Vinita (2007). "Famine in Bengal: A Comparison of the 1770 Famine in Bengal and the 1897 Famine in Chotanagpur". *The Medieval History Journal* 10.1–2: 143–81.

Damodaran, Vinita, Rob Allan, and James Hamilton (2015). "Climate Signals, Environment and Livelihoods in Seventeenth Century India in a Comparative Context". Unpublished paper. Food Security and the Environment in India and Britain Workshop. http://foodsecurity.exeter.ac.uk/wp-content/uploads/2015/09/17th-century.pdf.

Das, Suranjan (1991). *Communal Riots in Bengal: 1905–1947.* New Delhi: Oxford University Press.

Das, Suranjan (1995). "Nationalism and Popular Consciousness: Bengal 1942". *Social Scientist* 23.4/6: 58–68.

Dasgupta, Chittaranjan (2000). *Bharater Shilpa Samskritir Patabhumikaye Bishnupurer Mandir Terracotta.* Bishnupur: Sushama Dasgupta.

Datta, Rajat (1986). "Merchants and Peasants: A Study in the Structure of Local Trade in Grain in late Eighteenth Century Bengal". *Indian Economic and Social History Review* 23.4. Reprinted in *Merchants, Markets and State in Early Modern India.* Ed. Sanjay Subrahmanyam. New Delhi: Oxford University Press, 1990.

Datta, Rajat (1996). "Crises and Survival: Ecology, Subsistence and Coping in Eighteenth Century Bengal". *The Calcutta Historical Journal* 17.1: 1–34.

Datta, Rajat (2000). *Society, Economy and the Market. Commercialization in Rural Bengal, ca. 1760–1800.* New Delhi: Manohar Publications.

Datta, Rajat (2014). "The Rural–Urban Continuum and the Making of a Proto-Industrial Economy in Early Modern India: A View from the East". In *Cities in Medieval India.* Ed. Pius Malekandathil and Yogesh Sharma. New Delhi: Primus.

Datta, Rajat (2015). "Towards an Economic History of Rural Households in Early Modern India: Some Evidence from Bengal in the Eighteenth Century". In *Looking Within, Looking Without: Exploring Households in the Subcontinent Through Time. Essays in Memory of Nandita Prasad Sahai.* Ed. Kumkum Roy. New Delhi: Primus.

Davis, Mike (2002). *Late Victorian Holocausts: El Niño, Famines, and the Making of the Third World.* London and New York: Verso.

De-la-Noy, M. (2004). "Frances Donaldson". *Oxford Dictionary of National Biography.*

Djurfeldt, G. (1996). "Defining and Operationalizing Family Farming from a Sociological Perspective". *Sociologia Ruralis* 36.3: 340–51.

Dobson, M. (2004). "Shakespeare Performances in England, 2003". *Shakespeare Survey* 57: 258–89.

Dobson, M. (2007). "Shakespeare Performances in England, 2007". *Shakespeare Survey* 60: 318–50.

Drake, Michael (1968). "The Irish Demographic Crisis of 1740–1". *Historical Studies* 6: 101–24.

Drew, W. (2012). "Review, *The Serpent's Tooth,* Shoreditch Town Hall". 7–12 November. *Exeunt Magazine.* OWE and Fringe. www.exeuntmagazine.com/reviews/the-serpents-tooth.

Driver, Felix (1993). *Power and Pauperism: The Workhouse System, 1834–1884.* Cambridge: Cambridge University Press.

Dyer, Christopher (1998). "Did the Peasant Really Starve in Medieval England?". In *Food and Eating in Medieval Europe.* Ed. Martha Carlin and Joel T. Rosenthal. London and Rio Grande: Hambledon, pp. 53–71.

Dyer, Christopher, ed. (2007). *The Self-Contained Village? The Social History of Rural Communities, 1250–1900.* Hertford: University of Hertfordshire Press.

Eaton, Richard (1993). *The Rise of Islam and the Bengal Frontier, 1204–1760.* Berkeley: University of California Press.

Edkins, Jenny (2000). *Whose Hunger? Concepts of Famine, Practices of Aid.* Minneapolis: University of Minnesota Press.

Edwards, S. M. and H. M. O. Garrett (1974). *Mughal Rule in India.* London: S. Chand.

Englander, David (2013). *Poverty and Poor Law Reform in Nineteenth-Century Britain, 1834–1914: From Chadwick to Booth.* London: Routledge.

Farson, D. (1986). *Henry Williamson: A Portrait.* London: Robinson.

Federowicz, J. K. (1980). *England's Baltic Trade in the Early Seventeenth Century: A Study in Anglo-Polish Commercial Diplomacy.* Cambridge: Cambridge University Press.

Fitter, Chris (2000). " 'The Quarrel is between Our Masters and Us Their Men': 'Romeo and Juliet', Dearth, and the London Riots". *English Literary Renaissance* 30.2: 154–83.

Fitzpatrick, S., H. Pawson, G. Bramley, and S. Wilcox, with B. Watts (2013). *The Homelessness Monitor: Wales 2012.* Institute for Housing, Urban and Real Estate Research, Heriot-Watt University and Centre for Housing Policy, University of York.

Flinn, M. W., ed. (1977). *Scottish Population History from the 17th Century to the 1930s.* Cambridge: Cambridge University Press.

Friedmann, H. (1978). "World Market, State, and Family Farm: Social Bases of Household Production in the Era of Wage Labor". *Comparative Studies in Society and History* 20.4: 545–86.

Frohman, Larry (2008). *Poor Relief and Welfare in Germany from the Reformation to World War I.* Cambridge: Cambridge University Press.

Foucault, Michel (1965). *Madness and Civilization: A History of Insanity in the Age of Reason.* New York: Vintage Books.

Fumerton, Patricia (2003, 2004). "Making Vagrancy (In)Visible: The Economics of Disguise in Early Modern Rogue Pamphlets". *English Literary Renaissance* 33.2: 211–27. Reprinted in *Rogues and Early Modern Literary Culture: A Critical Anthology.* Ed. Craig Dionne and Steve Mentz. Michigan: University of Michigan Press, pp. 193–210.

Fumerton, Patricia (2006). *Unsettled: The Culture of Mobility and the Working Poor in Early Modern England.* Chicago: University of Chicago Press.

Gagnier, Regenia (2000a). "The Law of Progress and the Ironies of Individualism in the Nineteenth Century". *New Literary History* 31.2: 315–36.

Gagnier, Regenia (2000b). *The Insatiability of Human Wants: Economic and Aesthetics in Market Society.* Chicago and London: University of Chicago Press.

Gander, A. (2001). *Adrian Bell: Voice of the Countryside.* Wenhaston: Holm Oak Publishing.

George, David (2000). "Plutarch, Insurrection and Dearth in Coriolanus". *Shakespeare Survey* 53: 60–72.

Gergis, J. L. and A. M. Fowler (2009). "A History of ENSO Events since 1525: Implications for Future Climate Change". *Climate Change* 92: 343–87.

Ghose, Ajit Kumar (1982). "Food Supply and Starvation. A Study of Famines with Reference to the Indian Sub-Continent". *Oxford Economic Papers* (New Series) 34.2: 368–89.

Gole, Susan (1989). *Indian Maps and Plans from Earliest Times to the Advent of European Surveys.* New Delhi: Manohar.

Gommans, Jos (2002). *Mughal Warfare: Indian Frontiers and Highroads to Empire, 1500–1700.* Oxford: Oxford University Press.

Gordon, Stuart (1993). *The Marathas: 1600–1818.* Cambridge: Cambridge University Press.

Greenblatt, Stephen (1980). *Renaissance Self-fashioning: From More to Shakespeare.* Chicago: University of Chicago Press.

Greenblatt, Stephen (2004). *Will in the World: How Shakespeare Became Shakespeare.* London: Jonathan Cape.

Greenough, Paul (1980). "Indian Famines and Peasant Victims: The Case of Bengal in 1943–44". *Modern Asian Studies* 14.2: 205–35.

Greenough, Paul (1982). *Prosperity and Misery in Modern Bengal: The Famine of 1943–44.* Oxford: Oxford University Press.

Greenough, Paul (1983). "Indulgence and Abundance as Asian Peasant Values: A Bengali Case in Point". *Journal of Asian Studies* 42.4: 831–50.

Griffiths, C. (2010). "Socialism and the Land Question: Public Ownership and Control in Labour Party Policy, 1918–1950s". In *The Land Question in Britain, 1750–1950.* Ed. M. Cragoe and P. Readman. Basingstoke: Palgrave, pp. 237–56.

Grigg, D. (1989). *English Agriculture: An Historical Perspective.* Oxford: Blackwell.

Gronke, M. (1992). "The Persian Court between Palace and Tent: From Timur to 'Abbas I". In *Timurid Art and Culture: Iran and Central Asia in the Fifteenth Century.* Ed. L. Golombek and M. Subtelny. Leiden: Brill, pp. 18–22.

Grove, Richard H. (1994). *Green Imperialism: Colonial Expansion, Tropical Island Edens, and the Origins of Environmentalism, 1600–1860.* Cambridge: Cambridge University Press.

Grove, Richard H. (1998). "Global Impact of the 1789–93 El Niño". *Nature* 393: 318–19.

Grove, Richard H. (2002). "El Niño Chronology and the History of Socio-Economic and Agrarian Crisis in South and Southeast Asia, 1250–1900". In *Land Use – Historical Perspectives: Focus on Indo-Gangetic Plains.* Ed. Y. P. Abrol, S. Sangwan, and M. K. Tiwari. New Delhi: Allied Publishers.

Grove, Richard H. and John Chapell (2000). *El Niño: History and Crisis.* Winwick: White Horse Press.

Habib, I. (1963, 1999). *The Agrarian System of Mughal India.* Oxford: Oxford University Press.

Habib, I. (1990). "Merchant Communities in Pre-Colonial India". In *The Rise of Merchant Empires: Long Distance Trade in the Early Modern World.* Ed. James D. Tracy. Cambridge: Cambridge University Press, pp. 371–99.

Habib, I. (1996). "Notes on the Economic and Social Aspects of Mughal Gardens". In *Mughal Gardens: Sources, Places, Representations, and Prospects.* Ed. James L. Wescoat and Joachim Wolschke-Bulmahn. Washington, D.C.: Dumbarton Oaks.

Hagerty, B. (1994). "*Coriolanus* Review". *Today,* 10 June.

Hall-Matthews, David (1996). "Historical Roots of Famine Relief Paradigms: Ideas on Dependency and Free Trade in India in the 1870s". *Disasters* 20.3: 216–30.

Harrison, C. J. (1971). "Grain Price Analysis and Harvest Qualities, 1465–1634". *Agricultural History Review* 19: 135–55.

Hartocollis, Anemona (2015). "Greece Financial Crisis Hits Poorest and Hungriest the Hardest". *New York Times*, 11 July.

Haskell, Thomas L. (1985, 1992). "Capitalism and the Origins of the Humanitarian Sensibility". 2 parts: *American Historical Review* 90 (April 1985): 339–61; (June 1985): 547–66. Reprinted in *The Anti-Slavery Debate: Capitalism and Abolitionism as a Problem in Historical Interpretation*. Ed. Thomas Bender. Berkeley: University of California Press.

Heal, Felicity (1990). *Hospitality in Early Modern England*. Oxford: Oxford University Press.

Heal, Felicity and Clive Holmes (1994). *The Gentry in England and Wales 1500–1700*. Basingstoke and London: Palgrave.

Healey, Jonathan (2011). "Land, Population, and Family in the English Uplands: A Westmorland Case Study, *c.*1370–*c.*1650". *Agricultural History Review* 59: 151–75.

Healey, Jonathan (2014). *The First Century of Welfare: Poverty and Poor Relief in Lancashire, 1620–1730*. Woodbridge: The Boydell Press.

Higginbottom, M. D. (1992). *Intellectuals and British Fascism: A Study of Henry Williamson*. London: Janus.

Hindle, Steve (2001). "Dearth, Fasting and Alms: The Campaign for General Hospitality". *Past & Present* 172: 44–86.

Hindle, Steve (2004). *On the Parish? The Micro-Politics of Poor Relief in Rural England c.1550–1750*. Oxford: Oxford University Press.

Hindle, Steve (2008). "Dearth and the English Revolution: The Harvest Crisis of 1647–50". *Economic History Review* 61: 64–98.

Hipkin, Stephen (2008). "The Structure, Development, and Politics of the Kent Grain Trade, 1552–1647". *Economic History Review* 61: 99–139.

Hobsbawm, E. J. (1954). "The General Crisis of the European Economy in the 17th Century". *Past & Present* 5.1: 33–53.

Holderness, B. A. (1985). *British Agriculture since 1945*. Manchester: Manchester University Press.

Hoskins, W. G. (1964). "Harvest Fluctuations and English Economic History, 1480–1609". *Agricultural History Review* 12: 28–46.

Hoskins, W. G. (1968). "Harvest Fluctuations and English Economic History, 1620–1759". *Agricultural History Review* 16: 15–31.

Hoyle, R. W. (2010). "Famine as Agricultural Catastrophe: The Crisis of 1623–4 in East Lancashire". *Economic History Review* 63: 974–1002.

Hudson, Julie (2017). *The Environment on Stage: Scenery or Shapeshifter?* PhD Thesis, University of Warwick.

Hudson, Julie and Paul Donovan (2014). *Food Policy and the Environmental Credit Crunch: From Soup to Nuts*. London: Routledge.

Hutson, Lorna (1987). *Thomas Nashe in Context*. Oxford: Oxford University Press.

Ingram, J., P. Ericksen, and D. Liverman (2010). *Food Security and Global Environmental Change*. London and Washington: Earthscan.

Islam, M. M. (2007). "The Great Bengal Famine and the Question of FAD Yet Again". *Modern Asian Studies* 41.2: 421–40.

Israel, J. (1974). "Mexico and the General Crisis of the Seventeenth Century". *Past & Present* 63: 33–57.

Jefferies, M. and M. Tyldesley, eds (2011). *Rolf Gardiner: Folk, Nature and Culture in Interwar Britain.* Farnham: Ashgate.

Jones, P. (2007). "Swing, Speenhamland and Rural Social Relations". *Social History* 32.3: 271–90.

Kates, Robert W. and Sara Millman (1995). "On Ending Hunger: The Lessons of History". In *Hunger in History: Food Shortage, Poverty, and Deprivation.* Ed. Lucile F. Newman. Oxford: Blackwell, pp. 389–407.

Kaviraj, Sudipta. (2000). "Laughter and Subjectivity: The Self-Ironical Tradition in Bengali Literature". *Modern Asian Studies* 34.2: 379–406.

Kelly, Morgan and Cormac Ó Gráda (2014). "Living Standards and Mortality since the Middle Ages". *Economic History Review* 67: 358–81.

Kershaw, B. (2015). "Performed by Ecologies: How Homo Sapiens Could Subvert Present-day Futures". *Performing Ethos* 4.2: 113–34.

Khare, R. S., ed. (1993). *The Eternal Food: Gastronomic Ideas and Experiences of Hindus and Buddhists.* Delhi: Sri Satguru Publications.

Kinney, A. F. (1993). "Textual Signs in *The Merry Wives of Windsor*". *Yearbook of English Studies,* Early Shakespeare Special, 23: 206–34.

Klein, Bernhard (2001). *Maps and the Writing of Space in Early Modern England and Ireland.* Basingstoke: Palgrave.

Kolff, D. (1990). *Naukar, Rajput, and Sepoy: The Ethnohistory of the Military Labour Market in Hindustan, 1450–1850.* Cambridge: Cambridge University Press.

Kothiyal, Tanuja (2016). *Nomadic Narratives: A History of Mobility and Identity in the Great Indian Desert.* New Delhi: Cambridge University Press.

Kussmaul, Ann (1981). *Servants in Husbandry in Early Modern England.* Cambridge: Cambridge University Press.

Kussmaul, Ann (1985). "Time and Space, Hoofs and Grain: The Seasonality of Marriage in England". *The Journal of Interdisciplinary History* 15.4: 755–79.

Lal, Ruby (2005). *Domesticity and Power in the Early Mughal World.* Cambridge: Cambridge University Press.

Lamb, H. H. (1977). *Climate: Present, Past and Future. Climatic History and the Future.* Vol. 2. London and New York: Methuen.

Langelüddecke, Henrik (1998). "'Patchy and Spasmodic'? The Response of the Justices of the Peace to Charles I's Book of Orders". *English Historical Review* 113: 1231–48.

Laqueur, Thomas W. (1989). "Bodies, Details, and the Humanitarian Narrative". In *The New Cultural History.* Ed. Lynn Hunt. Berkeley: University of California Press.

Laslett, Peter (1965). *The World We Have Lost.* London: Methuen.

Lawson, P. G. (1986). "Property Crime and Hard Times in England, 1559–1624". *Law and History Review* 4: 95–127.

Le Roy Ladurie, Emmanuel (1971). *Times of Feast, Times of Famine: A History of Climate since the Year 1000.* New York: Doubleday.

Lee, A. (2013). "Coriolanus, Directed by Motoi Miura for the Chiten Theatre Company (Kyoto, Japan) at Shakespeare's Globe". In *A Year of Shakespeare.* Ed. Paul Edmondson, Paul Prescott, and Erin Sullivan. London: Bloomsbury, Arden, pp. 47–50.

Lee, Joo-Yup (2015). *Qazaqlïq, or Ambitious Brigandage and the Formation of the Qazaqs: State and Identity in Post-Mongol Central Eurasia.* Leiden: Brill.

Lefèbvre, Henri (1974, 1991). *The Production of Space*. Trans. Donald Nicholson-Smith. Oxford: Wiley-Blackwell.

Lentz, Thomas W. (1996). "Memory and Ideology in the Timurid Garden". In *Mughal Gardens: Sources, Places, Representations, and Prospects*. Ed. James L. Wescoat and Joachim Wolschke-Bulmahn. Washington, D.C.: Dumbarton Oaks.

Leonard, E. M. (1900). *The Early History of English Poor Relief*. Cambridge University Press.

Levy, P. (2010). "Age Shall Not Wither Her". *The Wall Street Journal*, 26 November.

Lovelock, J. (2006). *The Revenge of Gaia*. London and New York: Allen Lane.

Lucas, A. T. (1959). "Nettles and Charlock as Famine Foods". *Breifne* 1: 137–46.

Lustig, Robert (2012). *Fat Chance: The Hidden Truth about Sugar, Obesity and Disease*. London: The Fourth Estate.

Mann, Michael (2015). *South Asia's Modern History: Thematic Perspectives*. New Delhi: Routledge.

Marks, Robert V. (1998). *Tigers, Rice, Silk, and Silt: Environment and Economy in Late Imperial South China*. New York: Cambridge University Press.

Marshall, P. J. (1977). *East Indian Fortunes: The English in Bengal in the Eighteenth Century*. Oxford: Oxford University Press.

Marshall, P. J. (1982). *The Great Map of Mankind*. London: Harvard University Press.

Martin, J. (2000). *The Development of Modern Agriculture: British Farming since 1931*. Basingstoke: Palgrave.

Marvin, Julia (1998). "Cannibalism as an Aspect of Famine in Two English Chronicles". In *Food and Eating in Medieval Europe*. Ed. Martha Carlin and Joel T. Rosenthal. London and Rio Grande: The Hambledon Press, pp. 73–86.

McIntosh, Marjorie J. (2014). "Poor Relief in Elizabethan English Communities: An Analysis of Collectors' Accounts". *Economic History Review* 67: 331–57.

McKendrick, Neil, J. Brewer, and J. H. Plumb (1982). *The Birth of a Consumer Society: The Commercialization of Eighteenth-Century England*. Bloomington: Indiana University Press.

McNeill, John (2003). "Observations on the Nature and Culture of Environmental History". *History and Theory* 42: 5–43.

McRae, Andrew (1996). *God Speed the Plough: The Representation of Agrarian England, 1500–1660*. Cambridge: Cambridge University Press.

McRae, Andrew (2009). *Literature and Domestic Travel in Early Modern England*. Cambridge: Cambridge University Press.

McRae, Andrew (2015). "Early Modern Chorographies". *Oxford Handbooks Online*. Oxford University Press. www.oxfordhandbooks.com/view/10.1093/oxfordhb/978 0199935338.001.0001/oxfordhb-9780199935338-e-102.

Melchiori, G. (2000). "Introduction". *The Merry Wives of Windsor*. London: Bloomsbury, Arden, pp. 18–30.

Meuvret, J. (1988). "Food Crises and Demography in France in the Ancien Regime". In *French Studies in History, Vol. 1: The Inheritance*. Ed. Harbans Mukhia and M. Aymard. New Delhi: Orient Longman.

Miller, Sarah G. (2017). "Climate Change is Transforming the World's Food Supply". *Live Science*, 16 February.

Moore-Colyer, R. J. (2001a). "Rolf Gardiner, English Patriot and the Council for the Church and Countryside". *Agricultural History Review* 49: 187–209.

Moore-Colyer, R. J. (2001b). "Back to Basics: Rolf Gardiner, H J Massingham and 'A Kinship in Husbandry' ". *Rural History* 12.1: 85–108.

Moore-Colyer, R. J. (2002). "A Voice Clamouring in the Wilderness: H J Massingham (1888–1952) and Rural England". *Rural History* 13: 199–224.

Moore-Colyer, R. J. (2004). "Towards 'Mother Earth': Jorian Jenks, Organicism, the Right and the British Union of Fascists". *Journal of Contemporary History* 39: 353–71.

Moore-Colyer, R. J. and P. Conford (2004). "A 'Secret Society'? The Internal and External Relations of the Kinship in Husbandry, 1941–52". *Rural History* 15.2: 189–206.

Moosvi, Shireen (1987, 2015). *The Economy of the Mughal Empire, c.1595: A Statistical Study.* Oxford and New Delhi: Oxford University Press.

Moosvi, Shireen (2008). *People, Taxation, and Trade in Mughal India.* New Delhi: Oxford University Press.

Moran, W., G. Blunden, and J. Greenwood (1993). "The Role of Family Farming in Agrarian Change". *Progress in Human Geography* 17.1: 22–42.

Muir, Cameron (2014). *The Broken Promise of Agricultural Progress: An Environmental History.* London and New York: Routledge.

Mukerjee, Madhusree (2010). *Churchill's Secret War: The British Empire and the Ravaging of India During World War II.* New York: Basic Books.

Mukherjee, Ayesha (2015). *Penury into Plenty: Dearth and the Making of Knowledge in Early Modern England.* London and New York: Routledge.

Mukherjee, Janam (2015). *Hungry Bengal: War, Famine and the End of Empire.* London: Hurst & Company.

Mukherjee, R. K. (1938). *The Changing Face of Bengal. A Study of its Riverine Economy.* Calcutta: University of Calcutta Press.

Mukherjee, Tilottama (2013). *Political Culture and Economy in Eighteenth-Century Bengal. Networks, Exchange and Communication.* New Delhi: Orient Blackswan.

Mukherjee, Upamanyu Pablo (2013). *Natural Disasters and Victorian Empire: Famines, Fevers and Literary Cultures of South Asia.* Basingstoke: Palgrave.

Murdoch, J. and N. Ward (1997). "Governmentality and Territoriality: The Statistical Manufacture of Britain's 'National Farm'". *Political Geography* 16.4: 307–24.

Neukom, R., H. Wanner, J. Elbert, C. C. Raible, D. Frank, J. Gergis, D. J. Karoly, M. Curran, A. D. Moy, T. Van Ommen, M. Curran, T. Vance, F. Gonzalez-Rouco, B. K. Linsley, I. Mundo, R. Villalba, E. J. Steig, and J. Zinke (2014). "Inter-Hemispheric Temperature Variability over the Past Millennium". *Nature Climate Change* 4: 362–7.

Neumann, J. and J. Detwiller (1990). "Great Historical Events that were Significantly Affected by the Weather: Part 9, the Year Leading to the Revolution of 1789 in France (II)". *Bulletin of the American Meteorological Society* 71.1: 33–41.

Newman, Lucile F., ed. (1995). *Hunger in History: Food Shortage, Poverty, and Deprivation.* Oxford: Blackwell.

NHS (National Health Service) (2013). "Latest Obesity Stats for England Are Alarming". 2 February. www.nhs.uk/news/2013/02February/Pages/Latest-obesity-stats-for-England-are-alarming-reading.aspx.

Nielsen, Randall (1997). "Storage and English Government Intervention in Early Modern Grain Markets". *Journal of Economic History* 57: 1–33.

Nightingale, B. (1994). "*Coriolanus* Review". *The Times.* 26 May.

Ó Gráda, Cormac (2005). "Markets and Famines in Pre-Industrial Europe". *Journal of Interdisciplinary History* 36.2: 143–66.

Ó Gráda, Cormac (2007). "Making Famine History". *Journal of Economic Literature* 45.1: 5–38.

Ó Gráda, Cormac (2009). *Famine: A Short History*. Princeton: Princeton University Press.

Ó Gráda, Cormac (2011). "Famines Past, Famine's Future". *Development and Change* 42.1: 49–69.

Ó Gráda, Cormac (2015). "Neither Feast nor Famine: England before the Industrial Revolution". In *Institutions, Innovation and Industrialization: Essays in Economic History and Development*. Ed. Avner Greif, Lynne Kiesling, and John V. C. Nye. Princeton: Princeton University Press, pp. 7–31.

Ormsby, R. (2014). *Shakespeare in Performance: Coriolanus*. Manchester: Manchester University Press.

Ortlieb, L. (1998). "Historical Reconstructions of ENSO Events from Documentary Sources from Chile, Peru, Brasil, and Mexico: Evidence for Variability of the Teleconnection Regime in the Last Centuries". In *Abstracts of the Pole-Equator-Pole Conference on the Paleo-climate of the Americas*. Convenor V. Markgraf, University of Colorado. Merida, Venezuela.

Outhwaite, R. B. (1991). *Dearth, Public Policy and Social Disturbance in England, 1550–1800*. Basingstoke: Palgrave.

Parker, Geoffrey (2013). *Global Crisis, War, Climate Change and Catastrophe in the Seventeenth Century*. New Haven: Yale University Press.

Parker, G. and L. M. Smith, eds (1978, 1985, 1997). *The General Crisis of the Seventeenth Century*. London: Routledge.

Patterson, Annabel (1991). *Fables of Power: Aesopian Writing and Political History*. Durham, NC: Duke University Press.

Pemberton, Rita (2013). "Workhouse Medicine in the British Caribbean, 1834–38". In *Medicine and the Workhouse*. Ed. Jonathan Reinarz and Leonard Schwarz. Rochester and Suffolk: University of Rochester Press.

Perry, P. J., ed. (1973). *British Agriculture 1875–1914*. London: Methuen.

Peter, J. (1994). "*Coriolanus* Review". *Sunday Times*. 29 May.

Pritchard, R. E. (2011). *Peter Mundy, Merchant Adventurer*. Oxford: Bodleian Library.

Quinn, W. H. (1992) "A Study of Southern Oscillation-related Climatic Activity for A.D. 622–1900 Incorporating Nile River Flood Data". In *El Niño: Historical and Paleoclimate Aspects of the Southern Oscillation*. Ed. H. E. Diaz and V. Markgraf. Cambridge: Cambridge University Press, pp. 119–49.

Quinn, W. H., V. T. Neal, and S. E. Antunez De Mayolo (1987). "El Niño Occurrences over the Past Four and a Half Centuries". *Journal of Geophysical Research* 92 (C13): 14449–61.

Raj, K. N, N. Bhattacharya, S. Guha, and S. Padhi, eds (1985). *Essays on the Commercialization of Indian Agriculture*. New Delhi: Oxford University Press.

Ramachandran, V. K. (1998). "Documenting Society and Politics". *Frontline*. September.

Ray, A. and M. Kuzhippalli Skaria (2002). *Studies in the History of the Deccan*. New Delhi: Pragati.

Rayner, G. (2008). "Credit Crunch Time Line: From Northern Rock to Lehman Brothers". *Telegraph*. 15 September.

Reid, Anthony (1990). "The Crisis of the Seventeenth Century in Southeast Asia". *Modern Asian Studies* 24.4: 639–59.

Reinarz, Jonathan and Leonard Schwarz, eds (2013). *Medicine and the Workhouse*. Rochester and Suffolk: University of Rochester Press.

Richards, John (1990). "The Seventeenth Century Crisis in South Asia". *Modern Asian Studies* 24.1: 625–38.

Riley, M. and D. Harvey (2007). "Oral Histories, Farm Practice and Uncovering Meaning in the Countryside". *Social and Cultural Geography* 8: 391–415.

Robb, Peter (2007). *Peasants, Political Economy, and Law.* New Delhi: Oxford University Press.

Rotberg, Robert I. and Theodore Rabb, eds (1985). *Hunger and History: The Impact of Changing Food Production and Consumption Patterns on Society.* Cambridge: Cambridge University Press.

Roychowdhury, Binata (1993). *Ponchasher Monnontor O Bangla Sahitya.* Kolkata: Sahityalok.

Rudé, G. (1964). *The Crowd in History: A Study of Popular Disturbances in France and England 1730–1848.* New York: Wiley.

Ruiter, David (2003). *Shakespeare's Festive History: Feasting, Festivity, Fasting, and Lent in the Second Henriad.* Farnham: Ashgate.

Sayce, R. V. (1953/54). "Need Years and Need Foods". *The Montgomeryshire Collections* 53: 55–80.

Scholl, Lesa (2011). *Translation, Authorship and the Victorian Professional Woman: Charlotte Brontë, Harriet Martineau and George Eliot.* Farnham: Ashgate.

Scholl, Lesa (2016). *Hunger Movements in Early Victorian Literature: Want, Riots, Migration.* London: Routledge.

Schwyzer, Philip (2009). "John Leland and His Heirs: The Topography of England". In *The Oxford Handbook of Tudor Literature.* Ed. M. Pincombe and C. Shrank. Oxford: Oxford University Press, pp. 238–53.

Scott, James (1976). *The Moral Economy of the Asian Peasant.* New Haven: Yale University Press.

Sen, Amartya (1981a). *Poverty and Famines: An Essay on Entitlement and Deprivation.* Oxford: Oxford University Press.

Sen, Amartya (1981b). "Ingredients of Famine Analysis: Availability and Entitlements". *The Quarterly Journal of Economics* 96.3: 433–64.

Sharma, Sanjay (2001). *Famine, Philanthropy and the Colonial State: North India in the Early Nineteenth Century.* New Delhi: Oxford University Press.

Sharp, Buchanan (2007). "Shakespeare's Coriolanus and the Crisis of the 1590s". In *Law and Authority in Early Modern England: Essays Presented to Thomas Garden Barnes.* Ed. Buchanan Sharp and Mark Fissel. Newark, NJ: University of Delaware Press.

Sharpe, J. A. (1998). *Crime in Early Modern England, 1550–1750.* 2nd edition. London: Routledge.

Shi, Feng, Jianping Li, and Rob J. S.Wilson (2014). "A Tree-Ring Reconstruction of the South Asian Summer Monsoon Index over the Past Millennium". *Scientific Reports* 4: 6739.

Short, B. (2014). *The Battle of the Fields: Rural Community and Authority in Britain during the Second World War.* Suffolk: Boydell Press.

Short, B., C. Watkins, and J. Martin (2007). " 'The Front Line of Freedom': State-Led Agricultural Revolution in Britain, 1939–45". In *The Front Line of Freedom: British Farming in the Second World War.* Ed. B. Short, C. Watkins, and J. Martin. Exeter: British Agricultural History Society, pp. 1–15.

Singha, Radhika (1998). *A Despotism of Law: Crime and Justice in Colonial India.* New Delhi: Oxford University Press.

Sinha, N. K. (1956). *The Economic History of Bengal.* Calcutta.

Slack, Paul (1980). "Books of Orders: The Making of the English Social Policy, 1575–1631". *Transactions of the Royal Historical Society,* 5th series, 30: 1–22.

Slack, Paul (1988). *Poverty and Policy in Tudor and Stuart England.* London and New York: Longman.

Slack, Paul (1990). *The English Poor Law, 1531–1782.* Cambridge: Cambridge University Press.

Slack, Paul (1999). *From Reformation to Improvement: Public Welfare in Early Modern England.* Oxford: Oxford University Press.

Slavin, Philip (2014). "Market Failure and the Great Famine in England and Wales (1315–17)". *Past and Present* 222: 9–49.

Smith, Helen (2013). "Greece's Food Crisis: Families Face Going Hungry during Summer Shutdown". *Guardian,* 6 August.

Smith, M. J. (1989). "Land Nationalisation and the Agricultural Policy Community". *Public Policy and Administration* 4.3: 9–21.

Smith, M. J. (1990). *The Politics of Agricultural Support in Britain.* Aldershot: Dartmouth.

Smith, M. M. (2015). *The Smell of Battle, the Taste of Siege: A Sensory History of the Civil War.* Oxford: Oxford University Press.

Smith, Richard M. (2011). "Social Security as a Developmental Institution? The Relative Efficiency of Poor Relief Provisions under the English Old Poor Law". In *History, Historians and Development Policy: A Necessary Dialogue.* Ed. C. A. Bayly, Vijagendra Rao, Simon Szreter, and Michael Woolcock. Manchester: Manchester University Press, pp. 75–102.

Smith, Richard M. (2015). "Dearth and Local Political Responses: 1280–1325 and 1580–1596/7 Compared". In *Peasants and Lords in the Medieval English Economy: Essays in Honour of Bruce M. S. Campbell.* Ed. Maryanne Kowaleski, John Langdon, and Philip Schofield. Turnhout: Brepols, pp. 377–406.

Snyder M. G. (2005). "It Didn't Begin with Katrina". (US) *National Housing Institute, Shelterforce Online* 143. September/October. www.nhi.org/online/issues/143/beforekatrina.html.

Spencer, C. (1994). "*Coriolanus* Review". *Daily Telegraph.* 27 May.

Spufford, Margaret (1984). *The Great Re-Clothing of Rural England: Petty Chapmen and their Wares in the Seventeenth Century.* London: Hambledon.

Srivastava, Hari Shanker (1968). *The History of Indian Famines, 1858–1918.* Agra: Sri Ram Mehra & Co.

Steensgaard, Niels (1990). "The Seventeenth-Century Crisis and the Unity of Eurasian History". *Modern Asian Studies* 24: 683–97.

Street, P. (1969). *My Father, A. G. Street.* London: Robert Hale.

Sturmey, S. G. (1955). "Owner-farming in England and Wales, 1900 to 1950". *Manchester School* 23: 246–68.

Subrahmanyam, Sanjay (1990). *The Political Economy of Commerce: Southern India, 1500–1650.* New York: Cambridge University Press.

Subtelny, Maria Eva (1995). "Mīraki Sayyid Ghiyās and the Tīmurid tradition of Landscape Architecture". *Studia Iranica* 24: 19–60.

Subtelny, Maria Eva (2007). *Timurids in Transition: Turko-Persian Politics and Acculturation in Medieval Iran.* Leiden: Brill.

Sundar, Pushpa (2000). *Beyond Business: From Merchant Charity to Corporate Citizenship: Indian Business Philanthropy through the Ages.* New Delhi: Tata McGraw-Hill.

Sunderason, Sanjukta (2017). "Shadow-Lines". *Third Text* 31.2–3: 239–59.

Swaminathan, M. S. (2013). "From Bengal Famine to Right to Food". *The Hindu.* 13 February. www.thehindu.com/todays-paper/tp-opinion/from-bengal-famine-to-right-to-food/article4409557.ece.

Swanson, Scott (1997). "The Medieval Foundations of John Locke's Theory of Natural Rights of Subsistence and the Principle of Extreme Necessity". *History of Political Thought* 18: 399–459.

Thirsk, Joan (1967). *The Agrarian History of England and Wales, 1500–1640.* Vol. 4. Cambridge: Cambridge University Press.

Thirsk, Joan (2007). *Food in Early Modern England: Phases, Fads, Fashions, 1500–1760.* London: Bloomsbury.

Thomas, Keith (1983). *Man and the Natural World: Changing Attitudes in England 1500–1800.* London: Allen Lane.

Thompson, E. P. (1971). "The Moral Economy of the English Crowd in the Eighteenth Century". *Past and Present* 50: 76–136.

Thompson, E. P. (1975). "The Crime of Anonymity". In *Albion's Fatal Tree: Crime and Society in Eighteenth-Century England.* Ed. Douglas Hay, P. Linebaugh, J. G. Rule, E. P. Thompson, and C. Winslow. London: Verso, pp. 255–344.

Thompson, E. P. (1993). "The Moral Economy Reviewed". In *Customs in Common: Studies in Traditional Popular Culture.* New York: New Press.

Thorpe, Andrew (1992). *Britain in the 1930s: A Deceptive Decade.* Oxford: Blackwell.

Tichelar, M. (2003). "The Labour Party, Agricultural Policy and the Retreat from Rural Land Nationalisation during the Second World War". *Agricultural History Review* 51.2: 209–25.

Tilley, Morris Palmer (1950). *A Dictionary of the Proverbs in England in the Sixteenth and Seventeenth Centuries.* Ann Arbor: University of Michigan Press.

Tilly, Charles (1975). "Food Supply and Public Order in Modern Europe". In *The Formation of National States in Western Europe.* Ed. Charles Tilly. Princeton: Princeton University Press, pp. 380–455.

Trevor-Roper, Hugh (1967, 2001). *The Crisis of the Seventeenth Century: Religion, the Reformation and Social Change.* Indianapolis: Liberty Fund.

Turner, M. (1992). "Output and Prices in UK Agriculture, 1867–1914, and the Great Agricultural Depression Reconsidered". *Agricultural History Review* 40.1: 38–51.

van der Zee, Henri A. (1982). *The Hunger Winter: Occupied Holland, 1944–45.* Lincoln: University of Nebraska Press.

Vattimo, G. and A. Rovatti, eds (2018). *Weak Thought.* Trans. P. Carravetta. New York: SUNY Press.

Vernon, James (2007). *Hunger: A Modern History.* Cambridge, MA: Harvard University Press.

Waddell, Brodie (2012). *God, Duty and Community in English Economic Life, 1660–1720.* Woodbridge: Boydell and Brewer.

Wakeman, F. (1986). "China and the Seventeenth Century Crisis". *Late Imperial China* 7.1: 1–26.

Walsham, Alexandra (1999). *Providence in Early Modern England.* Oxford: Oxford University Press.

Walter, John (1989). "The Social Economy of Dearth in Early Modern England". In *Famine, Disease and the Social Order in Early Modern Society.* Ed. John Walter and R. S. Schofield. Cambridge: Cambridge University Press.

Walter, John (2001). "Public Transcripts, Popular Agency and the Politics of Subsistence in Early Modern England". In *Negotiating Power in Early Modern Society: Order, Hierarchy and Subordination in Britain and Ireland.* Ed. Michael J. Braddick and John Walter. Cambridge: Cambridge University Press, pp. 123–48.

Walter, John (2006). *Crowds and Popular Politics in Early Modern England.* Manchester: Manchester University Press.

Walter, John (2015). "The Politics of Protest in Seventeenth-century England". In *Crowd Actions in Britain and France from the Middle Ages to the Modern World.* Ed. Michael T. Davis. Basingstoke: Palgrave, pp. 58–79.

Walter, John and R. S. Schofield, eds (1989). *Famine, Disease and the Social Order in Early Modern Society.* Cambridge: Cambridge University Press.

Walter, John and Keith Wrightson (1976). "Dearth and the Social Order in Early Modern England". *Past and Present* 71: 22–42.

Wardle, I. (1994). *Coriolanus* Review. *Independent on Sunday.* 29 May.

Watt, Carey Anthony (2005). *Serving the Nation: Cultures of Service, Association, and Citizenship in Colonial India.* New Delhi: Oxford University Press.

Webster, Charles (1982). "Healthy or Hungry Thirties?" *History Workshop Journal* 13: 110–29.

Welch, Anthony (1996). "Gardens that Babur Did Not Like: Landscape, Water, and Architecture for the Sultans of Delhi". In *Mughal Gardens: Sources, Places, Representations, and Prospects.* Ed. James L. Wescoat and Joachim Wolschke-Bulmahn. Washington, D.C.: Dumbarton Oaks.

Wescoat, James (2007). "Questions about the Political Significance of Mughal Garden Waterworks". *Middle Eastern Garden Traditions.* Ed. Michel Conan. Washington, D.C.: Dumbarton Oaks, pp. 177–96.

Wescoat, James (2011a). "The Changing Cultural Space of Mughal Gardens". *A Companion to Asian Art and Architecture.* Ed. Rebecca M. Brown and Deborah S. Hutton. Oxford: Blackwell.

Wescoat, James (2011b). "Gardens, Pavilions and Tents. The Art of Shelter". In *Architecture in Islamic Arts: Treasures of the Aga Khan Museum.* Geneva: Aga Khan Trust for Culture.

Westerfield, Ray B. (1915, 1968) *Middlemen in English Business: Particularly between 1660–1760.* New Haven: Yale University Press.

Whetham, E. (1972). "The Agriculture Act 1920 and Its Repeal: The 'Great Betrayal' ". *Agricultural History Review* 22.1: 36–49.

Whetham, E. (1978). *The Agrarian History of England and Wales. 1914–1939.* Vol. 8. Cambridge: Cambridge University Press.

White, Sam (2011). *Climate of Rebellion in the Early Modern Ottoman Empire.* Cambridge: Cambridge University Press.

Whitney, Charles (1994). "Festivity and Topicality in the Coventry Scene of *I Henry IV*". *English Literary Renaissance* 24.2: 410–48.

Wiggins, S. and S. Keats, with E. Han, S. Shimokawa, J. A. Vargas Hernandez, and Claro R. Moreira (2015). *The Rising Cost of a Healthy Diet. Changing Relative Prices of Foods in High-Income and Emerging Economies.* London: Overseas Development Agency.

Willett, J. (1957, 1963, 1964). "Study of the First Scene of Shakespeare's *Coriolanus*". In *Brecht on Theatre.* London: Methuen.

Williams, Raymond and Marie Axton, eds (1977) *English Drama: Forms and Development.* Cambridge: Cambridge University Press.

Williams, W. (1977). "Social Environment and Theatrical Environment: The Case of English Naturalism". In *English Drama. Forms and Development*. Ed. M. Axton and R. Williams. Cambridge: Cambridge University Press, pp. 202–23.

Williams, W. M. (1963) *A West Country Village: Ashworthy. Family, Kinship and Land*. London: Routledge and Kegan Paul.

Wilson, Richard (1993). "Against the Grain: Representing the Market in *Coriolanus*". *Will Power: Essays on Shakespearean Authority*. Hemel Hempstead: Harvester Wheatsheaf.

Wilt, A. F. (2001). *Food for War: Agriculture and Rearmament in Britain before the Second World War*. Oxford: Oxford University Press.

Winter, Michael (1986). *The Survival and Re-Emergence of Family Farming: A Study of the Holsworthy Area of West Devon*. Unpublished PhD Thesis, Open University.

Winter, Michael (1996). *Rural Politics: Policies for Agriculture, Forestry and the Environment*. London: Routledge.

Winter, M. and M. Lobley (2016). *Is there a Future for the Small Family Farm in the UK?* London: Prince's Countryside Fund.

Wittfogel, Karl A. (1958). *Oriental Despotism. A Comparative Study of Total Power*. New Haven: Yale University Press.

Woodbridge, Linda (2004). "The Peddler and the Pawn: Why Did Tudor England Consider Peddlers to Be Rogues?" In *Rogues and Early Modern English Culture*. Ed. Craig Dionne and Steve Mentz. Ann Arbor: University of Michigan Press, pp. 143–70.

Wrightson, Keith (1980). "The Nadir of English Illegitimacy in the Seventeenth Century". In *Bastardy and its Comparative History*. Ed. P. Laslett, K. Oosterveen, and R. M. Smith. Cambridge, MA: Harvard University Press, 176–91.

Wrightson, Keith (2000). *Earthly Necessities: Economic Lives in Early Modern Britain*. New Haven and London: Yale University Press.

Wrigley, E. A. and R. S. Schofield (1981). *The Population History of England 1541–1871: A Reconstruction*. Cambridge: Cambridge University Press.

Yang, Anand A. (1987). "Disciplining 'Natives': Prisons and Prisoners in Early Nineteenth Century India". *South Asia*, N.S., 10.2: 29–45.

Yong, Tan Tai (2005). *The Garrison State: Military, Government and Society in Colonial Punjab*. New Delhi: Sage.

Zeeveld, W. Gordon (1962). "Coriolanus and Jacobean Politics". *Modern Language Review* 57: 321–34.

Zhang, Jiacheng, and Zhiguang Lin (1992). *Climate of China*. New York: Wiley.

Zins, H (1972). *England and the Baltic in the Elizabethan Era*. Manchester: Manchester University Press.

Zweiniger-Bargielowska, Ina (2000). *Austerity in Britain: Rationing, Controls, and Consumption, 1939–1955*. Oxford: Oxford University Press.

Index

For Product Safety Concerns and Information please contact our EU
representative GPSR@taylorandfrancis.com
Taylor & Francis Verlag GmbH, Kaufingerstraße 24, 80331 München, Germany

www.ingramcontent.com/pod-product-compliance
Ingram Content Group UK Ltd.
Pitfield, Milton Keynes, MK11 3LW, UK
UKHW021000180425
457613UK00019B/758